CAMBRIDGE STUDIES IN
INTERNATIONAL AND COMPARATIVE LAW

General Editors:
H. C. GUTTERIDGE, H. LAUTERPACHT, SIR A. D. MCNAIR

IV
GOVERNMENTAL LIABILITY
A COMPARATIVE STUDY

GOVERNMENTAL LIABILITY

A COMPARATIVE STUDY

BY

H. STREET

LL.M., Ph.D.

Professor of Law in the University of Nottingham
Solicitor of the Supreme Court

CAMBRIDGE

AT THE UNIVERSITY PRESS

1953

CAMBRIDGE
UNIVERSITY PRESS

University Printing House, Cambridge CB2 8BS, United Kingdom

Cambridge University Press is part of the University of Cambridge.

It furthers the University's mission by disseminating knowledge in the pursuit of
education, learning and research at the highest international levels of excellence.

www.cambridge.org
Information on this title: www.cambridge.org/9781107594715

© Cambridge University Press 1953

First published 1953
First paperback edition 2015

A catalogue record for this publication is available from the British Library

ISBN 978-1-107-59471-5 Paperback

PREFACE

In 1947–8 I was fortunate enough to be given by the University of Manchester a year's leave of absence in order to accept a Commonwealth Fund Fellowship in the United States. My subject of investigation was the civil liability of Governments, both within the Commonwealth, and American and European. This book is the product of the research which I was able to undertake in the United States. To write a book on the substantive law of countries other than one's own is a rash venture, and I hope therefore that foreign readers especially will be charitable.

I am grateful to the many judges of the United States courts, the lawyers in Federal Government service and American law teachers who so patiently and helpfully answered my numerous queries, and to the staff of the Law Library at Columbia University. I am particularly indebted to my friend, Professor Walter Gellhorn, for his guidance at all stages of this work. I thank the judges of, and lawyers practising before, the Conseil d'Etat, who explained to me the workings of that court. I am glad to seize this opportunity to thank my former colleagues, Professors Eastwood and Wortley, who have always encouraged me in every possible way. A. L. Goodhart, K.B.E., Q.C., was kind enough to make many helpful suggestions on reading the original manuscript. My friend, J. A. G. Griffith, rendered great assistance by reading the whole of the proofs. The editors of this series have aided me greatly in preparing the book for publication. Finally I wish to thank the officers of the Commonwealth Fund without whose support this work could not have been carried out.

In some chapters I have made use of articles previously appearing in the *Michigan Law Journal*, the *Modern Law Review* and the *University of Toronto Law Journal*. I am under an obligation to the editors of these periodicals for permission to make use of them.

H. STREET

THE DEPARTMENT OF LAW
THE UNIVERSITY
NOTTINGHAM

CONTENTS

Chapter I

HISTORICAL INTRODUCTION

I. ENGLAND

It has sometimes been asserted that before the reign of Edward I a writ lay against the Crown. This view, originating in an observation of a pleader before the Court of Common Pleas,[1] is now generally rejected. Holdsworth[2] and Pollock & Maitland[3] agree that proceedings against the King could never have been instituted by writ. Nor is the reason for this hard to discover once the impact of feudalism is remembered. Just as no lord could be sued in the court which he held to try the cases of his tenants, so the King, at the apex of the feudal pyramid and subject to the jurisdiction of no other court, was not suable. Subjects with claims against the King in the thirteenth century presented them informally to him, whereupon he might refer them to his courts. With the reign of Edward I a standard procedure of presenting claims against the King by petition of right was introduced,[4] and after the fourteenth century no important procedural changes were made.

Of course the subject had no right of action. If the petitioner had a claim which would have vested in him a legal right against a subject, then the King, through the *Curia Regis* or sometimes through particular officers, would adjudicate. A subject prejudiced by a royal refusal to consider a petition was remediless. A petition of right was available for all proprietary actions, in the wide sense in which that term was used in the medieval legal system, so that it was used not merely for recovery of land, but also on a claim for damages in respect of an interference with an easement.[5] It also lay for the determination of a claim to a corody[6] and for the recovery of chattels.[7]

It is usually said that the petition of right did not lie for torts. Yet the

---

1 Y.B. 33–5 Ed. I (470 Rolls Series, *per* Passeley).

2 *History of English Law*, IX, 12.

3 Pollock & Maitland, *History of English Law*, I, 515. Passeley's statement has deceived United States courts, e.g. *Chisholm* v. *Georgia* (1793), 2 Dall. 419; and for further examples see H. A. Walkup, 'Immunity of the State from suit by its citizens—Towards a more enlightened concept', in 36 *Georgetown L.J.* (1948), 310 at 314.

4 See *H.E.L.* IX, 12 ff. and Ehrlich, *Proceedings against the Crown* (1216–1377), *passim*, for full accounts of this procedure.

5 *Clifton's Case*, Y.B. 22 Ed. III, 12.

6 Y.B. 5 Ed. IV, 37.

7 Staunford, *Exposition of the King's Prerogative*, 72.

examples mentioned above would be covered by the modern actions of nuisance and detinue. The correct rule is that a petition of right would not lie for those torts normally outside the province of a real action. The principle, traceable back to Bracton,[1] that 'the King can do no wrong' accounts for this exception. Although it seems to rest on an insecure historical foundation,[2] the judges by formal legalistic reasoning have made it the basis for the royal immunity in tort. The judicial approach is perhaps best illustrated in the judgment of Cockburn C.J. in *Feather* v. *Reg.*:[3]

...a petition of right in respect of a wrong, in the legal sense of the term, shows no right to legal redress against the Sovereign. For the maxim that the King can do no wrong applies to personal as well as to political wrongs; and not only to wrongs done personally by the Sovereign, if such a thing can be supposed to be possible, but to injuries done by a subject by the authority of the Sovereign. For, from the maxim that the King cannot do wrong it follows, as a necessary consequence, that the King cannot authorise wrong.... As in the eye of the law no such wrong can be done, so, in law, no right to redress can arise; and the petition, therefore, which rests on such a foundation falls at once to the ground.

Many writers base the royal freedom from suit on this maxim:[4] others say that immunity from suit results in non-liability in tort.[5] Both arguments are demonstrably false, because they do not explain why a petition of right was available for actions other than pure tort. The feudal rule that a lord is immune from suit in his own court makes the Crown also immune from jurisdiction in the courts, but torts, whether of the King or his officers, are outside the scope of the petition of right because 'the King can do no wrong'.[6] This tortious immunity is then a judge-made rule. It does not establish that law is inapplicable to the King, but that different laws may govern him from those controlling the activities of private individuals.

From the fifteenth century onwards, petition of right fell into virtual disuse largely because of its complicated procedure, and it was superseded by the real actions, traverse and *monstrans de droit*. There is no trace of a petition of right from 1605[7] until the nineteenth century. Nevertheless a case in that period was of vast importance in the development of petition

1 F. 107a.
2 Ehrlich, *op. cit.* 42; Maitland, *Constitutional History*, 482.
3 (1865), 6 B. & S. 257 at 295–6.
4 E.g. Morgan, *Remedies against the Crown*, xviii.
5 E.g. *The Times* newspaper, editorial of 30 September 1946.
6 It is remarkable that, not only in England but throughout Europe, the inviolability of property has been acknowledged in law as a right, superior even to that of sovereignty itself. Cf. Duguit, *Traité de Droit Constitutionnel*, III, 463.
7 Rolls Chapel Series, bundle 4, no. 34.

of right. In the *Bankers' Case* (1700)[1] the Court of Exchequer Chamber, and Lord Somers in particular, made a thorough investigation of the history of petition of right. By this time, of course, the action of assumpsit had been developed and actions involving agreement were no longer clothed in their proprietary garb. The supreme importance of this case is that Lord Somers was able to treat, as precedents for the competence of the petition of right in contract, cases the facts of which corresponded to those in modern suits in contract but which had been decided as proprietary actions.

There is one other important development in this period. Although, with the establishment of constitutional monarchy, a distinction between the King in his public and private capacities could be perceived plainly, no legal acknowledgement of this was made. In consequence, the Crown, as the personification of the English State, was accorded all those immunities and prerogatives originally personal to the King.[2] Nor was the Crown vicariously liable for the torts of its servants—it could neither do wrong nor authorise others to do wrong.[3] Conversely, a petition of right would lie even though sovereign or governmental acts were called in question.

The nineteenth century witnessed a remarkable revival in the use of the petition of right. *Monstrans de droit* was no longer used, nor was the writ of *liberate*,[4] which had been used extensively by the Treasury for the settlement of accounts. There was a large increase in government contracts, disputes over which contractors sought to settle by petition of right. Not surprisingly, the rules of procedure which had been unaltered for 400 years were not suited to nineteenth-century conditions. Complaints by contractors led to the passing of the Petitions of Right Act, 1860,[5] which introduced a simpler procedure by way of alternative to that of the fourteenth century.

The scope of this revived petition of right had next to be ascertained. Some maintained that it was available whenever it was just and equitable that an individual should be compensated:[6] others held that it lay only when property was being recovered.[7] The courts rejected in 1848[8] the

1 (1700), 14 St. Tr. 1. Reversed by the House of Lords on other grounds.
2 Maitland, *Collected Papers*, III, 243 *et seq.*; E. M. Borchard, 'Governmental Responsibility in Tort' in 36 *Yale L.J.* (1926) 799.
3 See p. 2.
4 Clode, *Petition of Right*, 21.
5 23 & 24 Vict. c. 34.
6 E.g. Anstey, *Letter to Lord Cottenham as to the Petition of Right*, 8; Manning, *Exchequer Practice*, 84.
7 Halsbury, *Laws of England*, IX, 688; Robertson, *Civil Proceedings by and against the Crown*, 331.
8 *Baron de Bode* v. *Reg.* (1848), 13 Q.B. 364 at 378 n. 1.

first of these contentions. Blackburn J. in *Thomas v. Reg.* (1874)[1] relying greatly on the *Bankers' Case* rejected the plea of the Crown that it did not lie to claim unliquidated damages for breach of contract. Meanwhile the tortious immunity of the Crown had been confirmed in a series of decisions.[2] Then, in *Attorney-General v. De Keyser's Royal Hotel Ltd.* (1920), the House of Lords laid down this principle:[3]

> ...it [a petition of right] will lie when in consequence of what has been legally done any resulting obligation emerges on behalf of the subject. The petition of right does no more and no less than to allow the subject in such cases to sue the Crown. It is otherwise when the obligation arises from tort....[4]

One might have felt justified, after this case, in thinking that petition of right would be available generally whenever the petitioner claimed otherwise than for tort, and that the emphasis on restitution was ended. It was therefore surprising that in *Anglo-Saxon Petroleum Co. v. Lords Commissioners of the Admiralty* Scott L. J., in holding that an action for negligence would not lie against the Crown as salvor, should quote the following dictum of Cockburn C.J.:[5]

> ...the only cases in which the petition of right is open to the subject are, where the land or goods or money of a subject have found their way into the possession of the Crown, and the purpose of the petition is to obtain restitution, or, if restitution cannot be given, compensation in money, or where the claim arises out of a contract, as for goods supplied to the Crown or to the public service.

And should add:[6]

> This enumeration purports to be exhaustive, and the present claim cannot be brought within any of the enumerated heads.

It is suggested that this observation is *obiter*; since the action was for negligence it seems that without invoking this dictum the decision can be justified by the rule that the Crown could not be proceeded against for tort by petition of right.

1 (1874), L.R. 10 Q.B. 31.
2 *Viscount Canterbury v. Attorney-General* (1842), 1 Phill. 306; *Tobin v. Reg.* (1864), 16 C.B.N.S. 310; *Feather v. Reg.* (1865), 6 B. & S. 257.
3 [1920] A.C. 508 at 530-1 (*per* Viscount Dunedin).
4 It is appropriate that this broad principle should be established in a case concerning the taking of land. It was held that a subject whose land was requisitioned under statutory authority could claim by petition of right any compensation payable under the statute. And see Scott and Hildesley, *The Case of Requisition*, ch. VI.
5 *Feather v. Reg.* (1865), 6 B. & S. 257 at 294.
6 [1947] K.B. 794 at 801-2.

The Crown had certain other advantages not possessed by the citizen. Some of these were procedural ones relating to discovery, venue and the like. Others were prerogatives given to the Crown whenever its interests conflicted with those of subjects,[1] e.g. with regard to estoppel and laches.[2] In addition, a petition of right could be filed only if the Attorney-General granted his fiat, and, despite dicta to the contrary,[3] there can be little doubt that he had an unqualified discretion to grant or refuse it.[4]

Protests both from the Bench[5] and in the Press[6] against these immunities, particularly that from proceedings in tort, have been frequent in this century. It had been Dicey's boast[7] that the great merit of the English constitution was that Rule of Law which allowed actions to be brought in the civil courts against the officer responsible in the same manner as against any other citizen. The serious defects of a system, which merely gave an action against an individual who would probably have no funds to satisfy a judgment, were now fully recognised. In 1921 the Lord Chancellor appointed a strong committee which in 1927 presented a draft bill[8] proposing to abolish the petition of right and make the Crown freely suable in tort. The report was however pigeon-holed.

Not for the first time legal fiction rather than legislation was resorted to as a means of amelioration. The Crown, having furnished the name of a servant against whom an action was nominally brought, stood behind him and paid any damages and costs awarded against him. In those actions where the plaintiff could never have sued the servant, e.g. where the liability was that of the owner of land towards licensees, the proceedings were obviously fictitious. The House of Lords condemned this practice in 1946[9] and shortly afterwards the Court of Appeal dismissed a case[10] on the ground that it had no jurisdiction over a suit against a nominal or fictitious defendant. This, together with outcries against the large number of

1 Cf. *H.E.L.* x, 356.

2 This attained apotheosis in the era of judicial subservience to the Stuart kings, e.g. *Sir Edward Coke's Case* (1624), Godbolt 295: 'The law amplifies everything which is for the King's benefit or made for the King.... Everything for the benefit of the King shall be taken largely as everything against the King shall be taken strictly' (*per* Hobart C.J.).

3 E.g. *In re Nathan* (1884), 12 Q.B. 461 at 479 (*per* Bowen); Chitty, *Prerogatives of the Crown*, 341.

4 *Ruffy-Arnell and Baumann Aviation Co. Ltd.* v. *Rex*, [1922] 1 K.B. 599 at 607 (*per* McCardie J.); *Lovibond* v. *Governor-General of Canada*, [1930] A.C. 717.

5 See Morgan, *op. cit.* lxxxi and Allen, *Law and Orders*, 272 for examples of judicial protests.

6 E.g. Sir Henry Slesser, *Sunday Times* newspaper, 20 January 1946.

7 Dicey, *Law of the Constitution*, 369 *et seq.*

8 Cmd. 2842 (1927).   9 *Adams* v. *Naylor*, [1946] A.C. 543.

10 *Royster* v. *Cavey*, [1947] K.B. 204.

accidents involving government vehicles during the War of 1939-45 and fears (in fact unfounded) that the nationalisation programme of the Government would increase these immunities, led to Viscount Jowitt introducing on 13 February 1947 in the House of Lords a government-sponsored Crown Proceedings Bill based on the 1927 Bill. This bill which became law on 31 July 1947[1] and came into operation on 1 January 1948[2] abolished the petition of right and made the Crown suable in tort. It may be summarised as an extension to the Crown of the private law liabilities of the citizen so far as the Government thought desirable.

2. THE BRITISH COMMONWEALTH

The Commonwealth inherited England's common-law rules on Crown proceedings. None the less, many members effected radical statutory reforms much sooner than the Mother Country.[3] Australia anticipated the Crown Proceedings Act by more than forty years.[4] The Commonwealth of Australia Constitution Act, 1900,[5] provided that the legislature of Australia 'may make laws conferring rights to proceed against the Commonwealth or a State in respect of matters within the limits of the judicial power'. Part IX of the Judiciary Act, 1903, entitled 'Suits by and against the Commonwealth and the States', gave a right to sue the Commonwealth both in contract and tort without petition of right and laid down this wholesome principle:[6]

In any suit to which the Commonwealth or a State is a party, the rights of parties shall as nearly as possible be the same, and judgment may be given and costs awarded on either side, as in a suit between subject and subject.

Unfortunately, the right to sue the State in the State courts has not been given so freely. In Western Australia until 1947 the tort had to concern 'public work'[7] and in Victoria there is no governmental liability in tort at all.[8]

The Canadian Petition of Right Act[9] renders the Crown suable in a separate court, the Court of Exchequer, on petition of right in contract

---

1 10 & 11 Geo. VI, c. 44.
2 Crown Proceedings Act (Commencement) Order, (1947), S.R. & O., 1947, no. 2527.
3 W. P. Kennedy, 'Suits by and against the Crown' in 6 *Can. B.R.* (1929) 329.
4 H. E. Renfree, 'A Brief Conspectus of Commonwealth Liability in Tort' in 22 *Aust. L.J.* (1948) 102.
5 63 & 64 Vic. c. 12, para. 78.   6 S. 64.
7 T. R. Ambrose, 'Claims against the Crown' in 8 *Aust. L.J.* (1935) 214.
8 C. J. Lowe, 'The Liability of the Crown in Tort' in 11 *Aust. L.J.* (1938) 402.
9 R.S.C. 1927, c. 158.

and tort.[1] Although a previous limitation in tort to 'public work'[2] was abolished by the Exchequer Act, 1938,[3] a petition of right is still required.[4] In New Zealand the Crown is now suable in contract and tort under the Crown Proceedings Act, 1950.[5] Under the Crown Liabilities Act, 1910,[6] the Union of South Africa may be sued without petition of right in contract, and for torts arising 'out of any wrong committed by any servant of the Crown, acting in his capacity and within the scope of his authority as such servant'.[7] In Ceylon, and in most colonies also, the liability of the Crown is approximately the same as that in England before 1948, although a right to sue the Attorney-General instead of proceeding by petition of right is given in Ceylon.[8] India is liable in tort in a proprietary but not in a governmental capacity.[9]

The development of this branch of the law in the Commonwealth has, therefore, been along lines similar to that in England. The English lawyer who studies their law on the topic has much to gain. Some of their statutes have made important innovations—Canada's separate Court of Exchequer is in point; often their common law has taken new and progressive steps; useful treatises on aspects of government liability have been written.[10] Nobody seeking the best rules of governmental liability for operation in England can disregard Commonwealth experience.

3. UNITED STATES

Article III of the Constitution extended the jurisdiction of the federal courts to 'controversies to which the United States shall be a party; to controversies between two or more states; between a state and citizens of another state...and between a state, or citizens thereof, and foreign states, citizens or subjects'. In *Chisholm* v. *Georgia* (1793)[11] it was held that

---

1 Only negligence; see e.g. *Palmer* v. *Rex*, [1952] 1 D.L.R. 259.
2 French legislation, too, first made the State liable for 'public works'; see p. 16 *infra*.
3 Substituting a new s. 19 (1) (c) in the Petition of Right Act.
4 Cf. D. P. Jamieson, 'Proceedings by and against the Crown in Canada' in 26 *Can. B.R.* (1948), 373. For an account of the defence of this system by the Dominion government and a reasoned attack on its injustices see *Divine Right of Kings (Suits Against the Crown)* (Winnipeg Free Press Pamphlet, no. 28).
5 See letter from H. G. R. Mason (Attorney-General) in 22 *Aust. L.J.* (1948) 122.
6 S.2.
7 H. D. J. Bodenstein, 'The Liability of the Crown for Torts of its Servants' in *South African L.J.* (1923) 277.
8 Fernando, *Actions against Public Servants in Ceylon*.
9 Iyer, *Law of Torts*, 582 *et seq*.
10 E.g. Barlow, *The South African Law of Vicarious Liability in Delict and a Comparison of the Principles of Other Legal Systems*; Friedmann, *Australian Administrative Law*.
11 2 Dall. 419 (U.S.).

a citizen of one State could sue another State. Against this decision, the States, heavily in debt, and apprehensive of the financial implications, protested, with the result that in 1789 the eleventh amendment was passed:

> The judicial power of the United States shall not be construed to extend to any suit in law or equity, commenced or prosecuted against any one of the United States by citizens of another state, or by citizens or subjects of any foreign state.

In *Hans* v. *Louisiana*[1] the Supreme Court of the United States held (*obiter*) that *Chisholm* v. *Georgia* was wrongly decided, and upheld the reasoning of the dissenting judgment that the cognisance of suits unknown to the law was not contemplated by the constitution when establishing the judicial power of the United States. The same case decided that a citizen could not sue his own State without its consent. The following common-law rules were laid down by other decisions: A defendant State might consent to the jurisdiction,[2] and in that event an appeal would lie at the instance of the plaintiff from the decision of the court of first instance.[3] A counterclaim might be made against a State, at least to the extent of the claim.[4] Although a foreign State might not sue a State,[5] the United States could,[6] and so could any of the United States[7] unless it were in fact suing on behalf of some of its citizens.[8] A State[9] and, *a fortiori* a citizen,[10] could not sue the United States.

Why this English theory of sovereign immunity, an immunity originally personal to the King, came to be applied to the United States is one of the mysteries of legal evolution. Singewalde suggests that it was received into the United States with the rest of our common law as a fact.[11] The obstacle to the acceptance of this theory is that other common-law privileges associated with sovereignty, such as the inability of military and civil servants to sue for breach of contract of service, have never been part of the law of the United States.

Perhaps 'its survival in the United States after the Revolutionary War is attributable...to the financial instability of the infant American states

---

1 (1890), 134 U.S. 1.
2 *Clark* v. *Barnard* (1883), 108 U.S. 436.
3 *Cohens* v. *Virginia* (1821), 6 Wheat. 264 (U.S.).
4 *Siren* v. *U.S.* (1868), 7 Wall. 152 (U.S.).
5 *Monaco* v. *Mississippi* (1933), 292 U.S. 313.
6 *U.S.* v. *North Carolina* (1890), 136 U.S. 211.
7 *S. Dakota* v. *North Carolina* (1904), 192 U.S. 286.
8 *New Hampshire* v. *Louisiana* (1883), 108 U.S. 76.
9 *Kansas* v. *U.S.* (1907), 204 U.S. 331.
10 *Moffat* v. *U.S.* (1884), 112 U.S. 24.
11 Singewalde, *The Doctrine of Non-Suability of the States in the United States*, 12.

rather than to the stability of the doctrine's theoretical foundations'.[1] The tendency of the Supreme Court in the early nineteenth century was to take sovereign immunity for granted.[2] Only in the latter half of that century did judges look for a theoretical justification for it. Their judgments reveal no unity of thought on the matter. In *Railroad Co.* v. *Tennessee*[3] it was said that it is 'a privilege of sovereignty'. Holmes, J. explained that 'a sovereign is exempt from suit, not because of any formal conception or obsolete theory, but on the logical and practical ground that there can be no legal right as against the authority that makes the law on which the right depends'.[4] Well might one American writer comment:[5]

It may seem strange that authority from the fifteenth, sixteenth and seventeenth centuries, intent on establishing the absolute supremacy of a secular king over a universal church, and of an absolute monarch as against popular government or chaotic particularism, should be invoked to support a legal doctrine for a twentieth-century democratic republic.

Equally strange is it that this doctrine, with 'its roots in feudalism',[6] should apply in a country where feudalism has never been known. It is submitted that Holmes ignores the fact that in the United States the government is not sovereign but rather 'sovereignty itself remains with the people by whom and for whom all government exists and acts'.[7] It is difficult to give to his *dicta* any meaning beyond the fact that the law-making authority can exempt any group of the community from the operation of a particular law.

It has also been suggested that the immunity 'rests on a policy imposed by necessity'.[8] In *U.S.* v. *Lee*,[9] after a full historical investigation, the Supreme Court reached the conclusion 'that it has been adopted in our courts as part of the general doctrine of publicists, that the supreme power in every state, wherever it may reside, shall not be compelled, by process of courts of its own creation, to defend itself from assaults in those courts'.[10] Others have based it on public policy.[11] In *Briggs* v. *Light Boats*, for instance, it was said:[12]

It would be inconsistent with the very idea of supreme executive power, and would endanger the performance of the public duties of the sovereign,

1 W. Gellhorn and C. N. Schenck, 'Tort Actions against the Federal Government' in 47 *Col..L.R.* (1947) 722.   2 E.g. *U.S.* v. *McLemore* (1846), 4 How. 286 (U.S.).
3 (1879), 101 U.S. 337 at 339.
4 *Kawananakoa* v. *Polyblank* (1907), 205 U.S. 349 at 353. Cf. *The Western Maid* (1922), 257 U.S. 419 at 433.
5 E. M. Borchard, *op. cit.* 758.   6 Gellhorn and Schenck, *loc. cit.*
7 *Yick, Wo* v. *Hopkins* (1886), 118 U.S. 356 at 370.
8 *Langford* v. *U.S.* (1879), 101 U.S. 341 at 346 (*per* Miller J.).
9 (1882), 106 U.S. 196.   10 At 206.
11 *Gibbons* v. *U.S.* (1868), 8 Wall. 269 (U.S.).
12 (1865), 11 Allen 157 at 162 (Mass.).

to subject him to repeated suits as a matter of right, at the will of any citizen, and to submit to the judicial tribunals the control and disposition of his public property, his instruments and means of carrying on the government in war and in peace, and the money in his treasury.

On this it is sufficient perhaps to reiterate the comment of Holmes J. in 1925 that 'public opinion as to the peculiar rights and preferences due to the sovereign has changed'.[1] Nor do judicial attempts to justify the doctrine on grounds of 'sovereign dignity',[2] or because the State will in any event do justice, carry conviction.

It was evident by the middle of last century that the people of the United States were not content that there should be no remedy against it. Public demand for this reform had to be satisfied. Specific powers are assigned by the Constitution to the Judiciary and the Executive, Congress possessing the remaining powers of government. The American citizen therefore addressed his petition for relief not to the Executive on the English model, but to the Legislature.[3] Congress, where it desired to compensate the petitioner, passed a private Act to that effect. The unsatisfactory nature of this system is well expressed in the following authoritative comment:[4]

Claimants, in fact, presented only *ex parte* cases, supported by affidavits and the influence of such friends as they could induce to appear before the committees in open session, or to see the members in private. No counsel appeared to watch and defend the interest of the government. Committees were, therefore, perplexed beyond measure with this class of business, and most frequently found it more convenient and more safe not to act at all upon those claims which called for much investigation, especially when the amounts involved seemed large. Moreover, when bills for relief in meritorious cases were reported, few of them were acted upon by either House, or, if passed by one, were not brought to a vote in the other House, and so fell at the final adjournment, and if ever revived, had to be begun again before a new Congress and a new committee, and so year after year and Congress after Congress.

Not surprisingly there was repeated and severe complaint that this method both perpetrated injustices and wasted Congressional time.[5]

1 *Davis* v. *Pringle* (1925), 268 U.S. 315 at 316.
2 *U.S.* v. *Lee* (1882), 106 U.S. 196 at 248. Cf. R. Pound, 'A Survey of Public Interests' in 58 *Har. L.R.* (1944), 909 at 916, who there bases the immunity on 'a public interest in the dignity of the political organisation of society'.
3 E. Freund, 'Private Claims against the State', in 8 *Pol. Sc. Qu.* (1893), 625.
4 W. A. Richardson, 'History, Jurisdiction and Practice of the Court of Claims of the United States' in 7 *Southern L.R.* (1882) 781 at 782.
5 *Memoirs of John Quincy Adams* (1876), VIII, 480; R. C. Benton, 'The Distinction between Legislative and Judicial Functions' in 8 *A.B.A. Reps.* (1885), 261 at 264-5;

This led to the enactment in 1855[1] of the Court of Claims Act which set up a tribunal of three members appointed by the President to investigate the facts on claims (except torts) against the Government and submit a report of the facts and their reasoned opinions to Congress. Since this Court of Claims had also to submit the briefs of counsel and the evidence, the Committee on Claims of Congress assumed the duty of re-reading the entire case. Little improvement, therefore, was made by this statute. Lincoln in his Message to Congress of 3 December 1861 requested further reform, and in 1863[2] an Act was passed creating five judges of the Court of Claims, and authorising them to render judgments. In 1868[3] a further Act reversed a Supreme Court ruling[4] that there was no appeal to the latter court from the Court of Claims. The Court of Claims had jurisdiction over contracts and claims founded on the constitution, but not over torts.

The fifth amendment prohibited the taking by the United States of property for public use without compensation; compensation could be claimed under this Act. One sees here, as in England, a zealous regard for the rights of property. There has been much litigation and discussion on the meaning of 'taking'.[5] While English courts could rely on the 'real' nature of actions concerning property, the United States had to interpret the wording of the amendment. The theory has been that 'taking' implies an agreement to pay; the difficulties of affording relief, against indirect injury, or when the Government asserts a claim of right, are manifest. Nevertheless, so zealous is the Judiciary in the protection of rights of property that the Supreme Court has recently held that if the flying of aircraft is 'so low and frequent as to be a direct and immediate interference with the enjoyment and use of the land', the owner of a poultry farm who complains of the interference with his farm by noise and glare of aircraft has a cause of action.[6]

The view of judges of the Court of Claims and members of the Bar practising before it seems to be that it functions satisfactorily. The big

R. Luce, 'Petty Business in Congress' in 26 *Am. Pol. Sc. R.* (1932), 815 at 818–19; R. V. Shumate, 'Tort Claims against State Governments' in 9 *L. & C.P.* (1942), 242 at 249 ff.

1 10 Stat. 612.   2 12 Stat. 765.
3 14 Stat. 9.
4 *Gordon* v. *U.S.* (1864), reported in (1886), 117 U.S. 697.
5 See Note, 'The Fifth Amendment and the Tucker Act' in 32 *Yale L.J.* (1922) 725; Note, 'Grounds for Recognition of Implied Contracts under the Tucker Act' in 43 *Yale L.J.* (1934) 674; L. L. Anderson, 'Tort and Implied Contract Liability of the Federal Government' in 30 *Minn. L.R.* (1946) 133; J. A. Crane, 'Jurisdiction of the United States Court of Claims' in 34 *Har. L.R.* (1920) 161.
6 *U.S.* v. *Causby* (1946), 328 U.S. 256.

disadvantage, in so large a country, is that it sits only in Washington.[1] It demonstrates above all that one may channel all cases within the regular hierarchy, by allowing appeals from it to lie to the Supreme Court. The only substantial modification since 1868 was effected by the Tucker Act of 1887[2] which gave concurrent jurisdiction in claims not amounting to more than $10,000 to the Federal District Courts.

This century has witnessed a gradual increase in the range of governmental liability. Suits for patent infringement have been permitted since 1910,[3] and Federal liability for admiralty and maritime torts[4] and for damage caused by dredging activities[5] has been statutorily acknowledged. Extensive provision for administrative settlement of claims has been made. Acts dealing with such varied matters as federal employees' compensation,[6] war damage,[7] postal claims,[8] small torts[9] and claims against the Federal Bureau of Investigation[10] have been passed. All have a similar pattern, the head of the department being authorised to settle claims below a specified amount informally without a hearing, but after investigation by the legal staff of the department and receipt of affidavit evidence. In addition many public corporations have been set up to carry out governmental functions. Although the cases are conflicting the judicial tendency is to deny these corporations any immunity.[11]

Not even these palliatives have prevented a flood of applications to Congress for private Bills. For instance, the seventy-fourth and seventy-fifth Congress each considered more than 2300 private claim bills demanding relief exceeding $100,000,000. Congress felt that it was devoting a disproportionate amount of time to non-legislative matters, and the public complained of injustice and political favouritism. Since 1929 Congress has had under consideration a series of Bills proposing that the United States should be liable in tort, but not until 1946 was the Federal Tort Claims Act adopted as Title IV of the Legislative Reorganisation Act.[12] It is significant that the measure was introduced under the heading

---

1 Commissions take evidence in other places in the United States for suits in the Court of Claims.

2 24 Stat. 505.   3 36 Stat. 851.

4 41 Stat. 925 (1920).   5 49 Stat. 1049 (1935).

6 39 Stat. 742 (1916).

7 For a discussion of the many statutes, see Note, 'Liability of the United States and Canadian Governments for Tortious Conduct of their Military Personnel', in 53 *Yale L.J.* (1943), 188.

8 42 Stat. 63 (1921).   9 42 Stat. 106 (1922).

10 49 Stat. 1184 (1936).

11 *Keifer & Keifer* v. *Reconstruction Finance Corporation* (1939), 306 U.S. 381; *Federal Housing Administration* v. *Burr* (1939), 309 U.S. 242.

12 60 Stat. 842.

'More Efficient Use of Congressional Time'. This Act gives jurisdiction over certain tort claims against the United States to the Federal District Courts with an appeal to the Circuit Court of Appeals, or, by consent of the parties, to the Court of Claims.

Meanwhile, the States have not been idle.[1] Three, Alabama, Arkansas and West Virginia, still have constitutional provisions against suing the State. There is a bewildering diversity of rules among the rest, but at least twenty-seven allow the State to be sued in contract. Some, like New York, give the citizen unrestricted rights of suing both in tort and contract, while others like Arizona acknowledge limited tort liability. Others such as Iowa, Montana and Minnesota make provision for administrative investigation of claims, to be followed by reports to the Legislature.

4. CONTINENTAL EUROPE

A. *Influence of Roman Law*

The growth of the European law of governmental liability has been different from the Anglo-American.[2] To understand the European developments, one must first turn to Roman law. At first thought, it might seem that Roman law had little contribution to make to principles of governmental responsibility. It had no conception of protection of the individual against the group. Its *universitas*, whether in the form of the State or otherwise, could not be sued, and was not regarded as a separate person. Fault, the basis of responsibility for damages in Roman law, could be ascribed only to individuals.

Classical Roman law did, however, differentiate *ius publicum* and *ius privatum*,[3] although it is doubtful whether *ius publicum* could be regarded as law at all. If the State entered into commercial transactions, disputes could be settled only by administrative procedure controlled by officials, not by private law. Nor were the payments and receipts of the Republic, the *aerarium*, subject to private law. During the principate, the Emperor took over most of the financial direction of government. The funds now belonged not to the *populus* but to the *princeps*, with the result that more and more of them went to the *fiscus* or Imperial Treasury rather than to the *aerarium*.[4] By the time of Diocletian, the *fiscus* had swallowed up the

---

1 For fuller treatment of State liabilities, see E. M. Borchard, 'Government Liability in Tort', in 26 *C.B.R.* (1948) 399 at 408 *et seq.*; R. V. Shumate, *op. cit.*
2 Cf. L. Trotabas, General Report on 'La Responsabilité de l'Etat en Droit Interne'; *Mémoires de l'Académie Internationale de Droit Comparé*, book II, pt. III (Paris, 1935), 71.
3 Jones, *Historical Introduction to the Theory of Law*, ch. v; Borchard, *op. cit.* 1.
4 J. W. Jones, 'The Early History of the Fiscus' in 43 *L.Q.R.* (1927) 499 at 500.

aerarium. This enabled the State to enter private law domains. The Emperor, as a natural person, could be subject to private law, and for the first time the State, to the extent of the *fiscus,* acknowledged financial liabilities according to private law. The doctrines of agency in contract were held to bind the *fiscus.* A distinction, admittedly vague and ill-defined, was drawn between the commercial and pecuniary activities of the State on the one hand, and its political and governmental duties on the other. Only in the former case was there *fiscus* and legal responsibility. Nor did that responsibility then extend to delict, because a corporation was not liable for *culpa in eligendo* or *custodiendo.*

There is no agreement about the theoretical justification for *fiscus* in Roman law. Mommsen[1] suggested that the Emperor was the legal owner but under an obligation to apply funds to State purposes, and cited the contract *mutuum* by way of comparison. Mitteis[2] denied that the Emperor could even be the subject of rights and duties, and argued that the *fiscus* was itself an independent legal person, having either the property itself or the organised body of officials as its substratum. Borchard agrees that in late Roman times it was 'deemed theoretically a juristic person'[3] but Gierke denies this.[4] Jones puts forward the compromise view that the *fiscus* was at first the private property of the Emperor, but later, after its severance from *patrimonium privatum,* assumed the attributes of independent legal personality.[5] Certainly, whatever the philosophical basis, and notwithstanding the surviving immunities and privileges, the *fiscus* had for the first time subordinated the State in its commercial relations to rules of private law.

The *fiscus* survived the Holy Roman Empire, but in a very extended form, wherein its original meaning was almost lost. When the medieval towns arose, it fell to them, aided by the work of the post-glossators,[6] to resuscitate the Roman law notions of *fiscus.* Once the idea of state personality and property was reborn there, it soon spread to the new German territorial states.[7] Their organised system of self-government led them to distinguish the public funds or corporate revenue from private property, a distinction which Gierke has thought to have been established by 1495.[8] A source of confusion in the Middle Ages was the fact that feudal lords were deemed sovereigns as well as proprietors, and carried

---

1 *Römisches Staatrecht,* II, 556.   2 *Römisches Privatrecht,* I, 350.
3 E. M. Borchard, 'Governmental Responsibility in Tort' in 28 *Col. L.R.* (1928) 577 at 582 n.
4 *Das Deutsche Genossenschaftsrecht,* III, 60.   5 Jones, *loc. cit.* 504.
6 Hatschek, *Die Rechtliche Stellung des Fiskus,* 24 *et seq.*
7 Gierke, *op. cit.* I, 300. This is far from a solitary example of the medieval towns adapting a Roman idea to modern conditions.   8 *Op. cit.* III, 405.

their royal prerogatives in the performance of all their functions. The classical distinction between *imperium* and *dominium* had become blurred. The insistence of the publicists of the school of natural law in the seventeenth and eighteenth centuries led to a renewed recognition of the Roman division of state functions into corporate and governmental.

In the nineteenth century the effects on State liability of this distinction became evident. German and most other Central European states allowed the *fiscus* to be sued by the ordinary rules of private law, and at the same time denied a remedy for governmental matters. The content of *fiscus* has never been fixed,[1] but it may be said to cover the Treasury and fiscal relations of the State, and its private and public property, and the State when exercising corporate functions. In France, *fiscus* has played a relatively less important part: although the code distinguished *domaine public susceptible d'une propriété privée* from *domaine de l'Etat* held by the State *comme tout particulier*, this distinction was never logically carried out.[2] At the same time this concept of State property swallowed up that of *fiscus*. This Franco-German divergence has caused some writers to reach the erroneous conclusion that nineteenth-century French developments stem only from the Code and owe nothing to the influence of the postglossators and the European towns.[3]

B. *France*

Until the nineteenth century, France, in common with the rest of Europe, denied any State responsibility, so all-pervasive were the notions of divine right of kings and sovereignty. Dicey has argued that the innate superiority of English over French law in this field was shown by the Anglo-American device of allowing a private-law remedy against the individual officer who committed a wrong.[4] The French official was not, however, immune. On the contrary, a French jurist can write that 'it is, in fact, in the development of the rules as to this personal liability of the agent that we see the first beginnings in public law of actions for damages based on injuries caused by administrative acts'.[5]

Dicey did not perceive any objection to allowing complete freedom to sue officials. Yet to do so might interfere with effective administration or lead to abuse of process. Talented men might be dissuaded from entering the public service by the threat of exposure to a series of civil actions.

1 Primker, in the 9th *Deutscher Juristentag* (1878), III, 28.
2 Hatschek, *op. cit.* 36–41; J. M. Péritch, General Report on 'La Responsabilité de l'Etat en Droit Interne', *loc. cit.* 44.
3 Vauthier, *Etudes sur les Personnes Morales*, 305.   4 Dicey, *op. cit.* 387.
5 L. Trotabas, 'Liability in Damages under French Administrative Law' in 12 *J.C.L.* (1930) 44 at 49.

Over-caution and lack of initiative in the Administration might be encouraged. France sought a solution which would take account of these factors and yet not leave the citizen remediless. Her first method, embodied in statutes of 1789 and 1790, was to allow private citizens to sue officials only with the consent of the head of the Administration. By the Constitution of the Year VIII, 'government agents other than Ministers cannot be sued in respect of acts done in the discharge of their official duties except with the authority of the *Conseil d'Etat*'. Because the *Conseil d'Etat* in the early nineteenth century was under strict governmental control, only rarely and with difficulty was permission to sue obtained. This administrative guarantee was abolished in 1870 and now officials may be sued without the consent of the government for *fautes personnelles*.

In the nineteenth century, under the influence of the legacy of ideas left by the Revolution, there grew the conviction that sovereign responsibility should replace the outmoded concept of sovereign infallibility. A society pledged to democracy, self-government and social security and welfare as the ends of government was intolerant of the old order. In 1790, 1807 and 1836, statutes making the State responsible for injuries caused by the operation of public works were passed. Eminent domain, too, was considered. That land should be expropriated only for public purposes and subject to the payment of compensation had long been recognised in Anglo-American law,[1] but no similar right was afforded by the *ancien régime*.[2] The principle of protection against expropriation was embodied in the Declaration of the Rights of Man of 1793 and given statutory precision in 1810.

One group of administrative acts, *actes de gouvernement*,[3] has remained immune from court control. Their content has varied, but the criterion has been consistently political. Examples are acts of high executive officers, diplomatic acts and matters of war. They may be loosely compared with acts of State in English law. Those apart, administrative acts were divided into two groups, *actes d'autorité* and *actes de gestion*, corresponding to the classical distinction between *imperium* and *dominium*.[4] Jurists first

1 See ch. IV *infra*.
2 Marcq, *La Responsabilité de la Puissance Publique*, 278 et seq.; Picot, *De la Responsabilité de l'Etat du Fait de ses Préposés*, 26 et seq.
3 See 72 et seq. *infra*.
4 Although this distinction is not found in English law, rather surprisingly it applies to the liability of American municipal corporations, though with less force than hitherto: D. W. Doddridge, 'Distinction between Governmental and Proprietary Functions of Municipal Corporations' in 23 *Mich. L.R.* (1925) 325. For a successful attempt to abolish the distinction, see *Bernadise* v. *City of New York* (1944), 182. Misc. 609; W. J. Lloyd, 'Municipal Tort Liability in New York' in 23 *N.Y.U.L.Q.R.* (1948) 278.

emphasised the distinction in their desire to end the former State immunity in contract.[1] *Actes d'autorité*, for which there was no civil liability, included legislation, adjudication, execution of the laws and such other governmental acts as could not be performed by a private citizen. Liability for the remaining administrative acts, *actes de gestion*, was, on the other hand, favoured. It was tempting to equate the distinction with that between public and private law, and to hold that liability for all *actes de gestion* should be determined according to the Civil Code. Some decisions of the *Cour de Cassation* supported this view, and Michoud[2] and Berthélemy[3] agreed. The criteria of the distinction were not precisely defined,[4] but two categories of *gestion* were recognised. *Actes de gestion privée* were such acts of management as could be performed by a private person, for instance running a state commercial enterprise, managing property or making contracts. *Actes de gestion publique* included management of such utilities as the gas, water and electricity services, and the maintenance of health and fire services. The contention of Michoud that article 1382 of the Civil Code made the State liable as a corporation in private law for the acts of its *préposés* was strenuously resisted in respect of *gestion publique*,[5] and it seems that only rarely did the courts seek to apply it to such acts.

It is at this stage that the influence of the *Conseil d'Etat* began to be felt. One of the complaints against the *ancien régime* had been that the Judiciary had been too powerful. Accepting the principle of the separation of powers, and determined that the Executive should be free from judicial domination,[6] the French set up the *Conseil d'Etat*.[7] At first its judicial powers were limited. They were extended in 1848 and after curtailment under Napoleon III were put on their present wide basis by an act of 1872. The *Conseil d'Etat*, a body of lawyers trained in administration, was to exercise exclusive jurisdiction over administrative acts, and the *Cour de Cassation* was to retain its private law jurisdiction over the acts of individuals, any disputed question of jurisdiction being settled by the *Tribunal des Conflits*. A year later, the famous *Blanco Case*[8] confirmed that actions

1 Cot, *La Responsabilité Civile des Fonctionnaires Publics*, 137, and the early authorities there cited.
2 'De la Responsabilité de l'Etat à Raison des Fautes de ses Agents', 3 *R.D.P.* (1895) 401 at 419.
3 Berthélemy, *Traité Elémentaire de Droit Administratif*, III; cf. Picot, *op. cit.* 108–27.
4 Marcq, *op. cit.* 312; Hauriou, *Précis de Droit Administratif et de Droit Public*, 19.
5 E.g. Duez, 'La Théorie de la Gestion Privée', in 44 *Revue Critique* (n.s.) 337 at 340.
6 Uhler, *Review of Administrative Acts*, ch. 1.
7 H. Berthélemy, 'The Conseil d'Etat in France', in 12 *J.C.L.* (1930) 23.
8 Dall. Pér. 1873, 3, 17.

in damages against the central Administration were within the exclusive jurisdiction of the administrative courts. The rule was soon extended to suits against the *départements*[1] and *communes*.[2]

The *Blanco Case* is the great turning point in French administrative law. The *Conseil d'Etat*, not bound by any code, was free to build up special rules of administrative liability. The social justice and breadth of vision which have characterised its judgments commended themselves to French jurists and rapidly enhanced its prestige. Protests against the distinctions between *actes d'autorité, de gestion publique* and *de gestion privée* were renewed.[3] Exercising jurisdiction over *gestion publique*, the *Conseil d'Etat* rapidly widened the scope of this category at the expense of the other two groups. Soon these categories were abandoned, and instead there were a narrow category of *actes de gouvernement* free from judicial control, a narrow category of *actes de gestion privée* subject to private law in the civil courts and a broad class embracing all acts of the public service (*puissance publique*), whether *d'autorité* or *de gestion*. It is to the development by the *Conseil d'Etat* of new principles of public law for *actes de puissance publique* that one must now turn.

The broad principle first worked out was that of *faute de service*. Where the agent of the Administration was at fault in the carrying out of administrative responsibilities, then a person injured in consequence could sue the State in the *Conseil d'Etat* for this *faute de service*. This '*faute*' is not the same as that determining the liability of a *commettant* for the act of a *préposé* under the Civil Code. The *Conseil d'Etat* has freed itself from the Civil Code whenever it has thought fit. The broad test of liability was 'bad administrative practice';[4] whether or not the act was traceable to an individual officer was irrelevant. If the act were not linked with the Administration, if it were the act of an individual 'with his passions and weaknesses' then it would be a *faute personnelle* engaging only the liability of its perpetrator in the civil courts.

Inspired by this creative role of the *Conseil d'Etat*, writers sought a broader basis of responsibility than that of subjective fault. Should not the State be liable for special damage that it has caused to the citizen even though there was no fault, they argued.[5] Although the *Conseil d'Etat* did not lay down general principles, it gradually extended the responsibility of the state in that direction. It first gave practical expression to the theory of risk in the field of public works, but it is no longer so limited. Whether the theory of risk has completely superseded that of *faute* is much debated

1 *Terrier*, Dall. Pér. 1904, 3, 65.   2 *Fautry*, Dall. Pér. 1908, 3, 49.
3 L. Duguit, *Transformations du Droit Public*, ch. v *passim*.
4 Trotabas, *op. cit.* 219.   5 Duguit, *op. cit.* 250.

in France and will be best considered later. Simultaneously, there has been developed the theory of *cumul* whereby a *faute personnelle*, if committed in the course of administrative duty, might subject the State to liability. In short, the *faute personnelle* has become less and less important, whereas the State liability becomes increasingly wider in range.

Not in tort alone has the *Conseil d'Etat* developed rules of administrative liability. Special rules for determining the liability of the State in contract have been laid down.[1] If the contract relates to the execution of the public service, then, it is contended, it is of paramount public importance that the work should be completed, even if the Administration seeks variations from the original contract. This is, of course, not to deny the right of the contractor to be paid for his extra work. Where these or other special considerations not found in private contracts subsist, then the principles of *contrat administratif*, not of private law, must be invoked, and the *Conseil d'Etat* will apply them.

The *Conseil d'Etat*, therefore, maintains a wide control over the Administration. Its *contentieux de pleine juridiction* enables it to adjudicate on actions for damages against the Administration, whether sounding in tort or contract. In addition, its *contentieux d'annulation* authorises it to review the legality of acts of the Administration and if necessary to annul them *erga omnes*.

C. *Germany*

German states could be sued for breach of contract. If the State were affected in a proprietary or contractual capacity then it as *fiscus* could be sued for delicts also in the nineteenth century. This rule applied to the seventeen German states as well as to the Reich.[2] It was embodied in the German Civil Code, articles 31 and 89 providing that, in a private law capacity, the railway, postal or other appropriate *fiscus* could be sued for delictual injuries inflicted on third persons by its directing officials. For the acts of subordinate officials acting within the scope of their duties, the *fiscus* could also be sued if the accident were caused by faulty selection or supervision of the employee or the provision of defective equipment.[3] The *fiscus* could not then be sued for governmental acts.[4]

Only the *fiscus* could be sued, and then always according to private law in the civil courts, throughout the nineteenth century. At the turn of the

---

1 Péquignot, *Théorie Générale du Contrat Administratif, passim.*
2 See *Proceedings of the Section of International and Comparative Law of the A.B.A.* (1946), 117.
3 S. 831, s. 278.
4 *Staatsfiskus zu Weimar* v. B. (1884), R. G. Zivilsachen, II, 206.

century the writings of Gierke greatly influenced German legal development. He propounded the theory that a corporation was a real person,
having a will manifested by its organs. So convincing were his researches
and arguments that jurists throughout Europe commended his work.
His theory led to the conclusion that the State as a public corporation
should be liable according to private-law rules. Contending that if the
officer could be sued in the ordinary courts whatever the nature of his act,
then, since the officer was to be identified with the State, the State's
liability should be similar, he held that the old distinction between corporate and governmental acts should be abolished, and liability for both
types of act enforced.[1] The distinction between State and *fiscus*, he argued,
was outworn and useless. Jellinek[2] was soon to support him.

The first practical result of his teaching was that the courts gradually
extended the scope of the liability of *fiscus*. Since Gierke, jurists have
largely abandoned the view that state and *fiscus* are separate institutions.
Instead, many have taken up the half-way position that the State enters
into legal relations with citizens in two capacities, as a governing authority
or as a *fiscus*.[3]

The views of Gierke were implemented in the Weimar Constitution of
1919. Article 131 provided:

If an official in the discharge of the public power entrusted to him
violates his official duties due from him to a third party, the responsibility
rests in principle with the State or the body in the service of which he
stands. The right of recourse against the official is reserved. The resort to
the ordinary courts of justice shall not be excluded.

The remarkable result reached is that the State has a wider area of liability
for governmental than corporate acts. One jurist has said of it that 'it
would be difficult to think of a more liberal formulation of the rule of
liability'.[4] Although German law recognises the distinctions between
public and private law, actions under this article are brought before the
civil courts, not before administrative courts. By 1937 there had been an
extensive development of administrative tribunals, particularly for the
review of administrative discretion.[5] Some statutes under the Nazi
régime removed some actions against the State to administrative courts,
for example, to the Railway courts and the Labour courts. If, then, it must

1 *Die Deutsche Genossenschaftstheorie und die Deutsche Rechtsprechung*, 743 *et seq.*
2 Jellinek, *System der Subjektiven Öffentlichen Rechte*, 245.
3 Borchard, 28 *Col. L.R.*, 609 n. 84.
4 E. Freund, General Report on 'La Responsabilité de l'Etat en Droit Interne',
loc. cit. 40.
5 R. E. Uhlman and F. G. Rupp, 'The German System of Administrative Courts'
in 31 *Ill. L.R.* (1937) 847.

be conceded that administrative courts were making some inroads upon the jurisdiction of the civil courts, it still remained true that in Germany the State might be sued in the ordinary courts according to private-law rules whether the act were governmental or corporate, except where statute provided a substitute remedy in an administrative court. Wide though the range was of acts for which the German State might be sued, it must be noted that the basis of liability was largely fault; there has not been that development of risk so characteristic of French *droit administratif.*

D. *Other States*[1]

The extent of State liability in other European states varies considerably. Nevertheless, certain broad tendencies can be discerned.[2]

State liability in contract was generally conceded. All of them used to deny the right of the citizen to sue the State but allowed him some remedy against officers of the State. By the nineteenth century delictual liability, based on fault, for *actes de gestion privée* but not *de puissance publique* was enforced in civil courts. The next stage was a halting recognition, usually by statutes in limited fields, of liability for *actes de puissance publique.* Typical fields for this liability were eminent domain and judicial errors. Grudging and spasmodic acknowledgment of liability without fault has followed. On the whole, however, it is true to say that no European states have advanced so far along the road of liability as France and Germany. The reason varies from State to State: in some the cramping influence of a strict separation of powers;[3] sometimes lack of money; elsewhere the reluctance to adopt modern theories of liability; in others a denial that there is any distinction between public and private law.

A short statement of the position in various European countries can be given. In Italy the State can be sued in the civil but not in the administrative courts. The distinction between management and authority is abandoned there, but liability for other than fault is exceptional.[4] Finland, though liable when it acts in a proprietary capacity, can only be sued for governmental acts when specific statutes so provide, and when there is no successful recourse against the officer concerned; the rules of private law determine liability, and the civil courts have jurisdiction. Holland has endeavoured to extend private law concepts to State responsibility, but

[1] It has not always been possible to check developments since 1939. The best summary is contained in *Mémoires de l'Académie, op. cit.*

[2] J. W. Garner, 'Anglo-American and Continental European Administrative Law' in 7 *N.Y.U.L.Q.R.* (1929) 387.

[3] E.g. Oroveanu, *La Séparation des Pouvoirs Administrative et Judiciaire et le Contentieux Administratif en Roumanie.*

[4] P. B. Ravà, 'Italian Administrative Courts under Fascism' in 40 *Mich. L.R.* (1941) 654.

there are lingering traces of the old distinction between proprietary and governmental acts. Sweden applies private law, and with few statutory exceptions is not liable for *actes de puissance publique*. In Russia there is no right to sue the State; the citizen may only address a complaint to the head of the department or to the Prokuror, with a further right of complaint by way of appeal to the State Control Office.[1] Switzerland also favours this method of settlement of disputes with the State.[2] In Hungary the Civil Code makes the State liable for the delicts of its servants in the course of their employment and makes the State liable also for risk in the residuary cases where the harm to the citizen cannot otherwise be made good and equity demands that some compensation be given.[3] It is note-worthy that the countries with a separate *Conseil d'Etat*, for example, Greece[4] and Spain, do not usually give to it jurisdiction over suits against the State. All the Latin-American States except Argentina can be sued without consent; but they are liable generally for *actes de gestion*, not *actes d'autorité*.[5]

Belgium merits more detailed study both because the admirers of the French *droit administratif* have frequently compared its system unfavourably with that of France,[6] and because of recent statutory changes.

When Belgium framed its Constitution in 1830 the French administra-tive arrangements were faring badly. It is not surprising therefore that the French model was not followed. Articles 92 and 93 provided respectively:

Les contestations qui ont pour objet des droits civils sont exclusivement du ressort des tribunaux.

Les contestations qui ont pour objet des droits politiques sont du ressort des tribunaux, sauf les exceptions établies par la loi.

In Belgium the State could be sued in contract in the civil courts and its officers could be sued in accordance with civil law without the permission of the State. These constitutional provisions were interpreted in a rather surprising manner by the courts.[7] They confined their jurisdiction to where the State acted to meet individual as distinct from public needs; the

---

1 A. Nove, 'Some Aspects of Soviet Constitutional Theory' in 12 *Mod. L.R.* (1949) 12 at 34.   2 *Proceedings of the A.B.A. op. cit.* 121.
3 T. Ilosvay, 'La Responsabilité de la Puissance Publique et de ses Agents en Hongrie' in *Revue Internationale des Sciences Administratives* (1949) 269.
4 Andréades, *La Juridiction Administrative en Grèce*; Chariotis, *Conseil d'Etat en Grèce de 1830 à* 1930.
5 J. I. Y. Puente, 'The Responsibility of the State as a Juristic Person in Latin America' in 18 *Tulane L.R.* (1944) 408, 554.
6 Cambier, *La Responsabilité de la Puissance Publique et de ses Agents.*
7 Debeyre, *La Responsabilité de la Puissance Publique en France et en Belgique*, 39 *et seq.*

power to annul administrative acts was denied; and the French distinction between *actes de gestion* and *actes d'autorité* was followed. These interpretations have been the stick with which French administrative lawyers have beaten Belgium for its private-law approach. However, these were no necessary concomitants of a private-law system—they might be caused by unimaginative judges, a too literal interpretation, tenderness to the Executive, aping France, and a rigid conservatism—but the French critics conveniently ignored that possibility.

Under the influence of the Separation of Powers, the liability of the State as a *personne civile* but not as *puissance publique* continued until 1920. So, there was no action when a soldier damaged property while driving an army vehicle, but action would lie if the injury occurred while the army was assisting food distribution. An examination of the cases reveals a bewildering confusion of *autorité* and *gestion*. In 1920 a prominent Belgian lawyer, Wodon,[1] wrote an important book condemning these weaknesses of the Belgian system. His theory was that a citizen had three kinds of rights, the civil rights against fellow-citizens, public rights against the State, and political rights such as the right to vote and freedom of speech. In Belgium, he contended, the second of these rights was not enforced. Shortly after the publication of this book the Belgian courts renounced this distinction between *actes de gestion* and *actes d'autorité* and held the State liable for both.[2] In that case, Paul Leclercq did suggest that there was a wide field of *actes de gouvernement* covering all acts of a 'political' nature outside the scope of liability, but so wide a definition is supported neither by jurists[3] nor later cases.

Although the original basis of delictual liability was fault, by 1890 this had been extended by President Beckers to *respect des droits acquis* with a consequent emphasis on the damage rather than the fault. This tendency has suffered a serious setback in the last twenty-five years because many writers have propounded the theory that there is liability only *quand un acte illicite lèse un droit civil*. Thenceforth, the courts have oscillated between objective and subjective theories of State liability for delict. The courts are still unable to decide whether State liability rests on *la théorie de l'organe* whereby the State is assimilated to a human being and directly responsible for its acts, or whether its liability is vicarious by analogy to master-servant relationships. The two theories produce different decisions in the courts.[4]

1 Wodon, *Le Contrôle Juridictionnel de l'Administration et la Responsabilité des Services Publics en Belgique.*   2 *La Flandria*, Pasicrisie Belge, 1920, I, 193.
3 E.g. Vauthier, *Précis du Droit Administratif de la Belgique*, 514.
4 *Revue de Droit International et de Droit Comparé* (1950) 311 *et seq.* for recent conflicting cases.

Dissatisfaction with the handling by the civil courts of public law issues led to agitation for the setting up of a *Conseil d'Etat* on the French model. This was done by a law of 23 December 1946. Although the main purpose of the law seems to be the annulling of administrative acts, there is one article dealing with suits against the Government for indemnity which is of interest.[1] It enacts:[2]

La section d'administration connaît, dans les cas où il n'existe pas d'autre juridiction compétente, des demandes d'indemnité relatives à la réparation d'un dommage exceptionnel résultant d'une mésure prise ou ordonnée par l'Etat, la province, la commune ou le gouvernement de la colonie, soit que l'exécution en ait été normale, soit qu'elle ait été défectueuse ou différée. La section d'administration se prononce en équité par voie d'avis motivé, en tenant compte de toutes les circonstances d'intérêt public et privé.

The article has a narrow range and bristles with difficulties. It has been difficult enough for France, with its subjective distinction of *faute personnelle* and *faute de service*, to mark off the civil and administrative jurisdictions. It would seem much harder for Belgium with its emphasis in the civil courts on *droit civil* to do so. It is suggested that the basing of decisions on equity implies adoption of the theory of *l'égalité des administrés devant les charges*, compensation for exceptional damage. The *Conseil d'Etat* has advised the payment of compensation to a civil servant whose promotion was unjustifiably retarded, but has refused several claims for indemnity against losses suffered by general economic legislation.[3] Legislative control is retained because Parliament must grant the money. Moreover, the *Conseil d'Etat* under this article may only advise, not decide, although the Government has indicated that if the experiment is successful it would contemplate making that body competent to decide. Originally, it had been intended to limit the article to 'sovereign' faults, but that limitation is not contained in the final draft. It is to be observed that the Act applies to communes as well as to central government: this has led to some speculation whether public opinion will be forceful enough to compel the latter to accept the advice offered to them by the *Conseil d'Etat*.

1 Velge, *Le Conseil d'Etat*, 132 *et seq.*
2 Art. 7.
3 *Revue de Droit International et de Droit Comparé* (1950) 316.

Chapter II

TORT

It is proposed to compare in this chapter the provisions relating to substantive tortious liability contained in the Crown Proceedings Act, 1947, and the Federal Tort Claims Act, 1946.[1] The relevant French law will also be examined and some assessment of the relative worth of the Anglo-American and French law will be attempted.

I. ENGLAND AND THE UNITED STATES

A. *General Principles of Interpretation*

The task of interpreting the two Acts is made more difficult by the uncertainty about the principles of statutory interpretation to be applied by the courts. Both Acts for the first time impose upon the Government a more or less general liability in tort. Are they to be construed liberally in order to carry out the supposed intention of the Acts, namely, to end the former immunities, or are they to receive a strict construction? Sir Ivor Jennings foresaw this problem in 1932 when he warned that any Act passed would not succeed if the judges were hamstrung in their handling of it by private-law notions of contract and tort.[2] The problem is magnified because neither Act is clearly drafted.[3]

Writers on both sides of the Atlantic have asserted that the legislation will be liberally construed.[4] Friedmann, in the course of an analysis of modern methods of statutory interpretation, argues that the judge, whose task is to interpret the provisions of a statute reforming the law, should resolve any ambiguity by carrying out the general principles of reform envisaged by the statute. Taking the Crown Proceedings Act as his example, he says that since the purpose of this Act is to make the liability of the Crown correspond to that of the private individual, it will receive a liberal construction. There are, however, objections to

1 Part of the contents of this chapter was summarised in my article, 'Tort Liability of the State: The Federal Tort Claims Act and the Crown Proceedings Act' in 47 *Mich. L.R.* (1949) 341.
2 'The Report on Ministers' Powers' in 10 *Public Administration* (1932) 333 at 350.
3 Cf. Glanville Williams, *Crown Proceedings*, Preface.
4 E.g. W. Friedmann, 'Statute Law and its Interpretation in the Modern State' in 26 *Can. B.R.* (1948) 1277; Note, 'The Federal Tort Claims Act' in 56 *Yale L.J.* (1947) 534 at 538.

this argument. The Explanatory Memorandum to the Crown Proceedings Bill stated:[1]

> Part I of the Bill seeks, so far as practicable, to put the Crown in its public capacity in the same position, for the purposes of the law of torts, as a private person....But in regard to certain matters...the analogy breaks down, for in these spheres the functions of the Crown involve responsibilities of a kind which no subject undertakes.

A judge interpreting the Act in accordance with its general intention, if he could consult the *travaux préparatoires*, would therefore have to consider whether the matter in issue was beyond the point where 'the analogy breaks down'. But can one be sure that the courts will look for this broad legislative purpose? Too often they rely mechanically on presumptions or interpret legislation so as to leave the old law as little changed as possible.[2] Moreover, the recent trend of judicial decision shows a refusal to declare that the crown is bound by statutory liabilities which are not imposed on it either expressly or by necessary implication.[3]

Soon after the Federal Tort Claims Act came into force there were signs that the hopes of those desiring liberal interpretation of it would be dashed. The Federal District Courts held that the Act was to be construed strictly,[4] and another judge of the same courts expressed a similar view in an article.[5] The Supreme Court has, however, recently expressly rejected this view and held that the broad purpose of the Act to end sovereign immunity from suits is not to be frustrated by refinements of construction.[6] So far there is no pointer to the attitude of the English courts.

B. *Who are government servants?*

Both Acts seek to make the Government vicariously liable for the torts of its servants by analogy with the common-law rules of vicarious liability. The initial problem was to define the class of servants or agents for whose acts the Government would assume responsibility.

---

1 P. 5528, House of Lords, 13 Feb. 1947, i; cf. Viscount Jowitt, Hansard, vol. 146, col. 61.
2 *Rose* v. *Ford*, [1937] A.C. 826 at 846 (*per* Lord Wright).
3 See ch. VI.
4 *Maryland* v. *U.S.* (1946), 70 F. Supp. 982 at 984 (*per* Chesnut, J.); *Uarte* v. *U.S.* (1948), 7 F.R.D. 705.
5 Hon. R. M. Hulen, 'Suits on Tort Claims against the United States' in 7 *F.R.D.* (1948) 689 at 691; *ctra.* Note, 'Judicial Reception of the Federal Tort Claims Act' in 44 *Illinois L.R.* (1949) 212 at 220.
6 *U.S.* v. *Yellow Cab Co.* (1951), 340 U.S. 543; cf. *Brooks* v. *U.S.* (1949), 337 U.S. 49; *Larson* v. *Domestic and Foreign Corp.* (1949), 337 U.S. 682 at 703-4.

Section 2 (1) of the Crown Proceedings Act enacts:

Subject to the provisions of this Act, the Crown shall be subject to all those liabilities in tort to which, if it were a private person of full age and capacity, it would be subject: (*a*) in respect of torts committed by its servants or agents....

Section 2 (6) adds:

No proceedings shall lie against the Crown by virtue of this section in respect of any act, neglect or default of any officer of the Crown, unless that officer has been directly or indirectly appointed by the Crown and was at the material time paid in respect of his duties as an officer of the Crown wholly out of the Consolidated Fund of the United Kingdom, moneys provided by Parliament, the Road Fund, or any other Fund certified by the Treasury for the purposes of this subsection or was at the material time holding an office in respect of which the Treasury certify that the holder thereof would normally be so paid.

Section 38 (2) provides that 'officer' includes, in relation to the Crown, 'any servant of His Majesty, and accordingly (but without prejudice to the generality of the foregoing provision) includes a Minister of the Crown'.

English courts have long had difficulty in framing at common law a definition of a servant of the Crown. In particular, it has been difficult to determine which employees of public corporations are Crown servants.[1] Section 2 (1) leaves these problems unsolved. Even if the tortfeasor is a common-law servant, the Crown will not be liable for his torts unless he is also directly or indirectly appointed by the Crown and wholly paid out of the Consolidated or other funds set out in Section 2 (6).

The United States is liable only for the torts of 'any employee of the Government while acting within the scope of his office or employment'.[2] 'Employee of the Government' is defined as including 'officers or employees of any Federal agency, members of the military or naval forces of the United States, and persons acting on behalf of a Federal agency in an official capacity, temporarily or permanently in the service of the United States, whether with or without compensation'.[3] The two systems may be compared on several points of detail.

Military servants. The United States definition is vague, and, in the opinion of American writers, replete with 'latent ambiguities'.[4] The Supreme Court has held that two servicemen, injured while off duty by

---

1 W. H. Moore, 'Liability for Acts of Public Servants' in 23 *L.Q.R.* (1907) 12 at 23.
2 28 U.S.C. § 1346.   3 § 2671.
4 Gellhorn & Schenck, *op. cit.* 727.

the negligent driving of another serviceman, could sue the United States.[1] On the other hand, a serviceman has no remedy for injuries sustained while on service.[2] The reasons given for this denial are various: that the Act did not intend to compensate persons for whom adequate provision had otherwise been made; that to allow an action would disrupt service discipline; and that the relationship between Federal Government and soldier is different in kind from that found between Government and citizen.[3]

Australia has held that the Crown could not sue for the loss of services of a soldier because there is no master-servant relationship, the soldier only having a status compulsorily thrust on him.[4] English courts have not adjudicated on the liability of the Crown for soldiers under the Act, but it is submitted that for the following reasons the Crown is liable. First, although there can be no contract of service between Crown and soldier, a contract is unnecessary to establish the common-law relation of master and servant. Control is the test, and that the Crown certainly exercises over a soldier.[5] Secondly, the *raison d'être* of section 10 (1) (which prevents soldiers suing the Crown for (*inter alia*) the torts of other soldiers) is that otherwise the Crown would be liable for them under the Act. Thirdly, both Australia[6] and Canada[7] have dealt with actions against the Crown on the basis that there could be such a liability.

Public Corporations. In the nineteenth century there was a vast increase in the number of public bodies. Which of these bodies were to enjoy Crown immunities the courts found a most perplexing question. Even now no fixed criteria have been established. The matter is more complicated because the courts have had to consider it for various purposes— whether the body was exempt from rates;[8] whether it was liable for the torts of its servants;[9] did its servants make the Crown liable in contract;[10] were its servants public officers? Nor is it clear whether tests laid down are of general application or to be confined to the particular issue before the

1 *Brooks* v. *U.S.* (1949), 337 U.S. 49; *Santana* v. *U.S.* (1949), 175, F. 320; Note, 'Military Personnel and the Federal Tort Claims Act' in 58 *Yale L.J.* (1949) 615.

2 *Feres* v. *U.S.* (1951), 71 S.C. 153.

3 Cf. *U.S.* v. *Standard Oil Co.* (1947), 332 U.S. 301 at 305, holding that the United States has no action for the loss of services of a serviceman.

4 *The Commonwealth* v. *Quince* (1944), 68 C.L.R. 227. See Z. Cowen, 'The Consequences of *The Commonwealth* v. *Quince*' in 19 *Aust. L.J.* (1945) 2, for a powerful criticism of the decision.

5 Cf. Note, in 59 *Harvard L.R.* (1945), 137.

6 *Shaw Savill and Albion Co. Ltd.* v. *The Commonwealth* (1940), 66 C.L.R. 344.

7 *Rex* v. *Anthony*, [1946] 3 D.L.R. 577.

8 *Mersey Docks and Harbour Board Trustees* v. *Cameron* (1864), 11 H.L.C. 443.

9 *Gilbert* v. *Corporation of Trinity House* (1886), 17 Q.B.D. 795.

10 *Roper* v. *Public Works Commissioners*, [1915] 1 K.B. 45.

court.[1] The statutes setting up these bodies have been singularly unhelpful. To examine the large number of cases would be tedious, and the literature on the topic is voluminous.[2]

By way of summary, it may be said that there are several criteria which the courts have from time to time thought relevant. It is the function of the judge to select what he thinks are the dominant factors in the case before him. These criteria include the following: Is the body a substitute for private enterprise?[3] Has it independent discretionary powers?[4] Must it consult a Minister before it acts? Is it incorporated?[5] Is its function one which has been historically regarded as governmental?[6] Are its funds received from and to be returned to and audited by the Government? Is its authority general or local?[7] Is it a delegation by the Crown of its authority to individuals?[8] Is it a mere domestic body?[9]—Public interest on this point increased when it became governmental policy in 1945 to nationalise industries.[10] There was some apprehension whether nationalised industries possessed the immunities of the Crown.[11] These fears were thought by jurists to be groundless, because the corporations enjoyed some freedom from ministerial control and are clearly a substitute for private enterprise.[12] Nevertheless, there can be little doubt that the desire of the Government to avoid unpopularity on that account led to the passing of the Crown Proceedings Act.[13]

1 Cf. A. D. Hargreaves, 'The Crown as Litigant' in 122 *Nineteenth Century* (1937) 98; in *Victoria Railways Commissioners* v. *Herbert*, [1949] V.L.R. 211, it was suggested that a body may have the Crown priority in claiming debts and yet not be the Crown for the purpose of liability in tort.

2 E.g. Glanville Williams, *op. cit.* 21 *et seq.*; W. Sellar, 'Government Corporations' in 24 *Can. B.R.* (1946) 393, 489; Moore, *op. cit.* at 23; Note, 'Litigation with Nationalised Industry' in 96 *L.J.* (1946) 311; C. K. Allen, *Law and Orders*, 257; F. R. Scott, 'Administrative Law' in 26 *Can. B.R.* (1948) 268 at 284; W. Friedmann, 'Legal Status of Incorporated Authorities' in 22 *Aust. L.J.* (1948), 7.

3 *Mersey Docks and Harbour Board Trustees* v. *Gibbs* (1866), L.R. 1 H.L. 93 at 107 (*per* Blackburn J.).

4 *Metropolitan Meat Industry Board* v. *Sheedy*, [1927] A.C. 899 at 905 (*per* Viscount Haldane); Canadian courts have held this to be the determining test; e.g. *Bender* v. *Rex*, [1949] 2 D.L.R. 318; cf. *Yeats & Yeats* v. *Central Mortgage and Housing Corp.*, [1949] 2 W.W.R. 413.   5 *L.J. loc. cit.*

6 *Lane* v. *Cotton* (1701), 1 Raymond 646; *Bank voor Handel en Scheepvaart N.V.* v. *Slatford*, [1952] 2 All E.R. 956.

7 *Dunbar* v. *Guardians of Ardee Union* (1897), 2 Ir. Rep. 76.

8 *International Rly. Co.* v. *Niagara Parks Commission*, [1941] A.C. 328 at 342–3.

9 *Rowell* v. *Pratt*, [1936] 2 K.B. 226 at 242; reversed on other grounds, [1938] A.C. 101.   10 See *The Times* newspaper, 21 and 30 Sept. 1946.

11 Editorial, *The Times* newspaper, 30 Sept. 1946.

12 E.g. *L.J. loc. cit.*; Wade & Phillips, *Constitutional Law*, 309; Glanville Williams, *op. cit.* 26.

13 Sir Hartley Shawcross, Attorney-General, on 2nd R. Hansard, vol. 439, col. 1675 *et seq.* (4 July 1947).

In *Tamlin* v. *Hannaford*[1] the Court of Appeal recently held that the British Transport Commission was not an agent of the Crown. The court followed previous practice by not laying down any precise test to determine whether public corporations were Crown agents. Among the factors influencing the court were: that previously transport had been carried on by private enterprise; that execution could be levied against the Commission; the comparative looseness of ministerial control; the Act setting up the Commission neither relieved it of the liability of its predecessors, nor declared it to be the agent of the Crown; the Commission did not exercise the normal functions of a government department. The case has been criticised because there is inadequate examination of the important, and perhaps crucial, question—the degree of control exercised over the Commission by the Minister.[2]

The United States, too, has created government corporations, both during the War of 1914–18, as a means of prosecuting the war, and during the 'New Deal'.[3] The courts there have found difficulty in deciding whether these bodies could be sued if not made expressly suable by the creating statute.[4] It has been suggested that three separate bases of liability are deducible from the cases:[5] 'That it is inherent in the corporate form; that the corporation is engaged in a commercial activity, and that the government has given its consent.'

Recent decisions, and particularly the leading case, *Keifer & Keifer* v. *Reconstruction Finance Corporation*,[6] emphasise statutory intention.[7] There Frankfurter J. in an illuminating judgment said that 'the present climate of opinion. . .has brought governmental immunity from suit into disfavour'. Admitting that there was no clear evidence of legislative intent, he found that the present climate of opinion 'reveals a definite attitude on the part of Congress which should be given hospitable scope'. It is noteworthy that the Supreme Court took a very broad view of legislative intent, refusing to be bogged down in a morass of detailed tests.

1 [1950] 1 K.B. 18.
2 J. A. G. Griffith, 'Public Corporations as Crown Servants' in 12 *Mod. L.R.* (1949) 496; for the view that ministerial control of commercial corporations is strict see E. C. S. Wade, 'The Constitutional Aspect of the Public Corporation' in *Current Legal Problems*, II, 172 at 176 *et seq.*
3 For a full account, see J. A. McIntire, 'Government Corporations as Administrative Agencies' in 4 *Geo. Wash. L.R.* (1936) 161.
4 *Sloan Shipyards Corp.* v. *U.S. Shipping Board Emergency Fleet Corp.* (1922), 258 U.S. 549; *Panama Railroad Co.* v. *Bosse* (1919), 249 U.S. 41.
5 E. S. J. Thurston, 'Government Proprietary Corporations' in 21 *Virginia L.R.* (1935) 351, 465, cited Hart, *An Introduction to Administrative Law*, 586.
6 (1939), 306 U.S. 381.
7 Cf. Hart, *op. cit.* 586; McFarland & Vanderbilt, *Cases and Materials on Administrative Law*, 38.

That approach is more likely to lead to the desirable result of holding the corporation suable.

With the statutory recognition of governmental liability, the nature of the problem changes. It is not whether anybody is to be vicariously liable for the torts of the servant of the public body, but rather which body, the State or the public corporation, is to be sued. If the corporation is a servant of the Crown, then its servants will also be servants of the Crown, and the Crown Proceedings Act will apply; the rule that one servant of the Crown is not liable for the torts of another[1] will normally prevent an alternative action against the corporation from being brought. If the body is not an agent of the Crown, then the action will lie against it alone. To the extent that there is uncertainty whether particular corporations are Crown servants the Act fails to achieve its obvious purpose of ridding the plaintiff of technical difficulties when seeking redress for the torts of public servants. It is true that section 17 authorises the Treasury to publish a list of authorised government departments against which actions can be brought, and that such a list has been issued.[2] This device is, however, merely procedural, and is relevant only when it is established that the tort is that of a servant of the Crown.

Whether certain bodies are Crown servants is still unsettled. To consider merely the public corporations set up in the last few years,[3] it may be assumed, in view of *Tamlin* v. *Hannaford*, that the commercial corporations, the National Coal Board, the Gas Board, the Electricity Board and the Airways Corporations, like the Transport Commission are not Crown agents. But what of the social service corporations, the Regional Hospital Boards,[4] the Central Land Board, and the New Towns Development Corporations? They are not substitutes for private enterprise, and are subject to a considerable measure of ministerial control. It is an open

---

1 *Lane* v. *Cotton* (1701), 1 Raymond 646; *Whitfield* v. *Lord Le Despencer* (1778), 2 Cowp. 754; *Raleigh* v. *Goschen*, [1898] 1 Ch. 73; *Bainbridge* v. *Postmaster General*, [1906] 1 K.B. 178.

2 *Law Journal*, vol. 102 (1952) 600 has current list.

3 W. Friedmann, 'The New Public Corporations and the Law' in 10 *Mod. L.R.* (1947) 233, 377.

4 There seems a striking difference in the point of view of Denning L.J. and the Ministry of Health. The former in *Freedom under the Law*, 74, says of the Crown Proceedings Act that 'it certainly means' that the Crown is liable for the negligence of doctors and dentists under the National Health Scheme, whereas the Ministry in a memorandum (R.H.B. 49 (28) H.M.C. 49 (108) B.G. 49 (113) dated 15 Sept. 1949) states that actions must be brought against Regional Hospital Boards and that applications may be made to strike out proceedings brought against the Minister. *Cassidy* v. *Ministry of Health*, [1951] K.B. 343 is no authority on this point, because the Ministry was there liable as the successor to the previous hospital authority under s. 6 (2) of the National Health Service Act, 1946.

question whether they are servants of the Crown. Some of them, for instance, the Regional Hospital Boards, have been made suable by the express terms of the enabling statute. On the liability of others, such as the Central Land Board, the relevant statute is silent. A scholarly and detailed examination of the liability of the various social service corporations has been made elsewhere.[1] Only a few generalisations will be essayed here.

If the corporation is a servant of the Crown, and the statute does not expressly make it liable, an action lies, if at all, against the Crown. Even if there is express statutory liability, it is arguable that the effect of the maxim *Leges posteriores priores abrogant* is that the Crown Proceedings Act has repealed those provisions of earlier Acts.[2] If the corporation is not a servant of the Crown, then any proceedings under the Act will be struck out. Lord Atkin pointed out in *Mackenzie-Kennedy* v. *Air Council*[3] that an incorporated department could be sued for its torts. He showed that where the corporation committed the tort itself and not vicariously, for example, authorising the tort by a resolution of the corporation duly minuted, it was suable. It is submitted that the Crown Proceedings Act does not affect this liability. Clearly, there will be many cases where the plaintiff will have to join both the Attorney-General (in accordance with section 17 (3)) and the corporation as defendants, and ask for a *Bullock* order as to costs.

Nor is the Federal Tort Claims Act any less ambiguous. 'Federal agency' includes 'the executive departments and independent establishments of the United States, and corporations primarily acting as instrumentalities or agencies of the United States....'[4] The Supreme Court has recently held that the United States can be joined as co-defendant.[5] Before that, it seemed that the ambiguity might have more serious consequences in the United States because it was uncertain whether the United States could be joined as co-defendant with another tortfeasor.[6]

Section 2 (6).[7] Even if the officer is a servant of the Crown at common

---

1 Glanville Williams, *op. cit.* ch. II, *passim.* Cf. Friedmann, 'Public Welfare Offences, Statutory Duties and the Legal Status of the Crown' in 13 *Mod. L.R.* (1950) 24 at 29 *et seq.*; Griffith, 'Public Corporations as Crown Servants' in 9 *U. of Toronto L.J.* (1952) 169.

2 *Ibid.*   3 [1927] 2 K.B. 517 at 532–3.

4 §2671.

5 *U.S.* v. *Yellow Cab Co.* (1951), 340 U.S. 543.

6 *Bullock* v. *U.S.* (1947), 72 F.Supp. 445; *Dickens* v. *Jackson and U.S.* (1947), 71 F.Supp. 753; *Drummond* v. *U.S.* (1948), 78 F.Supp. 730; *ctra. Englehardt* v. *U.S.* (1947), 69 F.Supp. 451. See G. F. Foley & M. M. Heuser, 'The First Year under the Federal Tort Claims Act' in 9 *Fed. B.J.* (1947), 23 at 28–9; I. M. Gottlieb, 'Federal Tort Claims Act' in 35 *Georgetown L.J.* (1946), 1 at 36.

7 See p. 27 *supra* for text.

law, the Crown will not be liable for his torts unless he is appointed directly or indirectly by the Crown and paid out of the Consolidated or other specified funds.[1]

English law has borrowed from the United States[2] the principle that a body which appoints an official is not liable for his torts committed while carrying out duties imposed on him by law. Thus, in *Stanbury* v. *Exeter Corporation*,[3] the defendants, who had appointed a sanitary inspector, could not be sued for his tort in seizing sheep, when delegated legislation imposed the duty upon him directly. Similarly, *Fisher* v. *Oldham Corporation*[4] held that a local authority could not be sued for a wrongful arrest by a police officer appointed by its watch committee. The few jurists who have dealt with this seem to be of the opinion that those officers are never servants of the local authority, but may be servants of the Crown.[5] One learned writer, however, has suggested that 'in England the divided authority exercised over the police would probably in itself be sufficient...to prevent an action being maintained against any of those authorities as employer'.[6]

It is submitted that neither view is correct. The test is not the status of the officer, but the nature of the particular duty during the performance of which he commits the tort. The essence of vicarious liability is control by the master, who cannot exercise the control where the officer is carrying out a legal duty.[7] English authorities are few, but Commonwealth cases may be considered with profit. In *Enever* v. *Rex*[8] the High Court of Australia held that 'a constable when acting as a peace officer, is not exercising a delegated authority but an original authority, and the general law of agency has no application'. In South Africa, too, the employer was adjudged not liable for a false arrest by a constable because there was no master-servant relationship in respect of a duty which the law required him to perform.[9] The reason for the decision is brought out by *Union Government* v. *Thorne*, which, while approving the last two cases, held the State liable for the tort of a policeman when, in carrying out a particular task, he was obeying the orders of his employer, and was not

---

1 Both Acts make the State liable for the acts of a servant in what is normally paid employment, but neither Act imposes a liability for unpaid volunteers, e.g. fire-watchers.
2 Beven, *Negligence*, I, 410. Yet some of the United States are now liable for the torts of their police officers, e.g. *Egan* v. *State* (1938), 255. App. Div. 825 (New York).
3 [1905] 2 K.B. 838; cf. the Local Fuel Overseer, Coal Distribution Order, 1945 S.R.O. 1138.　　4 [1930] 2 K.B. 364.
5 Salmond, *Torts*, 89 n. (k); Clerk & Lindsell, *Torts*, 277.　　6 Moore, *op. cit.* 26.
7 Cf. Jennings, *The Law Relating to Local Authorities*, 25.
8 (1906), 3 C.L.R. 969.
9 *British South Africa Co.* v. *Crickmore*, [1921] A.D. 107.

executing a duty imposed on him by law.[1] Recently, courts in the Commonwealth, following these decisions, have held that a magistrate carrying out his judicial function,[2] and a legal aid officer performing legal aid duties thrust on him alone,[3] did not engage the State in liability.

The issue then is whether English law ought to impose a liability on either the Crown or the employer for these independent duties of public officers. It is submitted that it ought to do so. These officers are independent so that they may perform responsible tasks free from political ties; they are not given a compensating increase in salary in return for accepting sole liability for their torts. Their independence is given in the public interest: that same interest no less insistently demands that inappropriate rules of private law should not hinder the citizen seeking redress for wrongs inflicted on him by members of the Administration. Section 2 (3) seems to accept this in principle by providing:

> Where any functions are conferred or imposed upon an officer of the Crown as such either by any rule of the common law or by statute, and that officer commits a tort while performing or purporting to perform those functions, the liabilities of the Crown in respect of the tort shall be such as they would have been if those functions had been conferred or imposed solely by virtue of instructions lawfully given by the Crown.

Yet the definition of 'officer of the Crown' in section 2 (6) excludes police officers, since they are neither appointed nor paid by the Crown. It is not obvious of what use section 2 (3) is going to be in practice; although the failure to deal with the police was pointed out to the Attorney-General on the second reading.[4]

Other serious criticisms of section 2 (6) must be listed. First, it only applies to torts within section 2. When clause 3, dealing with patent and copyright infringements, was added while the Bill was in the House of Lords, the draftsmen apparently forgot to extend section 2 (6) to it. Secondly, the subsection prevents application of the principle that a master may be liable for the tort of a borrowed servant.[5] Thirdly, since

---

1 [1930] A.D. 47; *Sibiya v. Swart*, [1950] (4) S.A. 515; cf. May, *The South African Constitution*, 108.

2 *Swarts v. Minister of Justice*, [1941] A.D. 181 at 189 (*per* Feetham, J.): 'The statute thus has the effect of depriving the Crown of the power to direct or control the magistrate in carrying out the duty imposed upon him.'

3 *Field v. Nott* (1939), 62 C.L.R. 660.

4 Hansard, vol. 439, col. 1730 (3 July 1947). Is Hart, *The British Police*, 11, correct in saying: 'In such a case the police authority would in fact probably make the plaintiff an ex gratia payment' and is such a payment *ultra vires*?

5 *Ctra.* Canada; *Farthing v. Rex*, [1948] 1 D.L.R. 385.

it applies only to 'an act, neglect or default of an officer of the Crown' it would seem that it does not apply to section 2 (1) (*b*) and (*c*) where the liability is that of the Crown itself not arising out of vicarious liability for the act of the officer. Fourthly, the effect of section 38 (2) and of section 40 (2) (*d*) is that the Crown is liable for the acts of independent contractors whenever a private person would be so liable, even though the independent contractor is not paid and appointed by it.[1] Fifthly, even if a public corporation is a servant of the Crown and not suable in tort, the Crown also cannot be sued if the corporation has its own stock from which fund it pays its staff.[2] Sixthly, this is an addition to those anomalous cases where it is material to define the boundaries between contract and tort.[3]

Before the Act the Crown could be sued by petition of right for detinue and nuisance because they were torts affecting property. Section 1 provides that where a petition of right was formerly available 'the claim may be enforced as of right'. Section 2 need not be invoked for these torts, and the definition of officer in section 2 (6) is inapplicable. Section 1 also preserves existing statutory rights to sue, and since the Ministry of Transport was suable in tort by the Ministry of Transport Act 1919,[4] actions in respect of those functions which it possessed at the date of the Crown Proceedings Act are unaffected by section 2 (6).[5]

Neither Act, then, has a sharp definition of those servants for whose acts it is to be liable in tort. Each purports to retain the common-law definition of a servant or agent. That is unsatisfactory in the case of public corporations. It is suggested that the initial mistake was the failure of the various creating statutes to state specifically whether the body created was to be treated as the State. Any future Acts creating public corporations should be explicit on this. The two Acts should themselves have declared which of the existing public bodies were agents of the Government. The United States has not made any further restriction on the definition of 'servant'. English law should leave the definition similarly unrestricted by repealing section 2 (6), which serves no worthwhile purpose. These

---

1 There was a serious omission in the United States Act as originally enacted. There was no mention of independent contractors, and only if 'employee' included them could the United States have been liable. The Act, as revised, excludes 'any contractor with the United States'. § 2671.

2 See Friedmann, 10 *Mod. L.R.* (1947) 249–51.

3 Presumably, a remedy might sometime be denied in such cases as *Bowmakers Ltd.* v. *Barnet Instruments Ltd.*, [1945] K.B. 65; cf. C. J. Hamson, 'Illegal Contracts and Limited Interests' in 10 *Camb. L.J.* (1949) 65.

4 9 and 10 Geo. V, c. 50.

5 Glanville Williams, *op. cit.* 42.

reforms, together with the extension of section 2 (3) to all public officers, would remove many of the present anomalies and injustices.

C. *Vicarious Liability*

'The liability of a body corporate is...in all cases a vicarious liability for the acts of other persons', says Salmond.[1] Is a corporation only liable when its servant has committed a tort? Or does the corporation owe a duty entirely separate from that of the servant, for breach of which alone it is liable? On the answer to these questions the interpretation of both Acts depends.

It is usually said that a master is vicariously liable for the torts of his servants. So the English Act makes the Crown liable for 'torts committed by its servants or agents',[2] and the United States is liable for the 'negligent or wrongful act or omission of any employee'.[3] There have been recent denials that this is the true basis of a master's liability. Glanville Williams argues:[4]

It is the master who owes a duty to the plaintiff, and who breaks it as a result of the acts and mental states of his servant. In discussing the liability of the master it is not necessary to consider whether the servant owes a duty to the plaintiff or has committed a tort.

It is submitted, however, that a master may be liable in two different ways. First, he may be vicariously liable because his servant has committed an unlawful act in the course of his employment. Secondly, in some circumstances the master but not the servant owes a duty, or the master owes a duty different from that of the servant. The master is liable for not discharging, either himself or through other agencies, his own duty.[5]

It is on *Twine* v. *Bean's Express Ltd.*[6] that Glanville Williams bases his opinion. In that case the driver of a van, contrary to his employer's instructions, carried the plaintiff as a passenger. The latter was killed owing to the negligent driving of the servant, and his personal representatives sued the employers. Uthwatt J. held that the servant's being liable did not in itself make the employers liable. Their duty, which was merely that of an occupier of property towards a trespasser, had not been broken. It is arguable, therefore, that Uthwatt J. did not base his decision on vicarious liability, but on the nature of the duty of occupiers of property.

---

1 Salmond, *Torts*, 54; *ctra.* Winfield, *Tort*, 107.
2 S. 2 (1) (a).   3 §1346.
4 *Op. cit.* at 43. Cf. J. P. Lawton, 'Vicarious Liability of Hospital Authorities' in 10 *Mod. L.R.* (1947) 425.
5 Cf. Jennings, *op. cit.* 23; Glanville Williams seems to recognise this distinction at 41.   6 [1946] 1 All E.R. 202.

In any event, there is little justification for relying on his dicta as authority for the principle laid down by Glanville Williams, when it is noted that the case went to the Court of Appeal.[1] There (not cited by Glanville Williams) Lord Greene M.R. confirmed that the employers were not liable, but on the ground that the servant was acting outside the scope of his employment and therefore there could be no vicarious liability. Uthwatt J.'s reasoning was not followed.

Perhaps the clearest judicial utterance on this twofold liability is found in a Canadian decision:[2]

> There may be a direct duty on the master toward the third person, with the servant the instrument for its performance. The failure on the part of the servant constitutes a breach of the master's duty for which he must answer as for his own wrong; but it may also raise a liability on the servant toward the third person by reason of which the master becomes liable in a new aspect. The latter would result from the rule of *respondeat superior*; the former does not.

The Crown Proceedings Act, unlike the Bill of 1927, and perhaps following The Remedy against the Crown as Occupier Bill, 1947, introduced by Viscount Simon, recognised this separate liability of the Crown itself by adding further subsections which make the Crown liable for breach of the duties of an employer to employees[3] and for breach of 'the duties attaching at common law to the ownership, occupation, possession or control of property'.[4] The State of New York has also perceived the distinction and provided for it in the Court of Claims Act, 1939.[5] Unfortunately, the United States is made liable only for the 'negligent or wrongful act or omission of any employee' and it is difficult to see how it can incur non-vicarious liabilities.

It remains to consider the following proviso to section 2 (1):

> Provided that no proceedings shall lie against the Crown by virtue of paragraph (a) of this sub-section in respect of any act or omission of a servant or agent of the Crown unless the act or omission would apart from the provisions of this Act have given rise to a cause of action in tort against that servant or agent or his estate.

I have suggested elsewhere[6] that the purpose of this proviso is to prevent the Crown from being made liable where act of State would have been a defence to the servant. This should be a warning to legislative draftsmen

---

1 (1946), 175 L.T. 131; cf. *Conway* v. *George Wimpey & Co. Ltd.*, [1951] 2 K.B. 266; *Young* v. *Edward Box & Co.*, [1951] 1 T.L.R. 789.
2 *Rex* v. *Anthony*, [1946] 3 D.L.R. 577 at 585 (*per* Rand J.).
3 S. 2 (1) (b).   4 S. 2 (1) (c).   5 S. 8 N.Y. Laws 1939, c. 860.
6 'The Crown Proceedings Act' in 11 *Mod. L.R.* (1948) 129.

not to borrow from another Bill. The 1927 Bill mentioned 'act neglect or default'[1] not 'tort' of the servant, and the proviso contained in the Bill might have been necessary to exempt the Crown from liability for act of State.[2] But, since the 1947 Act only renders the Crown liable for a servant's 'tort' the Crown cannot be liable for any act of the servant to which act of State would be a defence. There would then be no 'tort'. The 1927 Bill recognised no liability of the Crown other than a vicarious one. Perhaps the draftsmen of the 1947 Act thought that they could safely repeat the proviso when they were confining its operation to the paragraph dealing with vicarious liability. In that they were mistaken. Consider the case of a husband-servant negligently injuring his wife. The wife cannot sue the husband,[3] but if *Smith* v. *Moss*[4] is rightly decided,[5] she can sue his employer. This proviso exempts the Crown from an employer's liability in such a case. On the other hand, the United States is liable if its servant in the course of his employment injures the servant's spouse.

To the extent that section 2 (1) (c) does not include all cases of direct duty owed by the Crown then it also must be criticised. It is suggested that it is not sufficiently all-embracing. It would not, for instance, cover the situation in *Collins* v. *Hertfordshire C.C.*[6] A patient having died because he had been given the wrong drug, Hilbery J. held that it was sufficient to hold the hospital liable for permitting a dangerous system; whether it was vicariously liable for the negligence of its staff was a separate possible head of liability.[7] The failure of the master to provide an efficient system of drug administration does not seem to arise from a duty attaching to the control of property.

---

1 Cl. 11.
2 For a severe though not wholly justified criticism, see J. W. Gordon, 'The Crown as Litigant' in 45 L.Q.R. (1929) 186.
3 *Tinkley* v. *Tinkley* (1909), 25 T.L.R. 264.
4 [1940] 1 K.B. 424; cf. *Broom* v. *Morgan*, [1952] 2 All E.R. 1007.
5 I believe that the decision is sound, not for the reason given by Glanville Williams, *op. cit.* 43, that the duty is that of the master, but for the reasons given by Cardozo J. in *Schubert* v. *Schubert Wagon Co.* (1928), 249 N.Y. 253: 'The statement sometimes made that it [the master's liability] is derivative and secondary means this and nothing more, that at times the fault of the actor will fix the quality of the act. Illegality established, liability ensues. The defendant, to make out a defence, is thus driven to maintain that the act, however negligent, was none the less lawful because committed by a husband upon the person of his wife. This is to pervert the meaning and effect of the disability that has its origin in marital identity. A trespass, negligent or wilful, does not cease to be an unlawful act though the law exempts the husband from liability for the damage.' Cf. Jacobs, *Cases and Materials on Domestic Relations*, 615 *et seq.* For another failure in recent legislation to cover this type of liability, see the definition of 'fault' in s. 4 of the Law Reform (Contributory Negligence) Act, 1945; Glanville Williams, *Joint Torts and Contributory Negligence*, §76.
6 [1947] K.B. 598.   7 At 614.

D. *Acts done with Statutory Authority*

The United States is not liable for 'any claim based upon an act or omission of an employee of the Government, exercising due care, in the execution of a statute or regulation, whether or not such statute or regulation be valid'.[1] Here, as in the English Act, the concept of 'property' dominates so as to break the smooth symmetrical lines of the statute. Many interferences with property are within this exception. Nevertheless there is nothing to prevent an action being brought under the Tucker Act if 'taking' can be proved.[2]

On this the English Act is silent so that the common-law rules of statutory authority will prevent the Crown from being liable for doing that which a statute has authorised it to do. This is satisfactory, and there seems no need to introduce an express statutory provision. In the United States, only a negligent execution of a statutory power is tortious— although the range of acts done 'in the execution of a statute or regulation' will be only defined with difficulty by the courts.

One difference may be noted. Not wishing to deprive the Government of a defence if the statute should be found unconstitutional, Congress has exempted the United States from liability 'whether or not such statute or regulation be valid'. By contrast, if delegated legislation on which an officer of the Crown relied were *ultra vires*, then statutory authority would be no defence. It is suggested that the latter rule is most desirable, and, although delegated legislation is not so extensive in the United States as in the United Kingdom, that justice would be done there, too, if the extension were limited to provisions invalid on constitutional grounds.

E. *Breach of Statutory Duty*

At common law a person to whom a statutory duty is owed, and who suffers damage through breach of this duty, may be able to sue for damages. Section 2 (2) extends this liability to the Crown, but only where the statutory duty 'is binding upon persons other than the Crown and its officers'. It is submitted that there is no justification for this last requirement. The Treasury Solicitor, in the course of a not very convincing apologia for the Act, argued:[3]

...there are many Acts of Parliament which impose general duties upon particular Ministers, e.g. it is the duty of the Minister of Education to provide the education of the people of England and Wales. Clearly, if

---

1 §2680.　　　　　2 See p. 123 *infra*.
3 Sir Thomas Barnes, 'The Crown Proceedings Act 1947' in 26 *Can. B.R.* (1948) 387 at 391.

the Minister fails to perform this duty, he should be answerable in Parliament and not elsewhere.

This argument is hardly worth serious consideration, because the action lies only if the duty is owed to the plaintiff—it does not lie for breach of a public duty, such as the one instanced above. This principle is confirmed in the subsection by the declaration that the Crown shall only be liable for breach of statutory duty when a private person would be so liable. Nor does there seem to be adequate foundation for the argument of another writer that the words are required to prevent the creation of 'a new department of tort by turning constitutional and administrative law into a system of duties owed to individuals'.[1] If a statutory duty is imposed on public authorities other than the Crown and on no other persons, then there may be an action for breach of it. That rule is satisfactory: it gives to the courts a latitude in statutory interpretation which enables them to maintain a fair balance between the Administration and the citizen. Why should the Crown as an administrative unit be treated differently from other public bodies? Until our law relating to public authorities is homogeneous, it will remain a legitimate target for volleys of criticism. The United States Act is no better: for it denies liability for failure on the part of a Federal agency or employee to perform a duty.[2]

F. *Discretionary Acts*

The United States is not liable for 'any claim...based upon the exercise or performance or the failure to exercise or perform a discretionary function or duty on the part of a Federal agency or an employee of the Government whether or not the discretion involved be abused'.[3] Hence, the United States was not liable when War Department engineers, acting under general authority from Congress to develop the Missouri River, constructed dykes which flooded the plaintiff's land.[4] The section is so widely drawn that it is unnecessary to exclude expressly liability for judicial acts.[5]

England has no comparable statutory provision. Since at common law a public officer is not liable, in the absence of negligence causing additional damage, for the exercise of a discretion[6] the Crown also seems not liable.[7]

---

1 Glanville Williams, *op. cit.* 48.   2 §2680.   3 *Ibid.*
4 *Thomas* v. *U.S.* (1949), 81 F.Supp. 881; cf. *Sickman* v. *U.S.* (1950), 184 F. 2nd 616.
5 L. Kaminski, 'Torts—Application of Discretionary Function Exception of Federal Tort Claims Act' in 36 *Marquette L.R.* (1952) 88.
6 *East Suffolk Rivers Catchment Board* v. *Kent*, [1941] A.C. 74.
7 Denning, *op. cit.* 74, thinks it an open question whether the Crown would be liable 'if its officers exercise their powers oppressively or spitefully'.

G. *Judicial Acts*

Neither in English nor in American law is a judge liable for acts done in the performance of his duties.[1] This is because it is contrary to public policy that litigants should reopen suits by bringing personal actions against deciding them. The State has an interest in the ending of litigation. At the same time a judge sued in defamation for words spoken in court has a defence of absolute privilege. This latter immunity seems to rest on a basis different from the *chose jugée* or *res judicata* mentioned above. Its *raison d'être* is that the State interest in justice being done is best furthered if all the participants are able to speak freely without fear of the consequences. Separate though these two rules appear to be, they have so far in the cases been treated as identical. It is, indeed, an illustration of that fallacy of the logical form, the legal category of concealed multiple reference.[2] In any event, several ambiguities remain. Holdsworth has shown[3] how the rule at first applied only to courts of record, and how it is doubtful whether the later extension to inferior courts applies if there is not an error of law, but an excess of jurisdiction.[4]

The problem that has arisen in this century is whether the judges of the many and diverse administrative tribunals are also protected. Are they 'judicial'? The decisions are conflicting, and from them no consistent principle can be deduced. It has been held that a tribunal hearing applications for deferment from military service was judicial, Sankey J. suggesting that the test was 'Does it act in a manner similar to a court of justice?'.[5] Yet licensing justices are not judicial,[6] nor, according to *Collins* v. *Henry Whiteway & Co.*,[7] was a court of referees under the Employment Insurance Acts, because it was created 'for the purpose of deciding claims made upon the insurance funds. It is not a body deciding between parties, nor does its decision affect criminally or otherwise the status of an individual.' It has also been suggested that the question is whether the acts need to be performed in a court or whether merely a judicial mind is required, and that to extend the immunity to the latter category of cases would be contrary to public policy. The application of this test is difficult if not impossible, for surely the only cases which need be heard in court are those required by statute to be so heard, whereupon there remains the

1 Winfield, *The Present Law of Abuse of Legal Procedure*, ch. VII.
2 Stone, *The Province and Function of Law*, 174.
3 'Immunity for Judicial Acts', in *J.S.P.T.L.* (1924) 17.
4 Cf. E. G. Jennings, 'Tort Liability of Administrative Officers', in 21 *Minn. L.R.* (1937) 263, an excellent account of the law in the United States.
5 *Co-partnership Farms* v. *Harvey-Smith*, [1918] 2 K.B. 405.
6 *Attwood* v. *Chapman*, [1914] 3 K.B. 275.
7 [1927] 2 K.B. 378 at 383 (*per* Horridge J.).

unanswered question, 'What is a court?' Well might a judge in a court of first instance, bound by *Collins* v. *Henry Whiteway & Co.*, think the matter one fit for further consideration by the Court of Appeal.[1] A recognition of the true basis of this immunity would surely lead to its extension to administrative tribunals, for there is an interest in the termination of such hearings and in the rendering of full justice there.

Definitions of 'judicial' for other purposes must be looked at circumspectly if analogies for judicial immunity are sought. Newspaper reports of 'judicial' proceedings are privileged, it is suggested, because there is a public interest in the publication.[2] Certiorari lies to quash 'judicial' proceedings. Here, because the High Court wants to exercise as wide a control as possible, a body is 'judicial' if it is 'any body of persons having legal authority to determine questions affecting the rights of subjects, and having the duty to act judicially'.[3]

Faced with these various meanings of 'judicial',[4] one turns to section 2 (5):

No proceedings shall lie against the Crown by virtue of this section in respect of anything done or omitted to be done by any person while discharging or purporting to discharge any responsibilities of a judicial nature vested in him. . . .

Since the judge is himself immune from suit and section 2 merely makes the Crown vicariously liable for the torts of its servants, it is not obvious what is the purpose of the subsection.[5] There is a presumption against attaching no meaning to a statute; so one might argue that, taking account of the doubt whether administrative judges are immune, it absolves the Crown from liability for their torts.[6] Further, it might be intended to prevent actions against the Crown for acts of judges of inferior courts outside their jurisdiction.

The effect on cases like *Warne* v. *Varley*[7] must also be estimated. There a public officer, authorised at his discretion to seize undried leather, mistakenly seized leather later found by a jury to be dry, and was held to

---

1 *Mason* v. *Brewis Bros.*, [1938] 2 All E.R. 420.

2 *Perera* v. *Peiris*, [1949] A.C. 1 at 20 (*per* Lord Uthwatt).

3 *Rex* v. *Electricity Commissioners, ex parte London Electricity Joint Committee* (1920) *Ltd.*, [1924] 1 K.B. 171 at 205 (*per* Atkin L.J.).

4 For a detailed account, see J. Finkelman, 'Separation of Powers: A Study in Administrative Law' in 1 *U.T.L.J.* (1935–6) 313; J. Willis, 'Three Approaches to Administrative Law: the Judicial, the Conceptual, and the Functional', *ibid.* 53. Cf. H. R. W. Wade, 'Quasi-Judicial and its Background' in 10 *Camb. L.J.* (1949) 216 at 219 n.   5 Cf. Clerk & Lindsell, *op. cit.* 1st Supp. 2.

6 *Ctra.* Denning, *op. cit.* 74: 'It may mean that if the inspectors, who hold local inquiries, should make defamatory statements the State may be liable in damages for slander.'   7 (1795), 6 T.R. 443.

be a trespasser. Conscious of the harshness of such a rule, particularly where the officer acted reasonably,[1] American courts have in such cases held that the act was judicial and therefore not tortious.[2] English courts have not been equally zealous in protecting the official;[3] but might not section 2 (5) exempt the Crown from liability if the officer is 'purporting to discharge' such functions, even though the officer himself is liable in accordance with *Warne* v. *Varley*? The United States would be exempt even if the exercise of the discretion were not judicial. If, as seems possible, there are cases where the officer but not the Crown is liable for what the former does in the discharge of his duties, then this is surely a matter for further reform.

Equally uncertain is the reason for section 2 (5). The Treasury Solicitor says of it:[4]

...the Crown ought not to interfere in the manner in which judicial functions are exercised.... The basis of a master's vicarious liability is the power of the master to control and direct the servant.

Yet why should the private-law concept of vicarious liability necessarily govern all questions of Crown liability for its servants, and how does the Treasury Solicitor explain away section 2 (3) which is the very negation of his argument? Moreover, the Crown controls the appointment, and, subject to some limitations in the case of High Court judges, the dismissal of these 'judicial' officers.

The Act, of course, completely ignores the fact that the personal immunity of a judicial officer is not necessarily inconsistent with the acceptance by the State of the duty to compensate those who suffer loss unjustly at the hands of the judicial machine, even if the loss has not been caused by the fault of any employee of the Crown. When Adolf Beck was sent to prison for a crime which he did not commit, and released with a free pardon ten years later,[5] surely his right to compensation should not have depended on the passing of a private Act for his benefit.[6] The same is true of Oscar Slater who served nineteen years of a life sentence (a commuted death sentence) for a murder of which he was innocent.[7]

1 Gellhorn, *Administrative Law*, 297 *et seq.*
2 E.g. *Fath* v. *Koeppel* (1888), 72 Wis. 289.
3 Many English statutes exempt the official from liability, but impose on the Crown a duty to pay compensation; e.g. Public Health Act, 1936, Pts. III, V and XII, Food and Drugs Act, 1938, Pt. VI.
4 Barnes, *op. cit.* at 391.   5 See Watson, *Trial of Adolf Beck.*
6 Parliamentary Papers (1905), vol. 62, Cmd. 2315.
7 For an account of some sixty-five cases of this type in Europe and the United States, see Borchard, *Convicting the Innocent, passim.* Cf. Hansard, vol. 449, 5 s. cols. 1941–4 (Mr Paget K.C.).

No one would saddle the trial judge with pecuniary liability, but that the convicted innocent should still be remediless is deplorable.

Over a hundred years ago Bentham[1] and Romilly[2] wrote tracts in protest at this long standing injustice. Meanwhile, the rest of the civilised world affords a remedy, most European countries having devised one in the nineteenth century.[3] Due mainly to a campaign fanned by the writings of Borchard, the United States, too, now provides a remedy by a 1938 statute, which lays down:[4]

Any person who, having been convicted of any crime or offense against the United States and having been sentenced to imprisonment and having served all or any part of his sentence, shall hereafter, on appeal or on a new trial or rehearing, be found not guilty of the crime of which he was convicted, or shall hereafter receive a pardon on the ground of innocence, if it shall appear that such person did not commit any of the acts with which he was charged or that his conduct in connection with such charge did not constitute a crime or offense against the United States...and that he has not, either intentionally or by wilful misconduct, or negligence, contributed to bring about his arrest or conviction, may,... maintain suit against the United States in the Court of Claims for damages sustained by him as a result of such conviction and imprisonment.

Several of the United States have followed this Federal lead.[5] The juristic basis for the liability seems to be liability for risk. Just as the Crown may be sued under *Rylands* v. *Fletcher* for damage caused without negligence, so here could the Crown accept liability. The reasonable safeguards of the United States legislation, a maximum liability of five thousand dollars, liability for pecuniary damage only, and 'clean hands' of the plaintiff, could be adopted in England too.[6]

Some European countries have gone further in providing damages for detention preceding acquittal on first hearing[7] or for reduced sentences on appeal.[8] Without proposing that extended liability, one may legitimately demand reform of the present position in England, where freedom of property seems so much better protected at the hands of the State than freedom of the person.

---

1 Bentham, *Traité de Législation Civile et Pénale*, vol. II, 378.
2 Romilly, *Memoirs*, II, 245–7.
3 E.g. Sweden (1886), Denmark (1888), France (1895), Belgium (1894).
4 52 Stat. 438.
5 E.g. Wisconsin, North Dakota, California.
6 For a comprehensive description of the Act, see E. M. Borchard, 'State Indemnity for Errors' in 21 *Boston U.L.R.* (1941) 201.
7 E.g. Holland, Norway.   8 Denmark, Mexico.

H. *Execution of Judicial Process*

Most jurisdictions not merely exempt the judge from liability for his judicial acts but also exempt officials from liability for acts done in the execution of judicial process. The two should not, however, be equated, for different policy considerations apply. A court officer is protected by statute when seizing property by way of execution, but this is not because there is a public interest in making the legality of his authority from the Court outside the scope of judicial review. On the contrary, the victim of an illegal execution can raise in court that illegality.[1] The official is protected because he, a ministerial officer carrying out his duty, is entitled to rely on what seems on its face to be a valid authorisation—to hold otherwise would be to subject him to a liability inconsistent with the nature of his job and his probable financial resources.

This protection is, then, one which should be personal to the official. Nevertheless, the Crown also has that immunity by that same section 2 (5) 'in respect of anything done or omitted to be done by any person while discharging or purporting to discharge any responsibilities... which he has in connection with the execution of judicial process'. The excuse that the Crown would not wish to interfere with those duties seems even flimsier here. Nor has the subsection the compensating virtue of clarity. Is arrest or imprisonment 'the execution of judicial process'?[2]

The only comparable provision in the United States act is an innocuous one. The act does not apply to 'any claim arising in respect of... the detention of any goods or merchandise by any officer of customs or excise or any other law-enforcement officer', an exemption of little importance because there is a separate statutory means of redress.

I. *Legislative Acts*

When a statute provided compensation there was a right to claim either by petition of right or under the Tucker Act. This right is unaffected, and a plaintiff under the Crown Proceedings Act would rely not on section 2 but on section 1. Expropriating statutes usually provide a compensation,[3] but in the United States there would be a constitutional right to it even if the statute did not provide it.[4]

1 Halsbury, *op. cit.* x, 476.
2 One can hardly, as does Bickford Smith, *op. cit.* 63, rely on the interpretation of 'process' contained in the definition section of the Summary Jurisdiction (Process) Act, 1881 !
3 E.g. the British statutes nationalising industries, 1945–8; see W. Friedmann, 'The New Public Corporations and the Law' in 10 *Mod. L.R.* (1947) 233, 377.
4 See ch. IV *infra*.

A person injured by an English legislative Act which affords no compensation is without remedy.[1] A United States victim is in no better case, if the statute does not expropriate.

J. *Post Office*

Section 1346 of the Federal Tort Claims Act excepts 'any claim arising out of the loss, miscarriage, or negligent transmission of letters or postal matter'. There is a similar provision in section 9 (1) of the English Act, which compares unfavourably with its American counterpart in that it adds: '...nor shall any officer of the Crown be subject, except at the suit of the Crown, to any such civil liability for any of the matters aforesaid'.[2] That a person witnessing his letter being torn to pieces by the postmaster should not even have a remedy against the postmaster has been the subject of protest by Viscount Simon in Parliament.[3] The latter Act also provides for the first time that a person registering a postal packet shall have a cause of action against the Government for the market but not the replacement value, subject to the maximum amounts laid down in Post Office regulations.[4] Loss or damage to a postal packet is presumed to be due to a wrongful act or default, until the Crown proves the contrary. Since Congress justified the exception by stressing the ease with which postal matter is registrable,[5] it is to be regretted that the opportunity was not taken to impose a clear-cut liability for registered mail.

The English exemption extends also to 'anything done or omitted to be done in relation to a telephonic communication by any person while so employed'.[6] In the United States the telephone service is not operated by the Government.

K. *Armed Forces*

Section 10 prevents a member of the armed forces from suing either the Crown or another member of the armed forces for personal injury suffered by him while on duty, or, even if not on duty, while on premises for the time being used for the purposes of the armed forces when the alleged tort has been committed by a member of the armed forces while on

---

1 *The North Charterland Exploration Co.* (1910) Ltd. v. *Rex*, [1931] 1 Ch. 169 at 189.

2 The common-law rule, laid down in *The Winkfield*, [1902] P. 42 that the bailee of mails may recover the whole value of lost mails still applies, so that the Crown as bailee could sue its servant for his negligence.

3 Hansard, vol. 146 (1947), col. 76; *ctra.* the Attorney-General, Hansard, vol. 439, (1947), col. 2631.   4 S. 9 (2).

5 Hearings before the Senate Committee on the Judiciary on S. 2690, 76th Cong. 3rd Sess. (1940), 38.

6 The Government paid £20 *ex gratia* to the Metropolitan Police Rugby Club when a delayed telegram caused them expense—Hansard, 497 H.C. 5 s. col. 2320.

duty. There is a similar immunity if death or personal injuries are caused in consequence of the condition of such premises or equipment or supplies. In short, where a member of the armed forces is injured in circumstances which would be attributable to service for purposes of pensions, he may sue neither the Crown nor the member of the armed forces.

The section refers to 'death or personal injury' and to no other heads of damage. This expression, no novel one in legislation, has been interpreted in the case of the Workmen's Compensation Acts to extend to nervous shock.[1] On the other hand, if the tort is one which in its nature can hardly result in personal injury, for example, defamation, the right to sue both the Crown and the member of the armed forces responsible is unaffected. Presumably, if a soldier is the victim of a tort involving personal injury he can still sue for other heads of damage such as damage to property arising out of the same tort.

The appropriate service department is authorised to issue a conclusive certificate, if satisfied that it is the fact, certifying whether a person was or was not on duty,[2] or whether premises were or were not used for the purposes of the armed forces. In the absence of a certificate, the court decides the issue, and it always decides whether 'the act or omission was not connected with the execution of his duties' as a member of those forces for the purposes of the proviso to section 10 (1).[3]

There seem to be several objections to the section. To absolve the officer from liability is contrary to the Dicey tradition of individual responsibility. The reply that it 'was clearly necessary in order to avoid a return to the practice of suing a servant of the Crown in the expectation that the Crown would "stand behind" him'[4] prompts the rejoinder that the Act has done that elsewhere. A joint tortfeasor with the Crown will be responsible for the whole of the damages awarded to a soldier without a right of contribution. The principle of the section that a soldier must rely on his pension rights is subject to the following criticisms. A soldier never has a legal right to a pension.[5] Secondly, the provision compares unfavourably with the Law Reform (Personal Injuries) Act, 1948,[6] whereby a civilian

1 *Yates* v. *South Kirkby Collieries Ltd.*, [1910] 2 K.B. 538; *ex parte Haines*, [1945] K.B. 183; cf. *Drinkwater* v. *Kimber*, [1951] 2 All E.R. 713.

2 For a discussion of some of the problems raised by this section, see Note, 'The New Legal Liability in Tort and Contract' in *Scottish L.R.* (1948) 81 at 88.

3 The member of the armed forces is then personally liable.

4 Bickford Smith, *op. cit.* 31.

5 Nevertheless, in *Romeo Meloche* v. *Rex*, [1948] Ex. C.R. 321 a soldier could not recover from the Crown because of the principle of statutory interpretation that a special statutory remedy (pension) excludes a general one. *Sed quaere*. Disapproved and not followed in *Oakes* v. *Rex*, [1951] 3 D.L.R. 442.

6 11 & 12 Geo. VI, c. 41 S. 2 (1).

entitled to social insurance benefits may still recover damages subject only to a maximum deduction of one half the value of those benefits received during a period of five years.

The United States has accepted a larger degree of responsibility for the acts of the armed forces than has the British Government. True, the former exempts 'any claim arising out of the combatant activities of the military or naval forces, or the Coast Guard, during time of war',[1] but in administrative regulations and interpretations 'combatant activity' has been restrictively interpreted so as not to extend to practice manœuvres or to any operations not directly connected with engaging the enemy. That exemption apart, the United States accepts liability for acts of military and naval personnel performed 'in line of duty'.[2] These provisions seem much to be preferred to their English counterpart.

L. *Prerogative and Statutory Powers*

Section 11 (1) provides that nothing in Part 1 of the Act shall extinguish or abridge the prerogative or statutory powers of the Crown. Section 11 (2) authorises the appropriate service department to furnish a conclusive certificate to the effect that an act was necessary for any purpose mentioned in section 11 (1) where 'it is material to determine whether anything was properly done or omitted to be done in the exercise of the prerogative'. Despite the certificate, the courts will decide whether any particular prerogative has any legal existence or not. Although both statutory and prerogative powers are saved by the section, a conclusive certificate cannot be given where it is material to determine whether anything was done in the exercise of a statutory as distinct from a prerogative power.

The reason for the section is obscure, and it seems to make little change in the law. Not unexpectedly, there is no like provision in the Federal Tort Claims Act.

M. *Foreign Torts and Aliens*

The Federal Tort Claims Act excepts 'any claim arising in a foreign country'.[3] Furthermore, it is the legislative practice of the United States

---

1 §2680.
2 In *Campbell* v. *U.S.* (1948), 75 F. Supp. 181, soldiers who knocked down a woman while they were running for a troop train were held to be 'in line of duty'; *Rutherford* v. *U.S.* (1947), 73 F. Supp. 867; cf. *Morin* v. *Rex*, [1949] Ex. C.R. 235 where the Crown was held liable for injuries to spectators at a wrestling bout organised by the armed services when the inefficient control of military policemen led to a *mêlée*.
3 §2676.

to deny aliens an action against it unless the country of that alien grants reciprocal rights to United States citizens as plaintiffs.[1]

The English Act is silent on both points, and English commentators on it have assumed that there are no such restrictions.[2] Since section 1 only confers a right of action where previously a petition of right lay it is submitted with respect that those restrictions (if any) which were imposed on the right of an alien to proceed by petition of right remain for the purposes of this section. Whether at common law an alien could proceed by petition of right does not seem to have been the subject of an authoritative decision, and the text-book writers offer no clear guidance. Fitzherbert[3] and Brooke[4] accord the right to 'persons', whereas Staunford,[5] Blackstone[6] and Chitty[7] limit it to 'subjects'. Section 7 of the Petitions of Right Act 1860 uses the word 'subject'. Robertson[8] believes that an alien may sue and Clode[9] thinks it doubtful.

Aliens have sometimes used the petition of right since 1860[10] but their right to do so does not seem to have been challenged.[11] In two Commonwealth cases, however, the point has been the subject of decision.[12] In each it was decided that 'subject' connoted a local allegiance, and that it included, therefore, a friendly resident alien. It would seem that they would have denied the right of other aliens to proceed. These decisions may well be sound, and in that case they should, it is submitted, govern section 1.

Whether the Act is available to aliens not relying on section 1 or for foreign torts is a problem of statutory interpretation.[13] The courts will have to consider the intention of the legislature,[14] and decide what weight (if any) to attach to the presumption against extra-territorial operation of

---

1 28 U.S.C. §261: 'Aliens who are citizens or subjects of any Government which accords to citizens of the United States the right to prosecute claims against such Government in its courts shall have the privilege of prosecuting claims against the United States in the Court of Claims, whereof such court, by reasons of their subject-matter and character, might take jurisdiction.' Now revised in 28 U.S.C. § 2502.

2 Glanville Williams, *op. cit.* 12. 3 *Abr.* Error 8.
4 *Abr.* Prerog. 2. 5 Staunford, *op. cit.* 72.
6 Blackstone, *Commentaries*, III at 246.
7 Chitty, *Prerogatives of the Crown*, 340.
8 Robertson, *op. cit.* 364. 9 Clode, *op. cit.* 35.
10 E.g. *The Amphitrite Case*, [1921] 3 K.B. 500.
11 In *U.S.* v. *O'Keefe* (1871), 11 Wall 178 (U.S.) the United States Supreme Court found as a fact of foreign law that an alien could sue under the Petitions of Right Act.
12 *Massein* v. *Rex*, [1935] 1 D.L.R. 701; *Arnerich* v. *Rex*, [1942] N.Z.L.R. 380; cf. Note in 16 *Aust. L.J.* (1942) 205.
13 Cf. for example Lorenzen, 'Tort Liability and the Conflict of Laws' in 47 *L.Q.R.* (1931), 483 at 496.
14 Cf. *Davidsson* v. *Hill*, [1901] 2 K.B. 606 (Fatal Accidents Act); *Krzus* v. *Crow's Nest Pass Coal Co. Ltd.*, [1912] A.C. 590 (Workmen's Compensation Act).

statutes. It is thought that both matters remain doubtful. Perhaps the best provision would be one empowering the Government to make separate arrangements with foreign countries, allowing actions against each other on a reciprocal basis. The existing provisions with regard to income tax, death duties and extradition could serve as a model.

N. *Act of State*[1]

Anglo-American law does not recognise that there is an indefinite class of acts concerning matters of high policy or public security which may be left to the uncontrolled discretion of the Government and which are outside the jurisdiction of the courts. That principle was firmly established by the *General Warrant Cases* of the eighteenth century.[2]

Perhaps the best definition of act of State in the restricted meaning which it has in English law is that of Wade:[3]

An act of the executive as a matter of policy performed in the course of its relations with another state, including its relations with the subjects of that state, unless they are temporarily within the allegiance of the Crown.

Acts of State as defences may be divided into two classes: first, those acts which only a State can perform in the course of relationships with other independent States; secondly, acts committed by a private citizen outside the jurisdiction and previously authorised or subsequently ratified by the State, and damaging an alien.

The most important consequence of the first class is that citizens have no rights of action under treaties between nations even if money for their benefit has been received by the State of which they are nationals.[4] Nor have the courts any jurisdiction over questions of seizure or annexation of land or goods in right of conquest, or of rights or liabilities alleged to be acquired in consequence of such acts.[5] Although the position at common law in the United States was similar, a statutory right enforceable by mandamus has been given to those entitled to moneys received by the United States under treaties.[6]

1 See Moore, *Act of State in English Law*; Sir William Holdsworth, 'The History of Acts of State in English Law' in 41 *Col. L.R.* (1941) 1313; S. Gordon, 'La Théorie des "Acts of State" en Droit Anglais' in 53 *R.D.P.* (1936), 5.
2 *Leach* v. *Money* (1765), 19 St. Tr. 1001; *Wilkes* v. *Wood* (1763), 19 St. Tr. 1153; *Entick* v. *Carrington* (1765), 19 St. Tr. 1029.
3 E. C. S. Wade, 'Act of State in English Law: Its Relations with International Law' in 15 *B.Y.I.L.* (1934) 98 at 103.
4 *Baron de Bode's Case* (1851), 3 H.L. Cas. 449; *Rustomjee* v. *Reg.*, [1876] 2 Q.B. 69; *Civilian War Claimants Association* v. *Rex*, [1932] A.C. 14.
5 *West Rand Central Gold Mining Co. Ltd.* v. *Rex*, [1905] 2 K.B. 391.
6 P. 129 *infra*.

The effect of the second division is that neither the official nor the State itself can be sued for injuries inflicted outside the jurisdiction with State authorisation upon foreigners.[1] The defence is never available against a British subject.[2] In *Johnstone* v. *Pedlar*[3] the House of Lords rejected the contention that act of State was always a defence to an action brought by a friendly alien even if the act were committed within the jurisdiction. It has been deduced from this much misunderstood case 'that this defence is of no avail in any case where the wrongful act was committed in British territory'.[4] This deduction is open to criticism. In that case the House of Lords was careful to point out that counsel was not raising the different question of whether a resident alien who had broken his duty of allegiance to the State in which he was resident may be met by a plea of act of State. Both Viscount Cave[5] and Viscount Finlay[6] reserved that point. Holdsworth thought that act of State could then be pleaded.[7] This view has been confirmed by cases arising out of the recent war.[8] It has been decided that both the detention[9] and deportation[10] of enemy aliens in England by the Home Secretary are acts of State.

It may be that Sir Percy Winfield, too, has misinterpreted *Johnstone* v. *Pedlar*. He says that it was suggested there that the act of State must be by an official high in the hierarchy.[11] The point raised in the dictum quoted by him[12] seems not to be the status of the official, but the quality of the act. The question is 'Can act of State be pleaded as a defence to any act, however trivial, or must the act be "a catastrophic change, constituting a new departure"?' as Fletcher Moulton L.J. defined it in *Salaman* v. *Secretary of State in Council of India*.[13]

Since the United States has not until recently intervened much abroad, there has been little scope for the operation of the doctrine last described. Holmes J. seems to have been the first to introduce it there in three decisions.[14] That introduction has been deplored by some,[15] but it seems

1 *Buron* v. *Denman* (1848), 2 Ex. 167. 2 *Walker* v. *Baird*, [1892] A.C. 491.
3 [1921] 2 A.C. 262. 4 Clerk and Lindsell, *op. cit.* 78.
5 At 277. 6 At 274.
7 Note in 38 L.Q.R. (1922) 11; cf. Emden, *The Civil Servant and the Law of the Constitution*, 43. J. K. O'Sullivan, 'The Defence of Act of State in respect of Acts Committed on British Territory' in 4 *Res Gestae* (1950) 245.
8 Not cited in Clerk and Lindsell, *supra* n. 4.
9 *Rex* v. *Bottrill, ex p. Kuechenmeister*, [1947] K.B. 41 at 57 (*per* Asquith L.J.).
10 *Netz* v. *Chuter Ede*, [1946] 1 All E.R. 628 at 632 (*per* Wynn-Parry J.); *ctra.* *Commercial and Estates Co. of Egypt* v. *Board of Trade*, [1925] 1 K.B. 271 at 290; C.A. (*per* Scrutton L.J. *obiter*). 11 Winfield, *Tort*, 90.
12 At 277. 13 [1906] 1 K.B. 613 at 640.
14 *The Pacquete Habana* (1903), 189 U.S. 453 at 465; *O'Reilly de Camara* v. *Brooke* (1908), 209 U.S. 45 at 52; *Tiaco* v. *Forbes* (1913), 228 U.S. 549.
15 E.g. H. T. Kingsbury, 'The "Act of State" Doctrine' in 4 *Am. J.I.L.* (1910) 359.

that in general at least the United States follows the English principles of act of State.[1] Neither the Crown Proceedings Act nor the Federal Tort Claims affects them.

O. *Other Exceptions in the United States*

The main limitations on the tortious liability of the Crown have already been examined. In the United States, however, there are further important exceptions.

Perhaps most important is that[2] of 'any claim arising out of assault, battery, false imprisonment, false arrest, malicious prosecution, abuse of process,[3] libel, slander, misrepresentation, deceit or interference with contract rights'.[4] The arguments adduced in support of these provisions are unsatisfactory. Only in committee hearings on earlier Bills was any justification for them attempted, and it was then said that such suits were difficult to defend and likely to result in awards of high damages. The second point loses its force when it is noted that, unlike the English Act, the United States one prohibits jury actions.

The United States is liable only for 'money damages...for injury or loss of property, or personal injury or death'.[5] Why these words were introduced at all is perplexing,[6] for without them the United States would still be liable under the Act for torts alone. Perhaps a court seeking a meaning for them may say that a husband suing for the loss of his wife's society and services is not suing for property damage or personal injury.[7] So much is likely, but there is the further possibility that a court will decide that the Act, referring expressly to injuries to property and persons, ex-

1 Borchard, *Diplomatic Privileges of Citizens Abroad*, 174.
2 §2680.
3 Cf. s. 2 (5) of the Crown Proceedings Act.
4 Cf. the exception in the New Zealand statute of assault, false imprisonment, libel, slander, malicious prosecution, and any tort of which malice is an essential element.
5 §1346.
6 Some light on the matter may be thrown by the evidence of the Special Assistant to the Attorney General (A. Holtzoff) on an earlier Bill: Hearings before the Senate Committee on the Judiciary on S. 2690, 76th Congress, 3rd Sess. (1940), 36, where he indicates that the Small Claims Act, 1922, only included property damage and that the Bill was drafted so as to make it clear that claims for personal injury as well as property damage were included. New York State, which had a form of wording in the Court of Claims Act, 1922, similar to §1346 wisely avoids the pitfall in its 1939 Act, section 8 of which provides: 'The State hereby waives its immunity from liability and action and hereby assumes liability and consents to have the same determined in accordance with the same rules of law as applied to actions in the supreme court against individuals or corporations.'
7 *Wilson* v. *Grace* (1930), 273 Mass. 146 so interpreted a statute creating liability for 'injury to the person'.

cludes economic loss, e.g. the cause of action which is allowed in the United States to those suffering loss as the result of the making of negligent statements.[1] At least, a more precise form of wording should have been used. The English Act, by rendering the Crown subject to all the liabilities of the citizen, avoids any such ambiguity.

The United States statute provides that the United States shall not be liable for punitive damages.[2] This raises a most important point in the Anglo-American law of torts which has received little consideration either from judges or writers. It may be assumed that the basis of damages in tort is compensation. Yet if there is violence or malice on the part of the defendant, damages are often increased.[3] It is usually said that this increase is calculated to punish the defendant.[4] It does seem, however, that some of the damages loosely called 'punitive' may be awarded as compensation for the invasion of the right of personality, 'for a wanton outrage—an *iniuria* in the Roman sense'.[5] Where, then, the damages cease to be compensatory and become punitive it is difficult to determine.[6] At the same time, juries often award higher damages almost unconsciously when confronted with a defendant of whose conduct they disapprove.[7] The award of damages to punish the offender is anomalous in the law of torts.[8] One may then approve the exclusion of those from the Federal Tort Claims Act, and deplore the absence of a similar provision in the Crown Proceedings Act. What is doubtful is whether the American courts will classify as punitive those damages by way of aggravation which, it is contended, are truly compensatory, though often labelled by courts and text-books[9] as punitive.

The further exemptions in section 2680 of claims arising out of the administration of the Trading with the Enemy Act, the quarantine laws and the fiscal and monetary systems, have no English parallel. No clear and conclusive explanation for them is traceable in the legislative history.[10]

---

1 The Supreme Court has recently held that the words include claims for contribution which would be due from the Government if it were a private individual. *U.S.* v. *Yellow Cab Co.* (1951), 340 U.S. 543.
2 §1346.
3 Mayne on *Damages*, 41.
4 *Butterworth* v. *Butterworth*, [1920] 126 at 136 (*per* McCardie J.).
5 Paton, *A Text-Book of Jurisprudence*, 333.
6 *Ley* v. *Hamilton* (1935), 153, L.T. 384 at 386 (*per* Lord Atkin).
7 Cf. Shulman & James, *Cases and Materials on the Law of Torts*, 244.
8 Salmond, *op. cit.* 127; Stone, *op. cit.* ch. 21; cf. Glanville Williams, 'The Aims of the Law of Tort' in 4 *Current Legal Problems* (1951) 137.
9 E.g. Gahan, *The Law of Damages*, 18.
10 One or two further exceptions for which there is separate statutory provision have not been cited.

It certainly appears harsh that the victim of a quarantine imposed by gross negligence should have no action against the United States.

P. Res Judicata

The judgment in an action against the United States 'shall constitute a complete bar to any action by the claimant, by reason of the same subject matter',[1] not merely against the United States but also against the employee. The common-law rules of *res judicata* provide that a judgment is a bar to a subsequent action between the same parties on identical subject matter and in respect of the same cause of action. This Act extends these rules by providing that actions against the United States bar actions against the employee. Beyond that, it seems to bar subsequent suits even though based on a different cause of action on the same subject matter. For instance, it was held in *Brunsden* v. *Humphrey*[2] that 'the real test is not. . . whether the plaintiff had the opportunity of recovering in the first action what he claims to recover in the second', and that a driver of a cab who had in a previous action recovered for damage to the cab caused by the defendant's negligence was not barred from further proceedings for personal injuries, since actions for property damage and personal injuries constitute separate causes of action. Under the Act, it seems that the plaintiff could not bring this second action.[3] On the other hand, the Crown Proceedings Act leaves untouched the above common-law rules.

Q. Admiralty

The English statute but not the American one has some special enactments about His Majesty's ships.

Section 2 (1) is drawn widely enough to make the Crown liable for the torts of members of the crew of Crown ships.[4] The rules for apportioning damage contained in the Maritime Conventions Act, 1911, 'apply in the case of vessels belonging to His Majesty as they apply in the case of other vessels'.[5] Actions against the Crown in respect of damage caused by warships or Post Office ships must be brought within the period of one year fixed by the Limitation Act, 1939, for public authorities. Actions in respect of damage caused by other Crown ships are to be brought within the period of two years[6] laid down by the Maritime Conventions Act.[7]

1 §2676.
2 (1884), 14 Q.B. 141 at 151 (*per* Bowen L.J.).
3 Cf. H. R. Baer, 'Suing Uncle Sam in Tort' in 29 *North Carolina L.R.* (1946) 119 at 126.
4 S. 6.   5 S. 30(1) (2).
6 S. 30(2).   7 S. 8.

At common law it seems that salvage actions could not be brought against the Crown,[1] but by section 8 of the Act the ordinary law of salvage is applied to it, except that the immunity of the Crown from actions *in rem* remains.

Thus, without regard to any particular social theory, force of circumstances has compelled both England and the United States to acknowledge their liability for wrongs inflicted on the citizen through the functioning of governmental agencies. Both Acts do this by extending private-law concepts of agency and vicarious liability to the Government.

It may be said that the object of both is to assimilate the subject suing the Government and him suing fellow-citizens, so far as reasonably practicable. This assimilation is far from complete in either case. The English Act is too tender to the Executive, and gives indications throughout of compromises with government departments. The latter have long been opposed to such legislation, and lingering traces of this hostility are seen in the rules relating to the armed forces and the postal services. Where, however, to give a complete remedy to the citizen would not interfere with the Executive, there seems a readiness in the English Act to grant him that remedy. Any further defects seem merely the result of careless draftsmanship. There is nothing to suggest that Parliament seized every chance to cut down financial liability; on the contrary the Act is marked by its generosity. One is struck, too, by its orthodoxy. It never carries liability beyond the limits of existing private law, and when it does not reach those limits, the explanation seems always to be executive pressure or erroneous drafting.

The United States statute shows less sign of executive interference. On the other hand, the determination of Congress to avoid what it thinks to be pecuniarily excessive liabilities is everywhere manifest. This difference between the two Acts perhaps reflects the greater British influence of the Executive on legislation. Moreover, as Borchard has said, the United States legislation suffers by being less comprehensive. Some procedural matters are left unsettled, and there is no dovetailing of it and the Tucker Act. Nor is its draftsmanship markedly superior to that of the Crown Proceedings Act.

Each Act could easily be improved by correcting drafting slips and by making it tally more exactly with the law operating between subject and subject, allowing the State a privilege for only the most compelling of reasons. Perhaps an examination of the good and bad features of each as

1 *Anglo-Saxon Petroleum Co.* v. *Lords Commissioners of the Admiralty*, [1947] K.B. 794 (C.A.); cf. *The Brabo*, [1947] 2 All E.R. 363 (C.A.) confirmed on other grounds, [1949] 1 All E.R. 294 (H.L.).

outlined herein would assist towards this end. The reforms would surely not be in advance of current lay and professional opinion, and could be expected to be brought about without serious public opposition.

2. FRANCE

A. *Jurisdiction of the* Conseil d'Etat

The keystone of the French law of governmental liability in tort is the separation of judicial and administrative authorities.[1] Before 1789 the Executive had been subject to undue interference by the Judiciary, and one of the purposes of the framers of the new Constitution was to end this. The Constitution of the Year VIII proclaimed therefore *la séparation des autorités* and denied the courts the right to exercise jurisdiction over acts of the Administration. Further, article 57 of the Constitution laid down that 'government agents other than Ministers cannot be sued in respect of acts done in the discharge of their official duties except with the consent' of the Government. The practical effect of these provisions was to deny the citizen any remedy against either the Government or the individual officer, for only rarely did the Government consent to suit being brought against its officer.[2]

Protests against this system led to the abrogation of this administrative guarantee in 1870. In 1874 the famous *Pelletier Case*[3] decided that a civil court could not adjudicate on the power of an army general to confiscate a newspaper, because civil courts had no jurisdiction over administrative acts. That jurisdiction was to belong to the *Conseil d'Etat*[4] and other administrative tribunals.

The *Conseil d'Etat* both participates in active administration (*sections administratives*) and adjudicates on suits arising out of acts of the administration (*section du contentieux*). All cases in the latter category go to the *section du contentieux*, consisting of a president and eighteen councillors who may be reinforced by councillors from the *sections administratives*. The *section du contentieux* is divided into nine subsections of three councillors

1 This theme is developed in Uhler, *Review of Administrative Acts, passim.*
2 E.g. *Lefèvre-Pontalis*, Sirey, 1864, 1, 248.
3 Dall. Pér. 1874, 3, 5.
4 For full descriptions in English of the organisation and procedure of this tribunal, see H. Berthélemy, 'The *Conseil d'Etat* in France' in 12 *J.C.L.* (1930) 23; Rokham and Pratt, *Studies in French Administrative Law*, pt. I, ch. II; and B. Schwartz, 'The Administrative Courts in France', in 29 *Can. B.R.* (1951) 381; C. J. Hamson, 'Le Conseil d'Etat Statuant au Contentieux' in 68 *L.Q.R.* (1952) 60; see also *Le Conseil d'Etat, Le Livre Jubilaire*, and *Etudes et Documents* of the *Conseil d'Etat*, vols. 1–4.

each, judgment being usually rendered by two of the subsections united. Cases of legal difficulty are heard by the *section du contentieux* consisting of the president of the *section du contentieux*, the presidents of the subsections and the two councillors of the subsection where the case arose, and the very important ones by the *assemblée plénière du contentieux* consisting of the vice-president of the *Conseil d'Etat*, the president of the *section du contentieux*, the other presidents and four councillors from the *sections administratives*.[1] The two most important divisions of this jurisdiction are *le contentieux d'annulation* and *le contentieux de pleine juridiction*. *Le contentieux d'annulation* enables the court to annul *erga omnes* any illegal administrative acts. The other enables the court to award damages against the Administration when a citizen is injured by an administrative act. The court has original jurisdiction over all suits against the Administration for damages other than those expressly assigned elsewhere.[2] Actions for damages caused by public works lie to the *Conseils de Préfecture*, with a right of appeal to the *Conseil d'Etat*.

Any dispute whether the matter is administrative and within the competence of the *Conseil d'Etat* or judicial within the competence of the *Cour de Cassation* is settled by the *Tribunal des Conflits* under the presidency of the Minister of Justice,[3] its other members being drawn in equal numbers from the *Conseil d'Etat* and *Cour de Cassation*. In 1873 this tribunal recorded a decision which is the basis of the present jurisdiction of the *Conseil d'Etat* over suits claiming damages against the Government. In *Blanco's Case*[4] the issue was the liability of the public service for an accident caused to a child by a truck used in a government tobacco factory. The tribunal held that this was within the exclusive jurisdiction of the administrative tribunals. Soon, the principle was extended to damage caused by *départements* and *communes*.[5]

France, after the liberation, has seen a growth of innominate public bodies such as food rationing organisations and *comités d'organisations*. Their acts, too, have been held to be within the jurisdiction of the *Conseil d'Etat* so that all administrative bodies, whether national or local, are subject to one and the same body of law and jurisdiction. Nationalised industries such as gas, electricity, rail and air transport are not generally subject to *droit administratif*.[6]

1 In 1948–9, of 4,777 cases determined by the *Conseil d'Etat* 69 were taken in *assemblée plénière* and 158 in the *section du contentieux*; Hamson, *op. cit.* 75.
2 *Cadot*, 13 Dec. 1889.
3 Where the other members are equally divided.
4 Dall. Pér. 1873, 3, 17.
5 *Terrier*, Dall. Pér. 1904, 3, 65; *Feutry*, Dall. Pér. 1908, 3, 49 (*Tribunal des Conflits*).
6 See law of 17 May 1946 and Waline, *op. cit.* 314 *et seq.*

For a long time it was contended that the *Conseil d'Etat* had jurisdiction over *actes de gestion* but not over *actes d'autorité* or *actes de puissance publique*.[1] Nevertheless, the *Conseil d'Etat* gradually extended its jurisdiction over this latter important category. Perhaps most decisive was the *Tomaso Greco* case in 1905.[2] There the *Conseil d'Etat* declared itself competent to adjudicate on the liability of the police service to a person wounded by a shot fired by a police officer at a mad bull which had escaped on to a highway. In the same year the State was held liable when a young soldier was killed in the course of military manœuvres by a live cartridge from a rifle thought to contain only blank cartridges.[3] Five years later the distinction between *actes de gestion* and *actes d'autorité* was treated as abandoned.[4]

B. *Faute de Service* and *Faute Personnelle*

Unhampered by any code, and not bound by civil law, the *Conseil d'Etat* was free to work out the principles of governmental liability. Of course, it did have regard to the principles of private law, and not surprisingly its starting-point was a liability based on fault, the *faute de service*.

If there is a *faute de service*, then the State is liable. If, on the other hand, there is a *faute personnelle* by the official then he can be sued in the civil court.[5] Both the *Tribunal des Conflits* and the *Conseil d'Etat* have found it difficult to decide when there is a *faute personnelle*. The former body has been faced with the problem when the Administration has raised a conflict for its decision; the latter body, when it has been determining its own jurisdiction. Only the Administration can raise a conflict, and if the *Conseil d'Etat* is seized of a case which might contain a *faute personnelle* only, the civil courts are powerless to raise a conflict before the *Tribunal des Conflits* if the Administration is unwilling to do so.[6] In fact, both the *Tribunal des Conflits* and the *Conseil d'Etat* have shirked the question of what are the criteria of *faute personnelle* and *faute de service*. Lacking clear guidance from them, jurists have themselves tried to discover these criteria in the light of the decided cases and logical principles.

1 Especially Laferrière, *Traité de la Juridiction Administrative*, 17.
2 Sirey 1905, 3, 113 and note of Hauriou; cf. Duguit, *Les Transformations du Droit Public*, 259.
3 *Auxerre*, Dall. Pér. 1906, 3, 81.
4 *Thérond*, Recueil, 1910, 197. Cf. J. W. Garner, 'French Administrative Law' in 33 *Yale L.J.* (1924) 597 at 619; E. M. Borchard, 'Governmental Responsibility in Tort' in 28 *Col. L.R.* (1928), 577 at 599 n. 63.
5 Originally only the official would be sued for a *faute personnelle*. In some cases the Administration can also be sued now; see pp. 63 *et seq. infra*.
6 Berthélemy, *Traité Elémentaire de Droit Administratif*, 1088.

'Nearly every French writer has suggested a criterion of his own.'[1] The most widely quoted test is that of Laferrière:[2] there is a *faute personnelle* if there is revealed *l'homme avec ses faiblesses, ses passions, ses imprudences.* Jèze, seeking a more precise definition, requires the proof either of *une intention mauvaise* or *une faute lourde*.[3] Hauriou denies that the gravity of the fault can affect the nature of the act, and declares that the test is whether, considered objectively, the fault is detachable from the agent's functions.[4] Colliard has said[5] that 'there is a *faute personnelle* every time the servant acts with the intention of satisfying his own interest and also when he acts without any interest in his service and has been very lazy or very imprudent'. De Laubadère thinks that there are no fixed criteria but that all the above are factors to be weighed by the court.[6]

Duguit[7] is dissatisfied with these various definitions.[8] Certainly, that of Laferrière seems vague, and it is hard to agree with Jèze that the gravity of the wrong can affect its nature. Nor is Hauriou's definition[9] above criticism. For example, if a mayor is empowered to ring the church bells, and does so during a funeral in order to annoy the priest, that act, though not detachable, has been held by the *Conseil d'Etat* to be a *faute personnelle*.[10] Duguit argues that there are two types of *fautes personnelles*. First, there is the *faute détachable*, performed upon the occasion of an administrative act, but quite distinct from it because it has neither an administrative purpose nor end.[11] For example, a mayor authorised to post a list of qualified voters, who maliciously posts alongside of it a notice that a certain person is bankrupt and is therefore disqualified, commits a *faute personnelle*.[12] Secondly, there is the *faute incluse*, an act inseparable from the administrative act, but containing in itself an element of personal fault 'lorsqu'il porte sur un objet ou est déterminé par un but étranger au domaine administratif'.[13] So, the mayor who rings the church bell for a civil burial

1 Garner, *op. cit.* 620 n. 86.   2 *Op. cit.* 648.
3 G. Jèze, Note in 26 *R.D.P.* (1909) 267 at 274.
4 '...le fait devient personnel à l'agent d'exécution lorsqu'il est accompagné d'une circonstance matériellement détachable, qui le met en dehors des instructions et des pratiques du service et qui fait présumer chez l'agent une volonté de ne pas agir conformément au service' (Hauriou, *Précis de Droit Administratif*, 320).
5 C. A. Colliard, 'Comparison between English and French Administrative Law' in 25 *Transactions of the Grotius Society* (1940) 119 at 127.
6 de Laubadère, *Manuel de Droit Administratif*, 117.
7 Duguit, *Traité de Droit Constitutionnel*, III, 302.
8 For a detailed examination of the several theories, see Dupeyroux, *Faute Personnelle et Faute du Service Public, passim.*
9 Adopted by L. Trotabas, 'Liability in Damages under French Administrative Law' in 12 *J.C.L.* (1930) 44 at 56.
10 Sirey, 1910, 3, 129.   11 Cf. Waline, 357.
12 Sirey, 1899, 3, 76.   13 Duguit, *op. cit.* 305.

to annoy the priest commits a *faute incluse*, whereas if he, in order to carry out a municipal ordinance controlling the import of meat, seizes meat, that is no *faute personnelle*.[1] Similarly, a policeman who arrests a person out of a spirit of vengeance commits a *faute personnelle*.[2] The analysis of Duguit seems logical and fair, but in view of the reluctance of the courts to lay down any principles, and its cold reception by French jurists,[3] it may not be an accurate statement of the law.

It is not enough to define a *faute de service* merely by contrast with a *faute personnelle*.[4] The *Conseil d'Etat* has not said that a citizen injured by any *faute de service* may sue; often it has employed the formula 'faute d'une gravité exceptionnelle de nature à engager la responsabilité de l'Etat'. It is left to the judge to decide in each case whether there is some administrative inadequacy for which the State should pay compensation. The *Conseil d'Etat* has exercised this discretion wisely in order to see that justice is done.

Hauriou[5] suggests that there is a *faute de service* whenever there is a *mauvaise habitude de l'Administration*. In order to determine whether the functioning is defective, the courts seem to require differing standards of gravity. An attempt has been made to frame rigid categories defining the degree of seriousness demanded.[6] According to this theory, extreme fault is required for a quasi-sovereign act, serious fault for a police function,[7] and light fault for an *acte de gestion*. These are irreconcilable with the cases and have not been generally approved.

Most in harmony with the decisions seem the views of Waline.[8] He first considers separately violations of law, and suggests that whereas *détournement de pouvoir* is a *faute de service*,[9] a mere *vice de forme* is not unless accompanied by bad faith. Turning next to the functioning of the services, he argues that in order to determine whether the fault has sufficient seriousness to render the State liable, these factors must be considered. The time, place and technical difficulties of the act are material. It is difficult to prevent a lunatic from escaping; so the Administration is liable only for gross fault if he does so and sets fire to a wood;[10] an act which is actionable in time of peace may give rise to no war-time liability. The

1 *Monpillié*, Sirey, 1918, 1, 17 (Cass. Crim.).
2 *Immenigeon*, Recueil, 1922, 185.
3 For what appears to be an attempt to fuse the views of Hauriou and Duguit, see de Laubadère, *op. cit.* 117 *et seq.*
4 Trotabas, *op. cit.* 218.   5 *Op. cit.* 322.
6 Appleton, *Traité Elémentaire de Contentieux Administratif*, S. 238.
7 Cf. *Lecomte et Daramy, Conseil d'Etat*, 24 June 1949.
8 *Op. cit.* 590 *et seq.*
9 Abuse by the Administration of its rights is also a *faute de service*; *Vaucanu, Conseil d'Etat*, 26 Oct. 1945.
10 *de Bony*, Sirey, 1933, 3, 95.

social importance of the service must be estimated, to decide to what extent interference in its administration is permissible; it would be easier to establish a *faute de service* in the weights and measures service than in the police. The relative importance of the roles of the individual and the State must be appreciated: the courts would be loath to hold the State liable for an accident occurring during a State driving test.[1] Further material considerations are whether the Administration had been warned of the danger, whether it had deliberately ignored some regulation; the seriousness of the consequences of the act, and its duration. If the State created the source of danger, then fault would readily be presumed. The Administration was therefore liable when a test tube in a school laboratory exploded.[2]

This last test suggested by Waline is what Hauriou calls the presumption of fault, which, he says, arises 'par suite des conditions particulièrement dangereuses de l'utilisation de la chose'.[3] The presumption is rebuttable by proof of a *cause étrangère, cas fortuit*, or *force majeure*. Hauriou emphasised that although it is a civil law notion, it rests here on utilisation, not on custody as in civil law. Motor vehicle accidents involving pedestrians are the most common example.[4]

Many writers subscribe to the doctrine of 'anonymous fault',[5] which lays down that *faute de service* is not necessarily a liability of the Administration for the wrong of a servant, but is a liability of the service itself. There may be fault by an unknown servant, or even no fault by any servant or just defective functioning of the service. Others, for example Duguit, say that all acts are those of individuals. Cases such as *Pluchard*[6] illustrate the problem well. There, a policeman, pursuing a criminal, accidentally knocked down a pedestrian, who successfully sued the Administration on the ground that there was a *faute de service*. Duguit denies[7] that there was any fault by the policeman, and asserts that the service functioned properly. His contention is, therefore, that the Administration cannot, on the basis of subjective fault, be liable for a *faute de service* not traceable to the fault of some individual or specific body of persons.[8] The conclusions which he refutes are, he contends,[9] based on fictitious theories of moral personality

1 *Perriot*, Dall. Pér. 1929, 3, 1.   2 *Lambert, Conseil d'Etat*, 28 April 1938.
3 *Op. cit.* 330.
4 *Société d'Assurance Mutuelle des Travailleurs Française*, Sirey, 1926, 3, 1; although *force majeure* is still a defence, these cases are now regarded as ones of liability without fault; *Beschon, Conseil d'Etat*, 18 Oct. 1946.
5 Rokham and Pratt, *op. cit.* 77; Duez, *La Responsabilité de la Puissance Publique, passim*.
6 Recueil, 1910, 1029.   7 *Traité*, 502.
8 He argues that liability is based on risk; see p. 66 *infra*.
9 *Traité*, 495.

or institutions ascribing to that aggregate, the public service, a reality and separate personality which it does not possess. Nor does Duguit accept the theory that liability for a *faute de service* may depend on the gravity of the fault.[1] For him it is enough to prove that the act was for an end of the *service public*; the degree of fault is irrelevant.

Failure to act or delay may be a *faute de service*. When the State was slow in demobilising an infant who had been illegally taken into the Foreign Legion without his father's consent, it was liable to the father in damages when the infant was killed during that delay.[2]

C. Damages

It is agreed that a victim suing the State for a *faute de service* must prove damage. Reparation against the State cannot, according to French theory, take the form of *restitutio in integrum*. The separation of judicial and administrative agencies within the Administration itself leads to the rule that the judicial elements cannot issue orders to the administrative. No injunction or *astreinte*[3] is possible. The demolition of buildings causing injury cannot be ordered.[4]

In short, the only reparation of the injury allowed is that which can be estimated in money; pecuniary damages only are given against the Administration. The plaintiff must prove that the *faute de service* has caused direct and certain money loss.[5] It is further argued that this loss must be material. Mere moral damage is not enough. Parents therefore may not claim damages for grief at the loss of a son.[6] Nor could a taxpayer upon whose goods execution has been levied for the non-payment of taxes which he did not owe recover damages for the loss of his reputation.[7] The damages are proportionately reduced if the claimant has been contributorily negligent.[8] Nor can anyone not entitled to claim for pension recover damage in respect of the death of another.[9]

One writer has sought to justify the rule about moral damage as follows:[10]

The moral damage is repaired 'morally' by the formal declaration on the part of the *Conseil d'Etat* that there has been an administrative fault.

1 *Traité*, 498.   2 *Brunet, Conseil d'Etat*, 18 July 1919.
3 *Gaz de Pézenas*, Lebon, 1919, 23, 5.   4 *Soubiran*, Lebon, 1916, 29, 7.
5 F. de Baecque, 'Règles de la Jurisprudence Administrative Relatives à la Réparation du Préjudice en Cas en Mise en Œuvre de la Responsabilité de la Puissance Publique' in 60 *R.D.P.* (1944) 197.
6 *Quénot*, Dall. Pér. 1922, 3, 22. Nor may a wife recover damages for grief at the death of her husband; *Société de Gaz et de l'Electricité de Marseille*, 1 May 1942 (*Conseil d'Etat*).   7 *Demoreuil*, Dall. Pér. 1928, 3, 21.
8 De Laubadère, *op. cit.* 119; cf. the *Stavisky-Bayonne Fraud Case*, 29 March 1946 (*Conseil d'Etat*); *Maignon, Conseil d'Etat*, 28 April 1950.
9 *Mongenot*, Sirey, 1945, 3, 8.   10 Trotabas, *op. cit.* 224.

To award money damages in such a case would not, as in private law, restore the balance between the estate of the wrongdoer and the estate of the victim: it would lay upon the public funds, that is to say, the funds of the taxpayers in general, who are not to blame for the fault and take no benefit by it, the burden of paying a sum arbitrarily fixed as equivalent to the moral damage sustained.

It seems, then, that French administrative law denies a remedy whenever the damages sustained are not capable of ready monetary assessment. It corresponds approximately to that distinction in English law between those damages, sometimes called 'special' damages, of which details must be given in the pleadings, and general damages which need not be specially pleaded. For instance, a victim of the French administrative machine may obtain damages for the cost of an operation on a broken leg but not for his pain and suffering.[1] This rule appears to make difficulty in assessing damages a reason for not awarding them at all, and to be contrary to the usual principle that the award of damages is an attempt to compensate for loss suffered.[2] There seems no convincing case for it.

Some inroads have been made on the rule. If a person's reputation is injured in the way of his business so as to produce pecuniary consequences, then moral damages may be awarded.[3] Singers whose gramophone records had been broadcast without mentioning their names were thus able to sue. A parent may recover damages for the loss of his child's potential wage-earning power.[4]

Three points of interest regarding damages may be noted. The *Conseil d'Etat* can reserve the right to try a further action if the plaintiff suffers more damage later.[5] An award of damages may take the form of an annuity. An award can take account of changes in the value of money between the date of the accident and that of judgment.[6]

D. *Cumul*

It has been shown that the basis of the development of the French law has been the distinction between *faute de service* and *faute personnelle*. By the start of this century French writers realised that in many deserving cases the citizen did not get compensation. If he sued the official for

---

1 In the *Morell Case*, Sirey, 1943, 3, 11, there is a tardy recognition that this rule is unsatisfactory. A person badly burned by a crashed aircraft during an aviation display was allowed damages for exceptional pain and suffering 'qui dépasse un certain degré d'acuité et de durée'. Cf. R. Bonnard, 'La Réparation de Préjudice Moral' in 60 R.D.P. (1943) 80; and *Michellet* C.E. 7 April 1944.
2 See p. 53 *supra*.   3 *Franz et Charny*, Dall. Pér. 1934, 3, 25.
4 De Baecque, *op. cit.*; *Nataf, Conseil d'Etat*, 6 January 1950.
5 *Guidicelli, Conseil d'Etat*, 7 Feb. 1934.
6 *Lefebvre, Conseil d'Etat*, 21 March 1947.

a *faute personnelle* and that official was judgment-proof, then reparation had not been made. Or the administrative courts might hold that there was no *faute de service* and the civil courts find no *faute personnelle*. Why, it was asked, should there not be *cumul des responsabilités de l'Administration et des fonctionnaires?*

In 1909 the *Conseil d'Etat* heard a case in which a colonial company claimed damages against the Administration because officials had interfered with the recruiting of native labour. Thwarting the attempt of the Administration to shelter behind the personal immunity of the officials, the *Conseil d'Etat* held that 'even if we admit that these acts constituted *fautes personnelles*, they were none the less acts done by an agent of the State in the exercise of his functions'.[1]

This encouraged jurists, and Jèze[2] in particular, to press for the unrestricted recognition of State liability for *faute personnelle* on the ground that the damage caused by it was usually much greater than that caused by a *faute de service*. Soon afterwards, the *Conseil d'Etat* heard the famous *Lemonnier Case*.[3] The mayor of a *commune* organised a duck-shooting competition in the course of which a walker along the river bank was shot. A civil court found that there had been a *faute personnelle* by the mayor, but the *Conseil d'Etat* held the Administration also liable. The court said:

...the fact that the accident in this case was the result of a personal act of such a character as to involve the liability of the agent, and even the fact that the agent has actually been found liable, cannot deprive the person injured of his right to bring a direct action against the public authority concerned to recover reparation for the loss which he has sustained.

Of course, this was hailed by Jèze[4] as the incorporation of his ideas into administrative law.

There seems, however, to be much force in the arguments of Duguit to the contrary. He stated that, usually, when a court holds the State liable even though there is a *faute personnelle*, it does so because there is also a *faute de service*. Two examples may be given. In the important *Anguet Case*[5] a person leaving a post office by the staff exit was jostled by an employee and injured. The Administration was liable, not for the *faute personnelle*, but for the *faute de service* in closing before the official time as a result of which the citizen had to use the staff exit. Where drunken soldiers in a private billet killed the child of the family the State was liable

1 *Cie Commerciale de Colonisation du Congo*, Lebon, 1909, 153.
2 Note in 31 *R.D.P.* (1914) 572.
3 Dall. Pér. 1918, 3, 9. Note the conclusions of L. Blum.
4 Note, 35 *R.D.P.* (1918), 42.   5 Dall. Pér. 1913, 3, 26.

for defective supervision despite the presence of a *faute personnelle*.¹ So too
the *Conseil d'Etat* has recently held the Administration liable for damages
caused by the negligent driving of a service vehicle, although the driver
was acting without authority at the time of the accident: the injuries
occurred 'à l'occasion du service et du fait d'un véhicule qui avait été
confié à son conducteur pour l'exécution d'un service public'.²
   There remain circumstances where there is only a *faute personnelle*.
Would Jèze argue that if a post office clerk shot a customer then the State
is liable?³ Duguit argues with conviction that the key is the distinction
between the *faute détachable* and the *faute incluse*. For the *faute incluse* the
theory of *cumul* is applied by the *Conseil d'Etat* so as to render the State
liable, but for the *faute détachable* the State is not liable. There are two
different types of cases. When there is both a *faute de service* and a *faute
personnelle* Duguit suggests that there is no *cumul* but a parallel responsi-
bility.⁴ Secondly, the *faute personnelle* may be so interwoven with the
administrative act that they are not separable. The *Lemonnier* decision
illustrates the second type of case, and there accordingly was *cumul* in the
strict sense.⁵ The arguments of Trotabas⁶ and others, that whenever there
is a *faute personnelle* then there is *cumul* because of presumed fault on the
part of the Administration, go further than the cases, and seek an undesirable end. The theory of Duguit is at once in accord with the authorities
and justice.
   One further problem of *cumul* must be considered. If there is a liability
on the part of both the official and the State, how is it to be shared? It
seems from the *Lemonnier Case* that the State and the official are each
liable for the whole amount of the damage, and that the *Conseil d'Etat*, by
the principle of subrogation, may authorise the State to recover full
contribution from the official. In practice this theory of subrogation is
unsatisfactory: until 1951 there was no reported case in which the Administration exercised its rights against the official. Therefore, an official
protected by *cumul* could be confident that he would suffer no pecuniary
loss for his *faute personnelle*. This solution did not commend itself to
Duguit,⁷ who thought that the virtual irresponsibility of the official might
have grave consequences. He agreed that the state and the official were

1 *L'huilier*, Recueil, 1919, 819; cf. *Baudelet*, Dall. Pér. 1920, 3, where a billeted
soldier, attempting to unscrew a bomb, caused an explosion which injured two
civilians.
2 *Mimeur, Defaux et Besthelsemer*, J.C.P. 1950, J. 5286.
3 Cf. Watkins, *The State as a Party Litigant*, 160.   4 *Traité*, S. 84.
5 L. Blum in his conclusions said that it depended on whether *le service a con-
ditionné l'accomplissement de la faute ou la production de ses conséquences dommageables
vis-à-vis d'un individu déterminé*.
6 Trotabas, *op. cit.* XIV, J.C.L. (1932) 84.   7 *Op. cit.* S. 84.

jointly liable for the whole damage, and that the victim might sue either for the whole amount at his whim.[1] He asserted that the *Conseil d'Etat* in the *Lemonnier Case* had no jurisdiction, because of the theory of separation of powers, to declare the official bound to give a full indemnity; for he was only liable civilly and was not even before the court. He thought that there should be contribution by the persons liable according to the degree to which each contributed to the injury. One might have thought that the separation of authorities in France would make it difficult for any one court to exercise this jurisdiction. Nevertheless, very recently the *Conseil d'Etat* has ordered a servant personally at fault to pay back to the State damages awarded against it to the victim.[2]

E. Risk

The liability so far discussed has been a subjective one based, however remotely, on subjective fault. French administrative law has not been content with this basis. So limited is fault in its scope that to found liability on it alone would leave many injured citizens remediless. Moreover, to search for fault in the Administration is unpalatable to judges bred in the tradition of separation of powers, and there has often been a reluctance to pronounce a judgment critical of the Administration. If, on the other hand, judgment may rest on the objective fact that damage has been sustained as a result of the functioning of the administrative machine, with or without fault, then the judges need have no qualms about finding the Administration liable. As will be seen shortly, the *Conseil d'Etat* has developed to a considerable extent such a liability.

In the past there has been some dispute among jurists over its jurisprudential nature. The *Conseil d'Etat* has shown no willingness to lay down any general principle, preferring to treat each case on its merits. Jurists at first sought a private law analogy. Hauriou, for instance, found it in unjust enrichment.[3] Those ideas have now been largely abandoned, and there is a large measure of agreement on the theory of risk. Teissier,[4] Jèze,[5] Duez[6] and Trotabas[7] all base it on the task of public law to ensure for all equality of public services and burdens. Just as no individual should receive preferential treatment from the Administration, so also he should not suffer special loss at its hands. If he does so, the balance should be restored by all persons sharing the burden equally. He who suffers an exceptional loss through the functioning of the governmental machine is

1 So held in *Delville*, Conseil d'Etat, 28 July 1951.
2 *Laruelle*, Conseil d'Etat, 28 July 1951.   3 *Op. cit.* 335.
4 Teissier, *La Responsabilité de la Puissance Publique, passim.*
5 Notes in *R.D.P. passim.*   6 Duez, *op. cit. passim.*
7 Trotabas, *op. cit.* XIII; *J.C.L.* (1931) 57.

entitled to have his loss repaired at the expense of the community in general. The very functioning of the service creates a risk which must be borne by the public equally. Duguit[1] and Waline[2] even assert that the State is the insurer of anyone injured in the course of its affairs.

There are two views of its origins. Duguit[3] and Duez[4] trace it back to the Revolution in this manner. None of the constitutions of that time declares any liability of the State, nor could this be expected in view of the dominance of the idea of sovereignty. At the same time the Roman concept of *dominium* lived on with the result that one thing, property, was superior even to sovereignty itself. Consequently, from the Revolution onwards, the State had to indemnify those whose property it expropriated. The extension of this notion to informal expropriation in the course of public works and even to indirect damage caused by the execution of public works was a smooth and easy one. Others like Trotabas[5] and Ponthus[6] regard expropriation under legislative authority as something quite different from risk, and think that the development of risk is attributable to the ingenuity of the *Conseil d'Etat*.

Both schools would agree that public works is the most important sphere in which liability for risk is recognised.[7] So, the owner of a well dried up through the tunnel excavations of the Public Works Administration on adjoining land could sue.[8] So could a café proprietor whose business suffered through highway obstructions.[9] The absence of fault will not prevent the State from being held liable for a permanent[10] and material loss caused by the execution of public works.[11] There are, as Waline has pointed out,[12] powerful reasons for this, the economic size of the State, the impossibility of *restitutio in integrum* and the difficulty of proving fault.

1 *Traité*, S. 81.
2 *Op. cit.* 580, he calls it *l'obligation de garantie de l'Etat*, 580.
3 *Traité*, S. 81.   4 *Op. cit.* 56 *et seq.*
5 *Op. cit.* XIII, 58.   6 *Op. cit.* 85.
7 For a detailed account of this branch of liability, see Mathiot, *Les Accidents Causés par les Travaux Publics*, *passim*, and R. Latournine, 'Dommages Causés par les Travaux Publics' in 60 *R.D.P.* (1945) 1. These actions against the Administration (unlike others) are tried by the *Conseil de Préfecture*, with a right of appeal to the *Conseil d'Etat*.
8 *Chamboredon*, Sirey, 1885, 3, 25.   9 *Lancelle*, Lebon, 1910, 486.
10 De Laubadère, *op. cit.* 122 suggests that if the damage were caused by a falling tree, *faute* would have to be proved. Cf. the English decisions in nuisance and negligence, *Noble v. Harrison*, [1926] 2 K.B. 332; *Cunliffe v. Bankes*, [1945] 1 All E.R. 459; *Caminer v. Northern and London Investment Trust Ltd.*, [1951] A.C. 88.
11 *Force majeure* (something extrinsic to the service) but not *cas fortuit* (intrinsic) is a defence—Duez, *op. cit.* 35.
12 *Op. cit.* 601.

Soon, the idea of risk penetrated other fields. In the *Cames Case*[1] of 1895 a workman obtained damages from his employer, the State, for injury sustained in the course of his employment through no fault of the State. Even more important was the extension to liability for explosions in ammunition dumps during the War of 1914–18 because they 'created risks in excess of such as result normally from neighbourhood'. The cases which made this extension, *Regnault-Desroziers*[2] and *Colas*,[3] are even more striking when it is noted that they are in flat contradiction of earlier decisions of the *Conseil d'Etat*,[4] an excellent illustration of the fact that that tribunal is not fettered by the doctrine of judicial precedent. Duguit thought these cases so important as to amount to a general acceptance of the idea of risk.[5]

Certainly, further new extensions were soon to follow. Prominent among them was the *Couitéas* decision.[6] The military authorities did not obey the requisition of the Minister of Justice to evict some Tunisian squatters from the land of the claimant in accordance with a judgment for trespass obtained by the claimant from a civil court. This refusal was in obedience to instructions from the Minister of Foreign Affairs that serious disturbances were to be feared if the eviction were carried out. Clearly the Government was acting within its powers in not evicting the natives, yet the claimant was awarded damages. In a later case[7] the mayor had ordered the destruction by fire of a contaminated building. The owner of an adjoining house damaged by the spread of the fire without negligence on the part of the Administration recovered on the basis of risk. Obviously the doctrine has pushed beyond the domain of *gestion* into that of *puissance publique*. Jèze[8] and Duguit[9] have argued that these cases are so wide in scope, and so representative, that the general recognition of risk must be conceded. None the less, the *Conseil d'Etat* has not yet recognised the universality of liability for risk. Certainly, it may happen in the future, and perhaps Waline is right when he says that only financial reasons are in the way of its general acceptance.[10]

If then risk has not superseded fault, one must look for some systematisation of the heads of liability for risk. Waline suggests[11] the following: *risque professionnel* (e.g. pensions claims by civil servants), *risque social*

1 Sirey, 1897, 3, 33. A statute of 1898 on this topic prevented the *Conseil d'Etat* from further developing it.
2 Dall. Pér. 1920, 3, 1; see now law of 28 Oct. 1946, art. 6.
3 Sirey, 1924, 3, 53.   4 E.g. *Ambrosini*, Sirey, 1912, 3, 161.
5 *Traité*, 506.   6 Dall. Pér. 1923, 3, 59.
7 *Walther*, Sirey, 1927, 3, 44.   8 Notes in *R.D.P. passim*.
9 *Traité*, 506.   10 *Op. cit.* 505 (4th ed.).
11 *Ibid.*

(e.g. liability for damage caused by riots), *risque anormal de voisinage*, and *refus d'exécution des sentences judiciaires.*[1] Ponthus[2] makes this division: *les travaux publics, l'inexécution des décisions de justice*, and *collaboration volontaire d'un particulier au fonctionnement d'un service public.* Neither these nor other attempts seem very successful: at best they seem artificial categories likely to be outmoded at any time by the latest decisions of the *Conseil d'Etat.* It has recently been asserted that 'anormalité' unites the apparent diversity of fault and risk.[3] However, it seems safest to say that risk remains a basis of liability subordinate to fault, that the categories of risk are not closed, and that their extension in an empirical fashion by the *Conseil d'Etat* can be expected. Perhaps also its power to deny a remedy if there is *force majeure*, or indirect or moral or remote damage will help the *Conseil d'Etat* to maintain a flexibility in this liability that will harmonise both with current juridical ideas and the state of the public finances.[4]

F. Limitations on Liability of the State

(i) *Judicial Acts.* A judicial officer is not freely suable for judicial acts. By a *prise à partie* he may, however, be sued for fraud, arbitrary conduct, extortion and wilful denial of justice.[5] The procedure is complicated, and the action may be brought only with the consent of the court having jurisdiction over it.[6] French jurists on the whole seem dissatisfied with its operation.[7]

In 1895 a statute for the first time allowed an appeal court acquitting a prisoner to grant him damages against the State for his wrongful conviction. Since 1933 there has been one further liability:[8] the State is secondarily liable for the gross fraud or negligence of a magistrate in connection with bail. These are the only exceptions to the general rule that the State is not liable for *actes juridictionnelles.* Until recently, at least, most French jurists approved of this general rule.[9] Justification is said to

---

1 *Couitéas*, Dall. Pér. 1923, 3, 59; *Société de Cartonnerie et d'Imprimerie Saint Charles*, Dall. Pér. 1938, 3, 65.　　　　2 *Op. cit.* 85–6.

3 R. Latournerie, 'Dommages Causés par des Travaux Publics' in 60 *R.D.P.* (1945) 1 at 5.　　　　4 Cf. Duez, *op. cit.* 66.

5 Criminal Code, arts. 505–16; the State is answerable in damages for them—law of 7 February 1933. Administrative judges are liable for *faute personelle*, but the State is not suable for their judicial errors; M. de la Roque, 'Essai sur la Responsabilité du Juge Administratif' in 67 *R.D.P.* (1952) 609.

6 Nesmes-Desmarets, *De la Responsabilité Civile des Fonctionnaires de l'Ordre Administratif et Judiciaire*, 207 et seq.　　　　7 E.g. Duguit, *Transformations*, 247 et seq.

8 Article 7 of law of 7 February 1933.

9 E.g. Teissier, *Répertoire de Droit Administratif*, 42; Garraud, *Précis de Droit Criminel*, 943; Rolland, Note in 26 *R.D.P.* (1909) 727.

be in theories of sovereignty, in the separation of powers, and in the need for the absolute independence of the judiciary and the maintenance of the principle of *res judicata*.

Duguit was one of the few jurists to protest at the absence of remedy against the State.[1] He contended that judicial acts should only confer immunity on the State where to hold otherwise would be contrary to the principle of *res judicata*. A judicial decision is a truth, a reality, which fixes finally the status and relations of the litigants, and to interfere with it would be contrary to the general interest. On the other hand, where there was a defective functioning of the Administration, he thought that the State should be suable if the principle of *res judicata* were not thereby affected. He distinguished between judicial decisions and other functions, such as execution of judicial process, granting of bail, and the like, which, though performed by judicial officers, were administrative in nature. There was no social interest in State immunity for those acts, and he demanded that the *Conseil d'Etat* exercise jurisdiction over them. This it has, however, refused to do.[2] He therefore supported the immunity for judicial decisions, and reinforced it by asserting that when an innocent man was found not guilty by a court of first instance, there was no administrative fault, no defective functioning of the service. He supported the 1895 statute on two grounds, that if the verdict had been successfully appealed against, to give damages for the original decision is not counter to the principle of *res judicata*, and that the appellate decision exposes the defects of the original verdict.

Perhaps the only signs that Duguit's arguments have been heeded are the *Couitéas* decision that the State is liable for not executing a judicial decision,[3] and the slight but discernible recent change of front on the part of French jurists.

(ii) *Legislative Acts.* As early as 1838 the *Conseil d'Etat* denied a remedy to manufacturers of artificial tobacco who sought compensation from the State for the loss sustained consequent on the prohibition of its manufacture.[4] For a hundred years that court pursued the policy. It did so because it regarded the legislature as sovereign, and because to do otherwise would contravene the doctrine of the separation of powers. In this it had the support of French jurists.[5]

Duguit, however, was dissatisfied with the situation.[6] Denying the validity of the theory of sovereignty, and seeing no obstacle in the

1 *Traité*, S. 85.   2 *Lambertin*, Recueil, 1919, 116.
3 See p. 68 *supra*.   4 *Duchatelier, Conseil d'Etat*, 11 Jan. 1838.
5 H. Berthélemy, Note in 24 *R.D.P.* (1907), 92; Arlet, *De la Responsabilité de l'Etat Législateur*; Giraud, *De la Responsabilité de l'Etat à Raison des Dommages Naissant de la Loi.*   6 *Transformations*, 234 et seq.

separation of powers, he argued as follows. Not everyone suffering damage through legislative acts should be entitled to damages. If the State prohibits an activity in itself injurious to it either physically or morally, then no damages should be given. So, the French legislature acted properly in refusing compensation when brothels and absinthe factories were prohibited, nor ought the courts to provide any. On the contrary, if the State nationalises some industry previously carried on by private enterprise, it ought to compensate those injured thereby. If the statute omits it, then the courts should fill the gap. Duguit prophesied that within a short time the *Conseil d'Etat* would recognise the validity of his arguments. There are many ambiguities in his proposals. Was not the manufacture of baby's feeding bottles until its prohibition just as legal as the manufacture of matches until it was made a state monopoly? Does not each amount to a decision that it is in the public interest that the manufacture should cease? Are the courts competent to decide whether the prohibited trade has this faint odour of non-respectability which is to disqualify its entrepreneurs from compensation? What, for instance, if the State forbids the sending through the post of gambling literature because there is a temporary paper shortage? Moreover, Duguit's renunciation of sovereignty carries him to the extreme position of authorising the courts to grant relief even if the statute contains an express prohibition.[1] The theoretical justification for his right of action is that an individual suffering a special loss in the public interest through no fault of his own must be compensated. When is the loss special?[2] Is it only when those suffering it are readily identifiable at the time of the legislation? If a ferry service is prohibited, and no compensation is given by the act, is the café proprietor on the quay as well as the ferry owner entitled to sue?

Duguit's prophecies have been at least in part accurate. In 1938 the *Conseil d'Etat* decided the *La Fleurette Case*.[3] A statute prohibited the manufacture of ice-cream substitute, and a manufacturer of it, given no compensation by the statute, recovered it in an action against the State before the *Conseil d'Etat*. This was followed by a similar decision in 1944.[4] In order to encourage cereal producers the percentage of sugar in beer was reduced. Damages were awarded to a sugar manufacturer compelled in consequence to close down his plant.

These cases have of course necessitated a re-examination of the position by French jurists. Jèze supports the decisions because they apply the principle of equality of burdens.[5] De Laubadère praises the principles for

1 *Traité*, 572.   2 Cf. Gellhorn & Schenck, *op. cit.* 739.
3 Sirey, 1938, 3, 25.   4 *Caucheteux et Desmont*, Dall. Analytique, 1944, J. 65.
5 G. Jèze, 'Préjudice Causé par une Loi' in 60 *R.D.P.* (1945) 366.

their flexibility, but thinks it essential to a right of action that a few readily identifiable people should suffer exceptional damage, and that the trade should be legal.[1] Waline (and surely he is right) denies the remedy if it is contrary to the clear intention of the statute.[2] He also holds that there is no remedy if the claimant is *turpis*. The developments are of recent growth, and are not fully worked out.[3] The problems posed in the preceding paragraph have not been faced by the *Conseil d'Etat*. One can expect that the *Conseil d'Etat* will decide each case on its own facts, and set its face resolutely against the laying down of any principle, at least for a long time.

(iii) *Actes de Gouvernement*. Governments everywhere are always zealous in secreting matters from the public gaze. There is a standing temptation to plead the public interest as a reason either for non-disclosure or even for denying the courts the right to review administrative acts. France is in no better case than other countries in this respect.[4]

There have long been and still are categories of governmental acts in France which the courts cannot control either by quashing for *excès de pouvoir* or by granting an indemnity.[5] Originally, it was contended that this exemption covered all *actes discrétionnaires*, but this claim is now abandoned.[6] To decide otherwise would of course make the Administration virtually free from any control.

Until 1872 there did, however, persist the dangerous theory of *mobile politique*. It was the motive not the nature of the act which determined whether the courts could adjudicate on it. If the end, in the opinion of the Government, were the security, whether internal or external, of the State then there was an *acte de gouvernement* immune from the jurisdiction of the courts.[7] Nineteenth-century French Governments under this cover seized lands and private documents, and even suppressed newspapers. Decisions of the courts in 1875[8] and 1887,[9] perhaps symbolic of the decline of sovereignty and of despotic government, marked the end of this theory of *actes de gouvernement*. The new criterion sought was in the nature of the

---

1 *Op. cit.* 126.   2 *Op. cit.* 513, 605.

3 See ch. III *infra* for the effect of subsequent legislation on contracts between State and citizen.

4 *Law Society*, Report of M. Hersant and H. Street, *Les Recours Contentieux contre l'Abus de Pouvoir Administratif*, 120, for French refusal to disclose in litigation documents the production of which is deemed contrary to the public interest.

5 By law of 24 May 1872, art. 26, ministers have the right to claim before the *Tribunal des Conflits* the withdrawal from the *Conseil d'Etat* of cases over which they have no jurisdiction.

6 *Annuaire de l'Institut International de Droit Public*, vol. XII, pt. II (1931, Paris), Rapport de P. Duez 35 *et seq.*; Hauriou, 395.

7 Dufour, *Traité Général de Droit Administratif Appliqué*, *passim*.

8 *Prince Napoléon*, Dall. Pér. 1875, 3, 18.

9 *Duc d'Aumale et Prince Joachim Murat*, Sirey, 1889, 3, 29.

act. A distinction was suggested between governmental or political acts and administrative ones. The attempt to establish this distinction failed. The broad differentiation of formation at high level of policy and its execution could not readily be applied to concrete cases. Aucoc[1] and Laferrière[2] insisted on the validity of the distinction, but they could not agree on its application to specific issues.

The search for a theory of *actes de gouvernement* was abandoned. As Hauriou pointed out,[3] to rely on an imprecise theory would be to run the risk of a return to categories as wide as those under the discarded theory of *mobile politique*.[4] It is now generally agreed that there is a list empirically arrived at by the *Conseil d'Etat*.

First on the list[5] are decrees summoning the legislatures or altering legislative procedure. Next are *actes diplomatiques*.[6] The scope of this immunity is wide; the State is not responsible for failure to pursue the claims of a French national abroad, or to effect the termination of his unlawful imprisonment by another state. No action may be brought in respect of a treaty, even when France may have received money from another state for distribution among its own subjects.[7] This widely drawn exemption is disapproved of by many French writers.[8] The third group covers matters of public security, a group which has been narrowly construed in recent years by the courts; it would cover for instance a state of siege. Opinions of twenty years ago, that it included acts *en matière de police sanitaire* such as anti-flood or anti-epidemic measures,[9] no longer represent the law, according to Jèze.[10] Fourthly are *les faits de guerre*, the justification for which is the right of the government to freedom of action in time of war.[11]

1 Aucoc, 92. 2 Laferrière, *op. cit.* 33.
3 *Op. cit.* 397.
4 Cf. P. B. Rava, 'Italian Administrative Courts under Fascism' in 40 *Mich. L.R.* (1941) 654 at 671, and the extension of *actes de gouvernement* there to cases involving 'the supreme interests of the State'. Sokol v. *Ministero dell' interno Foro Ammin*, 1927, I, i, 118, where the dissolution by government decree of a foreign gymnastic society was not reviewable because the aim was to curb foreign propaganda.
5 Duez, *Les Actes de Gouvernement*, is one of the best up-to-date monographs on the subject.
6 L. Trotabas, 'Les Actes de Gouvernement en Matières Diplomatiques' in *Revue Critique de Législation et de Jurisprudence* (1925) 342. There may be a detachable *faute personnelle* connected with *actes de gouvernement* in this group; *Giraud*, Sirey, 1942, 3, 21; cf. *Société Worms et Cie, Conseil d'Etat*, 7 Sept. 1945.
7 *Hutter*, Recueil, 1921, 127. 8 E.g. Appleton, *op. cit.* 293.
9 Hauriou, *op. cit.* 398.
10 Jèze, *Principes Généraux du Droit Administratif, passim*.
11 The reports in the *Annuaire, op. cit.* show how closely other European countries have followed the French lead in defining *actes de gouvernement*. See in particular the report of R. Laun, 87 *et seq.* and of M. Vauthier, 233 *et seq.*

These exemptions are substantial and there is the ever-present danger of their extension. Duguit[1] has shown that in the past, just when the *Conseil d'Etat* has seemed about to reject the notion of *actes de gouvernement*, it has extended the field of application. Most French jurists would support the continuance of *actes de gouvernement* in a restricted form on the ground that it is a necessary condition of harmony between the Administration and the Judiciary; without it *droit administratif* would be intolerable to the Government.[2] An English lawyer might be pardoned for asking why most of the acts listed above could not be justified on the plea that they were within the scope of the discretion of the officials, without having recourse to a theory of *actes de gouvernement*. Some think that the action for damages might lie on the theory of risk even though the annulment of an *acte de gouvernement* is rightly adjudged impossible,[3] and that decisions like those of *Couitéas*[4] and *Walthier*[5] are pointing in this direction.

G. *Voie de Fait*[6]

No account of the tortious liability of the Administration in France is complete without a description of the role of the *voie de fait* or administrative trespass. Little prominence is given to it by French administrative jurists. Certainly it is a prickly thorn in the side of those concerned to demonstrate the all-embracing and exclusive control of the administrative courts over the Administration.

Where there is a *voie de fait* the administrative courts have no jurisdiction; instead the civil courts have it. Sometimes the Administration purports to interfere with a citizen's rights under colour of authority when in the particular circumstances it has no authority to interfere; its action is illegal and outside the administrative domain. If then these acts have no administrative quality it is consistent with the theory of separation of powers to grant jurisdiction over them to the civil courts.

This usurpation of power is not the same as an excess of power. The difference is one of degree. So, a mere *violation des formes* would be an *excès de pouvoir* but would remain administrative; *l'absence totale de formes*, i.e. something outside the administrative sphere, would be a *voie de fait*. If an agent doing something within the power of his superior had himself no authority, his act could be challenged as a *voie de fait*.[7]

---

1 *Traité*, S. 99.   2 Hauriou, *op. cit.* 400.
3 Jèze, *Droit Administratif*, 411.   4 Dall. Pér. 1923, 3, 59.
5 Sirey, 1927, 3, 44.
6 For a recent description in English, see Uhler, *op. cit.* ch. 'Administrative Trespass'.
A recent French monograph is Goutagny, *La Théorie des Voies de Fait*.
7 Welire, *op. cit.* 432.

Some of the writers anxious to belittle *voie de fait* have said that *voie de fait* merely means that the Administration has not acted at all, and that there is thus only a *faute personnelle* for which the official may be sued. This conceals the important fact that there may be a *voie de fait* for which the Administration, and the Administration only, can be sued in the civil courts. For example, if the appropriate authority illegally constructed overhead electricity pylons on land, the landowner could sue the Administration civilly.[1] Sometimes there may be a *faute personnelle* in addition to this liability of the Administration.

To succeed in this civil action of *voie de fait* the litigant must show that the act is illegal, that it is outside the administrative sphere, and that it injures his private rights. The illegality may be either want of authority in the Administration or a defect of procedure. Any want of authority or a serious procedural error will deprive the act of its administrative character.[2] The private right may be either of property or of the person. To keep a person in prison illegally, to conscript him for military service, or to encroach[3] on his land may all be *voies de fait*. The remedies for a *voie de fait* are not only damages; the Administration may be ordered to desist from the continuance of the activity, and sometimes may be ordered to pull down illegal erections.[4] Whether the last can be ordered of *travaux publics* is doubtful: perhaps the rule is that the public interest is paramount.[5]

A decision in 1935[6] illustrates the operation of the *voie de fait*. A Paris newspaper had been seized and confiscated on the orders of the Paris prefect of police. In a civil action brought by the publisher it was held that there had been no *faute personnelle*. It was further agreed that in an emergency the Administration could seize a newspaper. Here, the order was not limited by the needs of public safety, because it authorised a seizure anywhere in Paris or its suburbs although no menace to public safety was either present or apprehended. There was therefore a *voie de fait* for which the Administration was liable in a civil court.

As De Laubadère says,[7] in view of decisions like this, it is futile to deny the existence of a *voie de fait* for which the Administration may be sued. Most administrative jurists[8] do at the same time condemn it as a historical

---

1 *Réalmont*, Sirey, 1935, 3, 97 (*Tribunal des Conflits*).
2 *Ponthus, op. cit.* 80.
3 If there is damage to land without an encroachment, the *Conseil d'Etat* has jurisdiction; Couzinet, *La Réparation des Atteintes Portées à la Propriété Privée Immobilière par les Groupements Administratifs.*
4 *Société Normande de Gaz et d'Electricité*, Dall. Pér. 1937, 3, 17.
5 Goutagny, *op. cit.* 107–8.
6 *L'Action Française*, Dall. Pér. 1935, 3, 25; ctra. *Société Immobilière de Saint Just*, Sirey, 1904, 3, 17.
7 *Op. cit.* 66.   8 E.g. Duez, Couzinet, *op. cit.*

survival of the time when there was no confidence in the *Conseil d'Etat*. Yet there is the evidence of a French practitioner[1] that since the 1939–45 war *voies de fait* have become increasingly numerous.

H. *Statutory Liability*

There is a common impression that administrative courts exercise a virtual monopoly of jurisdiction over cases involving the civil liability of the French State. Besides the exceptions already discussed, there is a wide field of statutory administrative liability within the jurisdiction of the civil courts.

By a law of 1899[2] the liability of the State for acts of teachers to pupils is a matter for the civil courts. All claims against the customs, railways,[3] and the postal and telegraph services[4] are dealt with in the same way.

There are elaborate war damage compensation statutes also vesting adjudication of disputes in the civil courts.[5] Liability for riots is a statutory liability,[6] and so is State liability for industrial accidents to its employees.[7] There is a civil liability for damage caused by army manœuvres.[8] A soldier, too, enforces his pension rights in civil courts. Always, of course, the detailed provisions of these statutes must be considered in a particular case, but they embody in general the principle of risk.

3. PROPOSALS FOR REFORM

Anyone accepting at their face value the panegyrics of French public lawyers on the French rules of administrative liability would unhesitatingly recommend their adoption *in toto* in Anglo-American law. However, it is submitted that there are too many defects in the system to allow that.

French legal administration is hamstrung by a blind unreasoning adherence to a 200-year-old doctrine of political conduct, the separation of powers. This produces several unsatisfactory results. Jurisdiction of judicial and administrative bodies must be rigidly separated. A special court has to be set up to resolve jurisdictional conflicts; yet only the administrative and not the judicial tribunal may raise a case before it. Once the administrative

---

1 Ponthus, *op. cit.* 79. Cf. *Livre Jubilaire, op. cit.* 156.
2 10 July 1899, and 5 April 1937.
3 E.g. *Groscœur*, Sirey, 1888, 1, 228 (*Cour de Cassation*).
4 No action lies for damages resulting from fault in the transmission of ordinary mail or telegrams, or in connection with telephonic communications; laws of 5 April 1897; 31 March 1931.
5 See de Vaulx, *La Responsabilité de l'Etat Française à Cause des Dommages Causés par les Faits de Guerre*.
6 Law of 16 April 1914.   7 Workmen's Compensation Law of 9 April 1898.
8 Law of 17 April 1901.

act amounts to a trespass on the rights of citizens administrative law ceases to be applicable; instead, it is an issue of civil law for the ordinary courts. Administrative courts are handicapped in handling matters affecting the Legislature and the Judiciary. Excessive devotion to the doctrine causes the administrative courts to deny their competence to pronounce on even the non-judicial duties of judicial officials.

Pervading this body of law is excessive respect for the political branch of the State. Ministers are incapable of doing wrong, *actes de gouvernement* are outside the jurisdiction, no injunction or other enforcement provisions are permitted against the State.

Moreover, there is too much uncertainty about the principles of liability. What degree of gravity is required for a *faute de service*? What are the categories of risk? These and many other fundamental questions are unsolved. Perhaps this illustrates the main defect of the French *jurisprudence*, the lack of precision consequent upon a denial of the binding force of precedent. Among other specific faults might be mentioned the following. A theory of damages omitting compensation for moral damage is inadequate. To exclude punitive damages is sound, but not those damages which, though they cannot be readily assessed, are none the less real and substantial. The theory of *cumul* leads to official irresponsibility with the attendant danger of a poor standard of public service. The procedure is slow;[1] long-delayed justice is never satisfactory justice. There is a lack of uniformity in the system; too many liabilities are statutory civil ones for no reason other than that statutes were passed before the present administrative law had been developed.

Advocates of the French system have sought to show its merit by comparing it with other systems. Existing material comparing it with Anglo-American law is of little value because it was written before the latter had accepted tortious liability. More useful is the literature on Belgium which, since 1920 at least, has recognised State liability based on principles of private law.[2] Many of the criticisms[3] are trivial, since they relate to matters not of the essence of a system of private law liability. Typical is the following argument: Vicarious liability depends on there being a contract between master and servant; there is no contract between State and servant; therefore a private law system of liability is impossible.[4]

---

1 E.g. *Jacquin*, Conseil d'Etat, 14 April 1948, was decided ten years after proceedings were started.

2 Vauthier, *Précis du Droit Administratif de la Belgique*.

3 Debeyre, *op. cit.* 39 *et seq.*; cf. P. Negulesco, 'La Responsabilité de la Puissance Publique' in 10 *Revista de Drept Public* (1935), 233; A. Teodoresco, 'Le Fondement Juridique de la Responsabilité dans le Droit Administratif', *Mélanges Paul Negulesco*, 751.   4 Duez, *La Responsabilité de la Puissance Publique*.

None the less, it is submitted that the French system embodies two principles of great merit, the adoption of which by common law countries deserves serious consideration. They are the tendency to base administrative liability on risk rather than fault, and the subjection of all administrative bodies, whether central or local, to the same law. How this principle of risk could be applied will now be investigated.

Where the functioning of the administrative machine inflicts on an individual an exceptional loss, even in the absence of fault, it is submitted that the State should be liable. So, the pedestrian knocked down by the municipal ambulance rushing a critically ill patient to hospital should have an action. The householder whose property is damaged by the dangerous lunatic who has escaped from the neighbouring mental home needs compensation. The motorist whose car axle is broken through a roadway being out of repair is entitled to a remedy. So is the tenant of a house, flooded while the fire brigade is extinguishing a fire next door. In each of these cases the Administration, functioning without fault, has inflicted exceptional damage on a citizen. The usual rules of causation in the law of tort should apply here to determine whether damage is too remote.

It is far more difficult when the damage is caused, not in the course of execution of a decision, but by the making of the decision. The levy of an additional tax on tobacco damages smokers but not others. Petrol rationing is more injurious to him whose livelihood depends on the use of a car. Yet few would suggest that the courts should have a power to award compensation to those victims of State policy. Whether general legislation shall give rise to individual claims for compensation seems a policy decision for Parliament to make. In doing so, it should consider whether any identifiable section of the community has sustained a loss for which there ought to be compensation.

What if the decision is at a lower level of administrative policy? During an epidemic the health authorities prohibit children from attending cinemas. Is the cinema owner entitled to damages? And the owner of the sweet shop in the *foyer*? The Ministry of Agriculture and Fisheries temporarily prohibits the transport of produce from a pest-infested farming belt. Is the farmer entitled to damages? Should it make any difference that the decision was an error of judgment, scientific investigation showing that the restriction was unjustified? The principle should be that only those suffering special loss should be compensated. Since many of these acts are local, they will cause special loss more often than legislation. The question is whether the courts should be given a general power to award compensation or whether that power should rest on specific authorisation contained in the Act of Parliament in pursuance of which the act was performed. The line between legislation and administration is hard to draw; to say that if the legislation were delegated then a general power should be vested in the courts, but not otherwise, seems arbitrary. Perhaps, again, it is the duty of Parliament to decide whether compensation should be payable. In some cases it could be specific, as it has been in expropriation statutes, and in others it might confer power on the courts to award compensation when the administrative act has inflicted an exceptional loss.

At the end of the comparison of English and American law several reforms within the framework of the existing private law system were proposed. What is eventually needed is a new code of administrative liability by which public authorities are liable for pecuniary damage directly caused in the course of the execution of their functions, provided that the damage suffered by the citizen suing is an exceptional loss exceeding that of his fellow-citizens. Whether there is a tort by an official would be irrelevant except to decide whether the public authority could recover from him a contribution. There would be liability for legislative acts to the limited extent set out above. Liability for judicial errors should be based on the United States statute. The other existing judicial immunities would continue but would not extend to the execution of judicial process. Breaches of statutory duty (including that to repair highways) owed either by the administrative body or by officials to citizens would entail administrative responsibility. In all cases performance of the duty could be compelled by mandamus. There would be no class of public officer for whom no administrative body would be liable. The body in control of him would be suable, and, in doubtful cases, the Crown would be liable. Existing doubts whether specific bodies were the Crown would no longer be material. The immunities of the armed forces and the savings for prerogative powers could be abolished. Act of State might remain as a defence, and the present postal immunities could be supported if the personal liability of officials for their own torts were reintroduced.

Who should adjudicate on these new issues? Belgium has entrusted disputes on its new grounds of liability to an administrative tribunal, leaving the old jurisdiction with the civil courts.[1] This seems an undesirable split, and one which will lead to difficult questions of jurisdiction.

The French argument, of course, is that these principles are essentially ones of public law, and must be worked out in special administrative tribunals.[2] One might have thought that France has this special jurisdiction

---

1 See p. 24 *supra*.
2 Cf. E. M. Borchard, 'French Administrative Law' in 18 *Iowa L.R.* (1932) 133 at 135.

largely because of the accident that she is committed to the separation of powers. Nevertheless, the contentions advanced by the supporters of her system of administrative tribunals must be examined.

It is complained that the citizen is reluctant to sue in civil courts because of the expense. But surely this points the need for reform of court procedure, not the innate superiority of administrative tribunals. Further, only administrative tribunals can strike a fair balance between private and public interests. Yet ordinary courts do not adjudicate in a vacuum where the issues of public interest cannot penetrate. And may not an administrative tribunal pay more attention to the public interest than the private? It is insisted that experienced administrators must be on the court to appreciate the peculiar problems of the Administration. This might be a valid argument for some aspects of administrative jurisdiction, for instance town planning or housing, but it is not evident what special administrative knowledge is called for to settle pecuniary liabilities of the Administration. Next it is argued that in this age of specialisation a specialised tribunal is essential. Even if this is granted, may there not be specialisation within the High Court, as in the English Commercial court? The incapacity of the ordinary courts to administer equity untrammelled by common law notions is further alleged. If the courts are so authorised, they can administer equity with the same ease and facility with which they have applied general standards of reasonableness, fairness and good faith in other spheres of their jurisdiction.

There seems therefore no reason why the development of this administrative liability should not be entrusted to the judges. Moreover, it is entirely in harmony with English traditions that this should be done. It also avoids problems of conflict of jurisdiction. It is not a case of unyielding opposition to any administrative tribunals—on the contrary the necessity for administrative tribunals for pensions, insurance and numerous other disputes is freely conceded. The suggestion is that there is a presumption that litigation should be fought out in the ordinary courts, and nothing in the circumstances of this case rebuts that presumption. The courts are no strangers to principles of strict liability in *Rylands* v. *Fletcher*, liability for animals, vicarious liability and the like, and they are quite competent to apply similar principles to litigation by citizens against the State.

Chapter III

CONTRACT

Section 1 of the Crown Proceedings Act provides:

> Where any person has a claim against the Crown after the commencement of this Act, and, if this Act had not been passed, the claim might have been enforced, subject to the grant of His Majesty's fiat, by petition of right, or might have been enforced by a proceeding provided by any statutory provision repealed by this Act, then, subject to the provisions of this Act, the claim may be enforced as of right, and without the fiat of His Majesty, by proceedings taken against the Crown for that purpose in accordance with the provisions of this Act.

Since proceedings for breach of contract could be instituted by petition of right[1] those may now be freely brought without using special procedures. The United States threw off the shackles of sovereignty from suits in contract much sooner.[2] The Tucker Act of 1887 provides that the United States can be sued upon its contracts. Suits are brought in a special court sitting at Washington, the Court of Claims.[3] This court, whose judges are appointed for life, exercises jurisdiction only over government suits. Its five judges sit together and only majority judgments are usually given. The Federal District Courts exercise concurrent jurisdiction over claims of not more than ten thousand dollars. There is an appeal to the Supreme Court from the Court of Claims. In France, too, since the Revolution, the State has been suable on its contracts.

I. GOVERNMENT CONTRACTS AS A SEPARATE BRANCH OF THE LAW

Government contracts are principally for the supply and procurement of materials and the execution of public works. Are these government contracts a legal category separate from private contracts? No one could answer this in the affirmative if he relied upon the English standard text-books on the law of contract. Nor is there, it is believed, a single monograph

---

1 For detailed accounts of the old law, see Robertson, *op. cit.* bk. III; Clode, *op. cit.* ch. X.

2 For a detailed account of the United States law of government contract, see Shealey, *The Law of Government Contracts, passim.*

3 W. A. Richardson, 'History, Jurisdiction and Practice of the Court of Claims of the United States' in 7 *Southern L.R.* (1882) 781.

on the subject.[1] The attitude to the topic in the United States is radically different. There are standard text-books on the subject.[2] Williston[3] treats the topic under a separate heading; 'Government Contracts' is a separate sub-title in the Index to Legal Periodicals, itself a witness to the abundant American periodical literature. At least one university law school has had a separate course in the LL.B. curriculum on 'Government Contracts' which occupied a whole semester.[4] No less than five of the fields of research suggested by Field in his *Research in Administrative Law* are on the topic.

The French are ranged on the side of the United States. For them *contrat administratif* is a separate subject. Jèze long advocated the need for this separation.[5] The effects of his pleading can be measured from the fact that the standard books on *droit administratif* now devote entire chapters to it,[6] and that a recent work entitled *Théorie Générale du Contrat Administratif*[7] has been published.

It is submitted that these contracts differ from ordinary contracts between individuals and should to some extent be governed by different legal rules. One writer has said:[8] 'In contract government enters the market place not as sovereign. On the other hand contract is a device that can be used as a method of coercion and to that extent it can be used to accomplish some of the regulatory ends of government.' If that is so, then it must have separate rules. One may show without difficulty that in England the Government does use contractual power for this purpose. For instance, since 1891 the House of Commons has required government contractors to comply with a fair labour standards resolution passed by it.[9] The current resolution was approved by the House of Commons in 1946.[10] Typical of the manner in which this resolution is introduced into government contracts is clause 51 of the General Conditions of Government Contracts for Building and Civil Engineering Works:[11] 'The Contractor shall, in the execution of the contract, observe and fulfil the

1 Cf. W. Friedmann, 'Changing Functions of Contract in the Common Law' in 10 *U.T.L.J.* (1951) 15 at 33 *et seq.*; J. D. B. Mitchell, 'A General Theory of Public Contracts' in 63 *Juridical Review* (1951) 60.
2 Shealey; L. M. Cherne, *Government Contract Problems.*
3 *Law of Contracts*, vol. IX, ch. XII.
4 University of Nebraska, by Dean Beutel. There is a mimeographed case-book for the course; Beutel and T. C. Billig, *Government Contracts.*
5 *Principes Généraux de Droit Administratif*, 15 *et seq.*
6 E.g. Appleton, *op. cit.* bk. IV, ch. I; Waline, *op. cit.* bk. IV, title I.
7 Péquignot.   8 Field, *op. cit.* 33.
9 O. Kahn-Freund, 'Legislation through Adjudication. The Legal Aspect of Fair Wages Clauses and Recognised Conditions' in 11 *Mod. L.R.* (1948) 269 at 272.
10 Hansard, 5 s. vol. 427, cols. 711–18.
11 Sept. 1948; Form CCC/Wks/1.

obligations upon contractors specified in the Fair Wages Resolution passed by the House of Commons on the 14th October 1946....' In consequence the contractor must pay the recognised rates of pay, observe the usual hours and conditions of labour, allow his employees to be members of trade unions, and see that his sub-contractors also observe these conditions. Indeed, he will not be allowed to tender unless he shows that he has in the past complied with these general conditions.

There are other differences of equal importance. If the Legislature is to maintain its traditional supremacy over the Executive and its financial control, the law of government contract must curtail the agency powers of executive officers to make contracts binding on the State. There is, moreover, in contracts made by all administrative authorities a public interest in the prevention of corruption, an interest normally safeguarded by special provisions regarding tenders, bids and disclosure of interest. French jurists contend that there is a special factor more important than any of these. To them *contrat administratif* is a device *pour assurer le fonctionnement régulier et continu des services publics, par des moyens juridiques plus faciles et plus énergiques que les moyens du droit privé.*[1] There is an overriding public interest in the State's getting its supplies and in its public works being executed, to which any niceties of private law must be subservient—in short, *le but de service public* is paramount.

Before comparing the English, American and French law of government contracts, it is desirable to examine a little more closely the French *contrat administratif.*

Not every government contract is subject to rules of public law. The contract must be *relatif à un service public*; one party to it must be an agent of the Administration, and it must be made in the exercise of an administrative function. If the function is merely *gestion privée*, for example a commercial lease,[2] it cannot be a *contrat administratif.* This test is not conclusive, but French jurists are imprecise about further criteria. It seems safest to say that the contract must contain provisions *exorbitantes du droit commun.* The form of the contract (when a *cahier des charges* is used), special terms such as one giving the Government a unilateral right to modify, ministerial control over the contract, direct participation by the contractor in the public service, for example, his claim for a reward after capturing stray dogs, and a submission to administrative jurisdiction —all these may evidence an intention to be governed by the *contrat administratif.*[3] Public works contracts are always in practice treated as

---

1 G. Jèze, 'Théorie du Contrat Administratif' in 60 *R.D.P.* (1943) 251.
2 *Compagnie Assurance 'Le Soleil'*, 4 June 1910 (*Conseil d'Etat*).
3 See Appleton, *op. cit.* 197; Péquignot, *op. cit.* 66 *et seq.*

administrative. One recent case decided that a contract for advertising in books of stamps was administrative, because it was contemplated that the Administration would be free to alter the design of their books even though to do so would involve an alteration in the advertising contract.[1] The same criteria are applied to determine whether the many recently created *entreprises d'intérêt public* have made administrative contracts. In what follows references to the French law will be to the *contrat administratif.*

2. LEGISLATIVE APPROPRIATIONS AND AGENCY[2]

Under both the English and United States constitutions the Legislature exercises control over the spending of moneys by the Executive. It is obvious that the maintenance of this principle presents some special problems in the field of contract. The Legislature must prevent contracts being made without its consent if they involve the spending of money.

This problem has been easily solved by the United States. A series of statutory provisions enacts that the United States shall not be bound by a contract purporting to be made on its behalf unless either the agent has express authority of statute to make it or there is 'an appropriation adequate to its fulfillment'.[3] The statute creates one exception: contracts for the subsistence and clothing of the armed forces for the current year.[4]

The common-law doctrine that the agent need only have ostensible authority does not apply;[5] his authority must be actual.[6] Nor can there be agency by estoppel.[7] Thus, Congress exercises adequate control without doing injustice to contractors.[8] Normally, a contract will be made by an authorised agent and with an appropriation, but if Congress has authorised an agent to make a contract, it would be harsh to withhold a right of action unless an appropriation had also been made. Recognising this, the Court of Claims has held that a professor at a military academy appointed by the Secretary of War under statutory authority could sue the United States even in the absence of an appropriation.[9] France also

1 *Courmont*, Recueil, 1940, 73 (*Conseil d'Etat*).
2 This section is a development of my article, 'The Provision of Funds in Satisfaction of Governmental Liabilities' in 8 *U.T.L.J.* (1949) 32.
3 R.S. §3732, 12 June 1906.
4 *The Floyd Acceptances* (1869), 7 Wall. (U.S.), 666.
5 P. E. Thurlow, 'Some Aspects of the Law of Government Contracts' in 21 *Chicago-Kent L.R.* (1942–3) 300; E. E. Naylor, 'Liability of the United States Government in Contract' in 14 *Tulane L.R.* (1940) 580 at 584.
6 *Whiteside* v. *U.S.* (1876), 93 U.S. 247 at 256; for a war-time relaxation of this rule see the Contracts Settlement Act, 1944, s. 17.
7 *Filor* v. *U.S.* (1869), 9 Wall. (U.S.) 45.
8 Katz, *Cases and Materials on Administrative Law*, ch. III, s. 2.
9 *Strong* v. *U.S.* (1925), 60 Ct. Cl. 627.

requires the agent to have actual legislative authority,[1] and ordinarily recognises no implied power to sub-delegate powers.[2] Central control in France is wielded by the provision that a *contrat administratif* is valid only when approved by a senior official of the Administration (*l'approbation*). In England, the law is not so just and unambiguous. Not until 1688 was this parliamentary control of expenditure a tenet of constitutional law, and not yet have its implications for crown-citizen relationships been worked out. Parliament itself has not intervened, and has left it to the courts to develop rules. Lacking legislative assistance, it seems that the courts have not appreciated the relative roles of agency and appropriation in securing the practical supremacy of Parliament. Nowhere in the cases is it suggested that different rules either apply or ought to apply when one seeks to make the Crown liable for the contracts made by agents. The problem has just not been tackled. So, a leading monograph on the law of agency states:[3] 'The Crown...may be sued...on any contract duly made on its behalf by a public agent.'

One might expect, as a corrective for this absence of a rule requiring actual authority of an agent, some special rule about appropriations. It is not surprising therefore that in modern text-books one finds the unanimous view that a government contract involving the payment of money by the Crown is invalid if Parliament has not made an express appropriation for the purposes of the contract. There is some disagreement about the basis for the rule; some ground it on incapacity of the Crown to contract without parliamentary appropriation;[4] others justify it for reasons of public policy;[5] but probably most would agree that 'there is an implied condition that the obligation is dependent upon the supply of funds by Parliament'.[6]

The authorities on which these statements are thought to be based warrant close examination. The earliest case cited, and the one chiefly relied on, is *Churchward* v. *Reg.*[7] The suppliant brought a petition of right alleging breach of a contract entered into with him by the Admiralty on behalf of the Crown. This contract provided that the suppliant was to maintain a mail service between Dover and the Continent for eleven years, the consideration to be 'a sum out of moneys to be provided by Parliament after the rate of £18,000 per annum'. The suppliant alleged that in 1863, the fourth year of the contract, the Admiralty ceased to employ him to carry the mails. The Appropriation Act, to its grant for

1 Péquignot, *op. cit.* 180.   2 Waline, *op. cit.* 571.
3 Bowstead, *Law of Agency*, 185.
4 E.g. Keir and Lawson, *Cases in Constitutional Law*, 220.
5 E.g. Keith, *The Constitutional Law of the British Dominions*, 387.
6 Dicey, *op. cit.*, Appendix by E. C. S. Wade, 528; Halsbury, *op. cit.* VI, 488.
7 (1865), 1 Q.B. 173.

the Post-Office packet service for that year, added this proviso:[1] 'No part of which sum is to be applicable or applied in or towards making any payment in respect of the period subsequent to the 20th June 1863 to the said Mr Joseph Churchward.' The *ratio decidendi* of this case is that a covenant subject to such a condition of payment[2] 'would be held to be binding on the covenantor only in the event of his being supplied with funds from the source which the covenant indicated'.[3] Since Parliament refused to provide these funds, the contract was void for non-performance of this condition precedent. It was quite unnecessary to consider the position where there was no such express condition, but Shee J. did add the following *obiter dicta*:[4]

In the case of a contract with Commissioners on behalf of the Crown to make large payments of money during a series of years, I should have thought that the condition which clogs this covenant, though not expressed, must, on account of the notorious inability of the Crown to contract unconditionally for such money payments in consideration of such services, have been in favour of the Crown implied....I am of opinion that the providing of funds by Parliament is a condition precedent to its attaching. A most important department of the public service, however negligently or inefficiently conducted, would be above the control of Parliament were it otherwise.

That is the only support afforded by the case to the views cited earlier; for none of the other three judges expressed similar opinions. Indeed, Cockburn C.J. said:[5]

I am very far, indeed, from saying, if by express terms, the Lords of the Admiralty had engaged, whether Parliament found the funds or not, to employ Mr Churchward to perform all these services, that then whatever might be the inconvenience that might arise, such a contract would not have been binding; and I am very far from saying that in such a case a petition of right would not lie, where a public officer or the head of a department makes such a contract on behalf of the Crown, and then afterwards breaks it....I agree that, if there had been no question as to the fund being supplied by Parliament, if the condition to pay had been absolute, or if there had been a fund applicable to the purpose, and this difficulty did not stand in the petitioner's way, and he had been throughout ready and willing to perform this contract, and had been prevented and hindered from rendering these services by the default of the Lords of the

1 S. 15.
2 When the matter was debated in the House of Commons, it was pointed out that the words 'out of moneys to be provided by Parliament' were inserted specially here contrary to the usual practice with the intention of making this contract subject to parliamentary ratification (Hansard, 3 s. vol. 157, col. 1370).
3 *Per* Shee J. at 209.　　　　4 *Ibid.*　　　　5 At 200-1.

Admiralty, then he would have been in a position to enforce his right to remuneration.

When the chief justice referred to 'absolute' promises to pay, it seems that he meant that if, in the case before him, there had been merely a covenant to pay without any condition that the funds were to be provided by Parliament, the contract would have been valid.

Do then, all the writers on constitutional law base their statement on the *obiter dictum* of one puisne judge (who cited no authorities whatever in support), those *dicta* being in conflict with the opinions of the chief justice expressed in the same case? No. But it will be shown that the other authorities alleged to 'confirm the decision' in *Churchward v. Reg.* are equally flimsy props for the statements of law expressed in the text-books.

From 1865 there is a gap of fifty years in which the *obiter dicta* of Shee J. are never examined by the courts. In *Commercial Cable Co. v. Government of Newfoundland,*[1] an observation on the subject was made by Viscount Haldane (it is noteworthy that in every subsequent relevant English decision the judgments are recorded by him) and perhaps, as a result, the defence has of late been raised not infrequently by the Crown.

In that case, an action against the Crown for breach of contract failed because the Governor-General of the Dominion had failed to observe some constitutional requirements in purporting to contract on behalf of the Dominion. Viscount Haldane added:[2]

What view the Legislature might have taken had it been properly submitted is a topic into which no court of law can enter, and no damages can be recovered for breach of any implied promise to submit it. For all grants of public money, either direct or by way of prospective remission of duties imposed by statute, must be in the discretion of the Legislature, and where the system is that of responsible government, there is no contract unless that discretion can be taken to have been exercised in some sufficient fashion.

A hasty perusal of this statement might lead to the conclusion that Viscount Haldane was supporting the contention that the provision of funds is a condition precedent to the validity of Crown contracts, but the following statement by him upon the hearing by the Judicial Committee of the Privy Council of an application for leave to appeal from the decision in *Commonwealth of Australia v. Kidman* exposes that as an erroneous conclusion:[3]

In that case [Commercial Cable Co.] we distinctly laid it down...that the Governor-General, as representing the Crown could enter into

1 [1916] 2 A.C. 610. 2 At 617. 3 (1926), 32 A.L.R. 1 at 2–3.

contracts as much as he liked, and even if he made the words clear, to bind himself personally. But he was presumed only to bind the funds which might or might not be appropriated by Parliament to answer the contract, and if they were not, that did not make the contract null and *ultra vires*; it made it not enforceable because there was no *res* against which to enforce it.

Clearly, then, the observation of Adams J. in *Rayner* v. *Rex*[1] that Viscount Haldane's words 'there is no contract', in the sentence quoted earlier from the *Commercial Cable Co.* decision, meant that 'there is no contract to pay' is sound.

Similar cases are *Mackay* v. *Attorney-General for British Columbia*,[2] and *Auckland Harbour Board* v. *Rex*,[3] in each of which contracts entered into by Crown servants on behalf of the Crown were held invalid because statutory restrictions on the authority of the agent were not observed. Although Viscount Haldane upheld in both instances the recognised principles of parliamentary control over expenditure, there is nothing in the judgments in either case to the effect that the Executive cannot lawfully impose on the Crown an obligation to pay money unless Parliament has furnished funds specifically therefor.

The next case, and the one apparently most relied on apart from *Churchward's Case*, is *Attorney-General* v. *Great Southern and Western Railway Co. of Ireland*,[4] a House of Lords' decision. The respondents had entered into a contract with the Board of Trade acting on behalf of the Crown to take up certain railway lines in Southern Ireland in consideration of the Government paying the cost of replacement after the end of the War of 1914-18. In 1922 an Order in Council made in pursuance of a treaty between Great Britain and Ireland transferred this liability (*inter alia*) of the Government in Southern Ireland to the provincial Government of the Irish Free State. The House of Lords dismissed the action of the appellant who sought enforcement of this contract against the British Government. The reason given by four of the five judges was that the liability had been transferred to the provincial Government and 'no petition of right can be brought in the High Court of Justice of England which has for its object a judgment against the Crown which is to be satisfied out of the Exchequer of a Dominion'.[5] Viscount Haldane spoke in the same sense as in his other judgments already cited, and after assuming the existence of a contract and citing *Churchward's Case*, he added:[6]

It is important that we should lay down clearly the restricted nature of the liability in modern times of the Crown under its contracts . . . the true

1 [1930] N.Z.L.R. 441 at 458.   2 [1922] 1 A.C. 457.
3 [1924] A.C. 318.   4 [1925] A.C. 754.
5 At 779-80 (*per* Lord Phillimore). 6 At 774.

view of any liability there was I take to be that it was a liability *in rem* which ceased to be operative when the *res* was transferred.

Again in *Kidman's Case*, after referring to this House of Lords' decision, he said:[1] '...whether these Crown contracts are enforceable depends upon whether there was an appropriation to answer them....'

These matters have not been considered in English courts for the last twenty years, but two Commonwealth cases have been directly in point. In *Rayner* v. *Rex*,[2] the Commissioner of State Forests was authorised by statute to enter into forestry contracts. The court considered whether an appropriation of public moneys was a condition precedent to the exercise of such authority. It was held that the contract was valid without such an appropriation, and, following Viscount Haldane, that the contract was conditional only in the sense that payment out of public funds was conditional on appropriation.

In *New South Wales* v. *Bardolph*,[3] the facts were as follows. An Officer of the Premier's department on the authority of the Premier entered into an advertising contract with the plaintiff for more than one State financial year. A parliamentary appropriation for 'Government advertising', exceeding the amount involved in the plaintiff's contract but not specifying particular contracts, was made. After a change of Government during the period covered by the contract, the new Administration refused to continue the contract, whereupon the plaintiff sued under the Judiciary Act for breach of contract. The Crown contended that no contract for the payment of money can expose it to suit unless and until Parliament has appropriated moneys therefor, and that without such a specific appropriation any contract is void for non-performance of a condition precedent. The High Court of Australia, affirming the decision of Evatt J., unanimously rejected these contentions.

Evatt J. summed up the law in the following masterly fashion:[4]

...in the absence of some controlling statutory provision, contracts are enforceable against the Crown if (*a*) the contract is entered into in the ordinary or necessary course of Government administration, (*b*) it is authorised by the responsible Ministers of the Crown, and (*c*) the payments which the contractor is seeking to recover are covered by or referable to a parliamentary grant for the class of service to which the contract relates. In my opinion, moreover, the failure of the plaintiff to prove (*c*) does not affect the validity of the contract in the sense that the Crown is regarded as stripped of its authority or capacity to enter into a contract....The enforcement of such contracts is to be distinguished from their inherent validity.

1 (1926), 32 A.L.R. 1 at 3.   2 [1930] N.Z.L.R. 441.
3 (1934), 52 C.L.R. 455.   4 At 474-5.

Starkie J. said:[1]

It is doubtless true, in modern times, that no money can be withdrawn from the public funds without a distinct authorization of Parliament itself. The Crown is dependent upon the supply granted to it by Parliament, and there is an express or implied term in its contracts that payment shall be made out of moneys so provided. But the existence of the contract is not conditional upon Parliamentary authority, or upon provision of funds by Parliament for the performance of the contract.

Besides rejecting the argument of the Crown that contracts are subject to the condition precedent of parliamentary appropriation, the court also dealt with the contention that specific appropriations are required. Had such a contention been upheld, the results would have been disastrous. In Appropriation Acts Parliament would have to itemise each contract before a right of action could vest in the contractor, clearly a practically impossible task. If, for example, an army unit wished to buy newspapers for its recreation room, only if the Appropriation Act mentioned this newsvendor's contract particularly could he sue for breach of contract. Very properly the court held that no such specific appropriation was ever needed.[2] A consideration of the treatises on parliamentary procedure confirms the correctness of this view. Durell, for instance, writes:[3]

If, as is the case, Parliament grants to the Crown a certain sum for a certain service in a given year, without any more definite appropriation in the terms of the grant, it is legally competent to the Executive to expend that sum at discretion in the year upon that service. That is to say, since the parliamentary enactment deals with the vote only, the Government is not legally bound to adhere to the details submitted to Parliament, provided the expenditure is restricted to 'the four corners of the vote'...if Parliament wishes to definitely prohibit the use of a vote for a service which would be covered by the terms of the resolution granting the vote, even though no mention is made of it in the details of the estimate, the resolution must contain a specific proviso to that effect. By this means only can Parliament ensure that a particular service is not carried out, for then there would be no funds which could legally be applied to it. In the absence of such a proviso there would be no technical incorrectness in charging the expenditure against the vote, even though the service were for a purpose for which Parliament had not wished to provide. This point is admitted by the Treasury, which points out that, even if the amount of a vote is reduced in supply, there is no guarantee that expenditure will not take place upon the object in respect of which such reduction is made.

---

1 At 501-2.

2 Cf. *Canadian Domestic Engineering Co. v. Ray*, [1919] 2 W.W.R. 762 at 777.

3 Durell, *Parliamentary Grants*, cols. 296-7; cf. Jennings, *Cabinet Government*, 138 *et seq.*

That *Churchward's Case* and the later decisions have been misunderstood is plain. The case itself is only authority for the extension to the Crown of the ordinary rule of private law that if a contract expressly provides that money payable thereunder is to come from one source only, then the provision of money from that source is a condition precedent to liability under the contract.[1] The tentative suggestion of Shee J. that there was an implied condition precedent that Parliament must have expressly allocated funds therefor has not been adopted anywhere in the British Commonwealth.[2]

Canadian cases in which the Crown has been held liable on a *quantum meruit* afford proof that the Crown may be liable even though Parliament has not made appropriations. When considering such a claim in *Hall* v. *Reg.*,[3] Burbridge J. noted that the Minister 'took or promised to take a vote of Parliament to compensate the plaintiff'. It is to be observed that his concern with this was only on the issue of whether the Crown had taken the benefit of the work; whether in fact the parliamentary vote was taken did not affect his judgment in holding the Crown liable on a *quantum meruit*.[4]

There might seem to be some conflict between the view of Cockburn C.J.[5] that absolute promises to pay are valid without parliamentary grant and that of Viscount Haldane[6] that a government agent 'was presumed only to bind the funds which might or might not be appropriated by Parliament to answer the contract, and if they were not...it made it not enforceable'.

It is suggested that the law is as follows. A contract made by an agent of the Crown acting within the scope of his ostensible authority is a valid contract by the Crown, in the absence of some controlling statutory provision. If there is also some parliamentary appropriation, whether general or specific, then the contract is enforceable. The trend of recent *dicta* is towards the view that without that appropriation the contract is 'unenforceable'.[7] It is supposed that 'unenforceable' is here given the

---

1 *Gurney* v. *Rawlins* (1836), 2 M. & W. 87; *Hallett* v. *Dowdall* (1852), 18 Q.B. 2.
2 The Irish cases are conflicting, however. In *Kenny* v. *Cosgrave*, [1926] Ir. R. 517, the *dicta* of Shee J. were cited in support of a finding that an action for breach of warranty of authority against the President of the Irish Free State, based on a promise by him that funds would be provided for the Parliament by the Government, failed. In another case in the same year, *Leyden* v. *Attorney General*, [1926] Ir. R. 334 at 367, doubts were expressed *obiter* about the merits of his *dicta*.
3 (1893), 3 Ex. C.R. 373 at 377.
4 And see *May* v. *Rex* (1913), 14 Ex. C.R. 341.
5 (1865), 1 Q.B. 173 at 201.
6 *Commonwealth of Australia* v. *Kidman* (1925), 32 A.L.R. 1 at 3.
7 Cf. also *Rex* v. *Fisher*, [1903] A.C. 158.

same meaning as for contracts within the Statute of Frauds. If, on the other hand, as some of the *dicta* of Viscount Haldane might suggest, 'unenforceable' merely implies that there is no legal right to execute against any property, it would only be restating the general rule applicable to all judgments against the Crown.[1] Moreover, on that interpretation, judgment (even though merely declaratory in effect) would be against the Crown, and that would not seem to be his intention.[2]

Lest anyone should think that parliamentary control is then inadequate, it should be noted that there is nothing to prevent the passing of a subsequent statute abrogating the contract. In *Reilly* v. *Rex*,[3] for instance, the plaintiff sued the Crown for breach of a contract of service. He failed because, a statute having abolished the office, the contract was void for subsequent impossibility. Lord Atkin said:[4] 'It will be important to bear in mind that a power to determine a contract at will is not inconsistent with the existence of a contract until so determined.' The unsatisfactory state of English law with regard to appropriations is due in part to not considering whether Crown agents should not be required to have express authority in order to bind the Crown.

An agent is normally only liable in contract where he has contracted personally. A Crown agent, too, cannot be sued if he has contracted on behalf of the Crown.[5] The cases show that the courts are most reluctant to find that a civil servant has contracted personally.[6] Indeed, there seems no reported case where a civil servant, legally capable of contracting as agent in the particular circumstances, and not having expressly contracted personally, has failed when setting up agency as a defence to an action for breach of contract. In the United States public officers 'are not personally liable unless they *intend* to assume such liability, and the presumption is that they do not so intend'.[7] That private agents would be liable in like circumstances is not conclusive; it is frankly acknowledged that the official relation is a factor making the private law of agency inapplicable.

1 P. 182 *infra*.
2 But see Meachem, *The Law of Agency*, 1034: 'Such a defect [the want of appropriation] seems to go rather to the question of damages than to the existence of a cause of action.'
3 [1934] A.C. 176.   4 At 179–80.
5 *Macbeath* v. *Haldimand* (1786), 1 T.R. 172; *Unwin* v. *Wolseley* (1787), 1 T.R. 674; *Gidley* v. *Palmerston (Lord)* (1822), 3 B. & B. 275.
6 *Palmer* v. *Hutchinson* (1881), 6 App. Cas. 619; *Wright & Co.* v. *Mills No. 2* (1890), 63 L.T. 186.
7 Hart, *An Introduction to Administrative Law*, 568.

3. BREACH OF WARRANTY OF AUTHORITY

The text-books are agreed that the common-law principle, that an agent who acts without the authority of his principal may be sued for breach of warranty of authority, does not apply to Crown servants.[1] All rely on *Dunn* v. *Macdonald*[2] as the sole authority for this. There, an action for breach of warranty of authority against an official who purported to engage another for a fixed term failed. This case is, however, not a binding authority for the proposition stated for the following reasons: first, the warranty was one of law and not of fact because whether a contract contains an implied term to dismiss at pleasure is a matter of interpretation;[3] secondly, if *dicta* to the effect that the Crown cannot enter into a contract for a fixed term are sound,[4] then the rule that this action lies only where one against the principal would lie on an agreement authorised by him would explain the decision;[5] thirdly, it may rest on the rule that the plaintiff must have relied on the misrepresentation, for here the plaintiff may have had notice of the inability of the agent to contract.

Although the case has been followed in Canada[6] and Ireland[7] English courts need not accept it as authority for the proposition that an agent of the Crown can never be sued for breach of warranty of authority. In the United States the question seldom arises, for there it is held that, since a public officer usually derives his authority from statute or other legal source, a third party must be presumed to know the law and cannot allege that he has been misled.[8] Had the authority of the agent depended 'upon the same sort of considerations as private agents' then the United States officer could be sued for breach of warranty of authority.[9] The United States rule seems based on sound principle, and the way is open for the English courts to copy it.

4. THE LIABILITY OF GOVERNMENT DEPARTMENTS

Before the Crown Proceedings Act a Government Department which, by statute, could be sued in that name, was liable in contract even though it contracted only as agent for and on behalf of the Crown.[10] Any defences

---

1 Pollock, *Contracts*, 87; Halsbury, 26 at 264; Mustoe, *Law and Organisation of the Civil Service*, 92.   2 [1897] 1 Q.B. 401, 555.
3 Glanville Williams, *op. cit.* 3 n. 11.   4 See p. 112 *infra*.
5 Cf. *Restatement*, Agency, S. 329. Comment.
6 *O'Connor* v. *Lemieux* (1926), 60 Ont. L.R. 365.
7 *Kenny* v. *Cosgrave*, [1926] Ir. R. 517 at 526.
8 *Perry* v. *Hyde* (1834), 10 Conn. 329.   9 Meachem, *op. cit.* §1371.
10 *Minister of Supply* v. *British Thomson-Houston Co. Ltd.*, [1943] K.B. 478 (C.A.); see also A. Smith, 'Liability to Suit of an Agent of the Crown' in 8 *U.T.L.J.* (1950) 218.

open to the Crown would also be open to the Department.[1] Some Departments not made suable expressly by statute, but which have been incorporated, have also been held by the courts to be capable of being sued.[2] One need not assume that incorporation *ipso facto* rendered a Department suable; it is not inconsistent with the cases to say that a Department was suable if that was the intention of the statute incorporating the Department.

The effect of the Crown Proceedings Act on these rules must now be considered. Its second schedule repeals the various 'sue and be sued' clauses with the result that actions against those Departments must now be brought in accordance with the procedures authorised by the Act. The position of incorporated Departments is not so clear. Glanville Williams disagrees[3] with the conclusion reached by the writer elsewhere[4] that the pre-Act right to sue them is unaffected. He argues that the Act applies to proceedings to which any officer of the Crown as such is a party, and that 'officer' includes servant, and therefore a Department. He says that this is so 'for all parts of the Act', but the sections cited by him in support do not, with respect, apply to Part I of the Act, that part which contains the substantive provisions of contractual liability. Therefore, 'Crown' in Part I of the Act does not seem to have that extended meaning. Even if the 'Crown' did include an incorporated Government Department there is nothing in the Act requiring proceedings against the Crown to be brought in accordance with the Act and not otherwise. It abolishes certain proceedings, namely petition of right and suits against Departments instituted under authority of those statutes repealed by the Act; beyond that it does not affect the existing rights of action in contract. Since the schedule of repealed statutes does not include these statutes incorporating Departments, presumably these Departments may be sued as they were sued before the Act.[5]

In France the rules for suits in tort discussed above also determine which Departments of the Administration are to be sued for *contrat administratif*.[6]

---

1 *The Brabo*, [1947] 2 All E.R. 363 (C.A.) affirmed other grounds H.L., [1949] 1 All E.R. 294.

2 *Graham* v. *Commissioners of Public Works and Buildings*, [1901] 2 K.B. 781; *Roper* v. *Commissioners of Public Works and Buildings*, [1915] 1 K.B. 45; cf. *International Railway Co.* v. *Niagara Parks Commission*, [1941] A.C. 328 (P.C.).

3 At 6.

4 H. Street, 'The Crown Proceedings Act' in 11 *Mod. L.R.* (1948) 129 at 132.

5 A study of the legislative history shows how this omission occurred. As originally drafted, the section covered incorporation, but it had to be altered on the Report Stage to meet another objection levelled against it by Viscount Simon. This alteration met his point, but unwittingly led to this error. Hansard, 5 s. vol. 146, cols. 363–4.   6 Ch. II *supra*.

Public corporations in the United States can be sued in contract if that is the legislative intent; the cases 'do not establish that the corporate form itself produces important results'.[1] The great majority of the statutes setting up these public corporations contain 'sue and be sued' clauses which are always interpreted by the courts as rendering the corporations liable in contract.[2]

5. THE MAKING OF THE CONTRACT

Here, above all, the futility of relying on the normal sources of law in this field of governmental contract is illustrated. We know from the Local Government Act, 1933,[3] that local authorities must in the case of contracts for the supply of goods or materials or for the execution of works frame standing orders providing for the publication of notice of their intention to contract and for tenders to be invited. Beyond that the legal sources tell us nothing. Yet there is a body of law on the making of governmental contracts, and it is largely the Public Accounts Committee, and the Estimates Committee of the House of Commons, which have fashioned it.[4] The usual practice is not to have an open system of tender but for Departments to draw up lists of approved contractors and to invite selected firms to tender. So, when the Ministry of Works is buying goods, or making building or civil engineering contracts, 'the open system...is now used only in a few special cases'.[5]

In France, on the other hand, the Administration must advertise its intention to contract, and tenders must be submitted to the *bureau d'Administration*. Normally, the lowest valid tender submitted must be accepted. To these rules three exceptions have been made by statute.[6] For certain small or urgent contracts, the procedure by way of *appel d'offres* is appropriate. Publicity is still demanded, but the Administration is free to choose its contractor. Where the contract involves matters of a secret

1 Gellhorn, *op. cit.* 219 n. 55.

2 Cf. Hart, *op. cit.* 586; *Keifer & Keifer* v. *Reconstruction Finance Corp.* (1939), 306 U.S. 381.

3 23 & 24 Geo. V, c. 51, s. 266.

4 Chubb, *The Control of Public Expenditure*, 143; see e.g. 2nd Report Public Accounts Committee 1888, 71–2, 1st Report Estimates Committee 1937, 4th and 14th Reports Select Committee on National Expenditure 1941–3, Select Committee on Procedure (1945–6) H.C. 189, Ev. Q. 4310 of Sir Gilbert Upcott, formerly Comptroller and Auditor General.

5 Report of the Committee on Intermediaries, Cmd. 7904 (1950) 19; see 11 for the similar Admiralty practice in the Directorate of Naval Contracts; H. A. Fox, 'British Government Contract Requirements' in 2 *Comparative Law Services* (U.S. Dept. of Commerce, 1939). For New Zealand practices, see articles by G. Curtis and D. B. North in vol. III (1940) at 17 and 139 respectively.

6 Décret of 6 April 1942.

nature, or of special technical or artistic competence, a contract *par entente directe* may be made, even with a person who has not tendered. A contract *de gré à gré* relating to day-to-day matters of trivial importance may be made informally. Public works contracts, except for small sums, must be in writing.

Statute controls tightly advertising of and bidding on United States contracts:[1]

All purchases and contracts for supplies or services, in any of the departments of the Government, except for personal services, shall be made by advertising a sufficient time previously for proposals respecting the same, when the public exigencies do not require the immediate delivery of the articles, or performance of the service. When immediate delivery or performance is required by the public exigency, the articles or service required may be procured by open purchase or contract, at the places and in the manner in which such articles are usually bought and sold, or such services engaged, between individuals.

The President has officially approved a standard form of invitation for bids.[2] To facilitate purchases or contracts for services of limited amounts, statutory exceptions to this section have been provided for many Government Departments.[3] The 'public exigency' must be 'a sudden and unexpected happening; a perplexing emergency or complication of circumstances; or a sudden or unexpected occasion for action'.[4] In *Goodroads Machinery Co. of New England v. U.S.*,[5] a Civil Works Administration contract for public works made at a particularly serious moment of the depression of the nineteen-thirties was held to be such a contingency. On the other hand, the emergency must not be merely the creation of the government agency;[6] it is not enough that it issues emergency purchase orders.

If it is clearly established that advertising for bids would serve no useful purpose,[7] as in the purchase of copyrighted or patented articles,[8] procurement of the goods without competitive bids is authorised. The provisions for bidding are contained in a series of standard forms having binding

1 R.S. s. 3709; cf. Beutel & Billig, *op. cit.* ch. v.
2 Standard form no. 20 of 19 Nov. 1926.
3 41 U.S. Code, arts. 6, 6a, 6b and 7, and Supplements.
4 Decision by Comptroller-General McCarl (1935), 14 Comp.-Gen. 875.
5 (1937) 19 F. Supp. 652.
6 *U.S. v. Sheridan-Kirk Contracting Co.* (1907), 149 F. 809; *U.S. v. Garbish* (1911), 222 U.S. 257.
7 Comptroller-General Warren to the Federal Security Administrator (1943), 23 Comp.-Gen. 395.
8 Attorney-General MacVeagh to the Postmaster-General, 17 Att.-Gen. Op. (1881) 84.

force which have been officially approved by the Secretary of the Treasury. There are standard government forms of instructions to bidders (construction and supplies),[1] of bid (construction contract),[2] of statement and certificate of award,[3] and of invitation, bid and acceptance (short form contract).[4] The instructions to bidders deal with such matters as withdrawals of bids, errors, samples and bonds. One important paragraph covers the award or rejection of bids. It provides:[5] 'The contract will be awarded to the lowest responsible bidder complying with conditions of the invitation for bids, providing his bid is reasonable and it is to the interest of the United States to accept it. . . .' These clauses have frequently been before the courts, which have held that the Government need not accept the lowest bid, and that its duty is to accept the most advantageous bid.[6] In reaching a decision it must consider the financial soundness, skill, capacity and integrity of the bidder.[7] As the Supreme Court has said, the provisions are for the benefit of the United States as a whole rather than of the bidder, and they are designed to prevent fraud.[8] There is a separate statutory provision entitling any bidder to be present when the bids are opened.[9] Once a bid is accepted there is a binding contract without further formality.[10]

On the whole, the courts have interpreted the statutes reasonably and realistically, with the result that they are effective instruments. As has been pointed out,[11] the danger in the United States is that, in stopping graft by framing elaborate rules about competitive bidding, there might result so much 'red tape' that higher bids and less competition would be an injury to the public as grave as fraud. Moreover, supervision of the performance of a contract might be more important in the suppression of graft than bidding requirements.

1 No. 22 of 13 July 1939.   2 No. 21 of 5 April 1937.
3 No. 1036 of 12 Nov. 1937.   4 No. 33 of 17 Jan. 1939.
5 S. 14.
6 *O'Brien* v. *Carney* (1934), 6 F. Supp. 761.
7 *William* v. *Topeka* (1912), 85 Kan. 857. The exercise of this discretion is not subject to judicial review.
8 *Perkins* v. *Lukens Steel Co.* (1940), 310 U.S. 113.
9 41 U.S.C. (1940) s. 8.
10 *U.S.* v. *Purcell Envelope Co.* (1919), 249 U.S. 313. There is, however, a mandatory requirement of writing: *Clark* v. *U.S.* (1877), 5 Otto 539 (U.S.).
11 James, *The Protection of the Public Interests in Public Contracts, passim.*

6. FREEDOM OF EXECUTIVE ACTION

In one case only, *Rederiaktiebolaget Amphitrite* v. *Rex*,[1] has the court suggested that the Crown can plead executive necessity by way of defence to an action for breach of contract. During the War of 1914–18, the British Legation at Stockholm on behalf of the Government gave a neutral shipowner an undertaking that one of his ships carrying a certain cargo for England would not be detained if sent there. Acting on this, the shipowner allowed the ship to proceed, but on its arrival the Crown nevertheless detained it. The shipowner took proceedings by petition of right for breach of contract, and Rowlatt J. dismissed the suit. He said:[2]

No doubt the Government can bind itself through its officers by a commercial contract, and if it does so it must perform it like anybody else or pay damages for the breach. But this was not a commercial contract; it was an arrangement whereby the Government purported to give an assurance as to what its executive action would be in the future in relation to a particular ship in the event of her coming to this country with a particular kind of cargo. And that is, to my mind, not a contract for the breach of which damages can be sued for in a Court of law. It was merely an expression of intention to act in a particular way in a certain event. My main reason for so thinking is that it is not competent for the Government to fetter its future executive action, which must necessarily be determined by the needs of the community when the question arises. It cannot by contract hamper its freedom of action in matters which concern the welfare of the State.

The case has not been followed in any decision in the common-law countries and only in *Robertson* v. *Minister of Pensions*[3] does it seem to have been carefully examined. It is possible to treat the case in any of four ways. The case may be regarded as an unsound decision at first instance. It may be said, as Denning J. (as he then was) said of it in *Robertson's Case*, that the *ratio* of the case is that there was no intention to contract[4] and that the further remarks were *obiter*. Thirdly, it may be regarded as deciding that the Crown can only make contracts of a commercial nature; with respect to Denning L.J., that does seem to be the *ratio* of the case. It has been suggested,[5] fourthly, that the rule is too wide, but that the case may be regarded as an example of a general rule of public policy[6] that a public

1 [1921] 3 K.B. 500.   2 At 503.   3 [1949] 1 K.B. 227. In many cases, e.g.
The Steaua Romana, [1944] P. 43, application of the decision would have led to an opposite result.
4 Cf. *Joy Oil Ltd.* v. *Rex*, [1951] 3 D.L.R. 582.
5 J. D. B. Mitchell, 'Limitations on the Contractual Liability of Public Authorities' in 13 *Mod. L.R.* (1950) 318, 455.
6 *Birkdale District Electricity Supply Co.* v. *Southport Corporation*, [1926] A.C. 355.

authority cannot be prevented by an existing contract from performing functions essential to its existence and for which it was created.

If the courts were to adopt this fourth and limited interpretation of the case many of the objections voiced against the case[1] would lose their force. It would be comparable, also, with the principle laid down in the United States that the United States in the exercise of its sovereign functions cannot be restrained by contracts made by it as a contractor,[2] and that it cannot by contract fetter its right to protect public health or morals.[3] France, of course, does not need a separate rule in view of its general right to rescind administrative contracts on payment of damages:[4] this raises the important point whether even in the suggested narrow field of application of the *Amphitrite Case* the Crown ought not nevertheless to pay damages.

7. STANDARD TERMS AND CONDITIONS

Although there are no legal restrictions on the contents of British government contracts, the same practical result is achieved because the Government only contracts on the basis of certain fixed standard terms and conditions. If a contractor wishes to contract with it, he can do so on those terms only; no alterations will be made.[5] These standard terms, in effect, acknowledge the overriding rights of the State as a contractor. The one for building contracts demonstrates this.[6] Clause 7 empowers the government supervising officer to give directions how the work is to be carried out, and gives him the right to uncontrolled supervision. If his directions are disobeyed, clause 8 enables the Government to have the necessary work done at the expense of the contractor. Clause 9 provides that where the supervisor requires alterations in the work done under the contract, the contract price shall be increased or reduced accordingly.

1 E.g. Sir William Holdsworth, 'A Case Book on Constitutional Law' in 45 L.Q.R. (1929) 162 at 166.

2 *Horowitz* v. *U.S.* (1925), 267 U.S. 458; see also *Ottinger* v. *U.S.* (1950), 88 F. Supp. 881.

3 *Stone* v. *Mississippi* (1879), 101 U.S. 814; cf. J. D. B. Mitchell, 'The Treatment of Public Contracts in the United States' in 9 *U. of Toronto L.J.* (1952) 194.

4 P. 101 *infra*.

5 Of course, the practice is widespread in many monopoly or large-scale industries, e.g. insurance, carriage, launderers. See Prausnitz, *The Standardisation of Commercial Contracts, passim*.

6 Form CCC/Wks/1 Sept. 1948. Cf. Standard Conditions of Government Contracts for Stores Purchases, Form CCC/Stores/1 Jan. 1949, which, the booklet states, 'has been adopted by the principal Government Purchasing Departments for the purpose of ensuring uniformity of Contract Conditions between themselves and Contractors, and also to achieve economy in time and paper'. For a case on variation of a building contract, see *Sir Lindsay Parkinson & Co. Ltd.* v. *Commissioners of Works and Public Buildings*, [1950] 1 All E.R. 208.

Clause 29 makes time the essence of the contract, and stipulates for the payment of liquidated damages in the event of default. Clauses 44 and 45 enable the Government to determine the contract at any time by notice in writing, leaving the Government liable only for work done, and discharged from future liability under the contract.[1]

Indeed, may one not say that if the Government only contracts on these terms, then, even though the terms have not the form of delegated legislation, nevertheless it is, indirectly, a recognition of a separate body of governmental contract law? The English lawyer to-day cannot advise his client solely by reference to the statutes, statutory instruments and law reports. This phenomenon of extra-legal rules having the practical force of law is even more obvious in other fields. There has sprung up what one writer has called administrative quasi-legislation.[2] Important examples are income tax concessions, War Damage practice notes, and the Motor Insurance Bureau.

In France these rules, which in England apply only when incorporated in government contract, are part of the law itself, not statutes, but the special principles of *contrat administratif* built up by the *Conseil d'Etat*.

The obligation of a contractor with the Government is that of strict execution. Paramount is the interest of the State in the proper completion of the work the subject-matter of the contract. There are three sanctions to secure this end. The contractor is liable in damages for delay, the State may do the work at the expense of the defaulting contractor, or it may determine the contract because of the failure to perform in accordance with the terms of the contract.

The contractor is entitled to be paid as the work proceeds. Secondly, he has the benefit of the civil law rule of contract, *l'imprévision*. This is given a wide interpretation most favourable to the contractor, in that, should prices of materials rise, he is entitled to have his contract price increased accordingly.[3] The reason for this is that performance of a public works contract must not be impeded by reason of hardships inflicted on those under an obligation to carry it out. Thirdly, he has a right to *l'équilibre financier* whereby if the State changes the terms of the contract he will be entitled to the same profit in the new circumstances.

At least four overriding governmental powers are part of the *contrat administratif*. The State has untrammelled power to supervise the execution

1 For a full analysis of 'break' clauses in England and the United States, see an unpublished dissertation by R. Bennett, 'The Termination of War Contracts in the United States and Great Britain' (1948), *passim* and R. Wienshink and F. Feldman, 'The Current Challenge of Military Contract Termination' in 66 *Har. L.R.* (1952) 47.

2 Note in 60 *L.Q.R.* (1944) 127.

3 Cf. Clause 11 B in Ministry of Works Contract.

of the contract. It can issue directions through its architects or other officers. It has the right of *mutabilité*, the right to effect unilateral modifications of the contract. This last power is subject to the right of the contractor to apply to a civil court for rescission if the changes alter the contract too fundamentally (*licite*) and to his right to a pecuniary indemnity for the changes (*la contrepartie*). Whenever the public interest demands it the State may rescind the contract on payment of compensation.[1] Any further special conditions are inserted in *le cahier des charges*.

Péquignot[2] mentions that there may be a temptation to equate the *contrat d'adhésion* of private law with the government contract, but he points out one important and significant distinction. The French civil court has a tendency to side with the weaker party to a *contrat d'adhésion*,[3] yet there is no such tendency in *contrat administratif*, based as it is on the subordination of all else to *le but de service public*.[4]

The United States is in an intermediate position.[5] Like France, some clauses are written in government contracts by law, and like England, many are dealt with by standard terms and conditions. Statute lays down:[6]

In all contracts entered into with the United States for the construction or repair of any public building or public work...a stipulation shall be inserted for liquidated damages for delay...in all suits commenced on any such contracts....It shall not be necessary for the United States...to prove actual or specific damages sustained by the Government by reason of delays, but such stipulation for liquidated damages shall be conclusive and binding upon all parties.

The condition in the standard construction contract implementing this statute authorises the Government to do the work at the expense of the defaulting contractor.[7]

Unlike Congress, the judges have not in the past recognised the exceptional position of the Government as a contractor. Their private law instincts have been so firmly rooted that they have consistently applied

1 Cf. O. W. Holmes, 'The Path of the Law' in 10 *Har. L.R.* (1897) 457 at 462: 'If you commit a contract, you are liable to pay a compensatory sum....'

2 At 66.

3 Perhaps because disputes go to arbitration, there are few cases showing the interpretative tendencies in England. See *Sir Lindsay Parkinson and Co. Ltd.* v. *Commissioners of Works and Public Buildings*, [1950] 1 All E.R. 208 and the unreported case of *Engineering (Educational) Trust Ltd.* v. *Rex* (1948), (C.A.), described at length by R. Bennett, *loc. cit.* 90–5. Recent cases on standard terms seem to follow the usual principles of documentary interpretation, e.g. *Beaumont-Thomas* v. *Blue Star Line Ltd.*, [1939] 3 All E.R. 127 (C.A.); *Alderslade* v. *Hendon Laundry Ltd.*, [1945] A.B. 189; and on governmental contracts see *Canada Steamships Lines Ltd.* v. *Rex*, [1952] A.C. 192.

4 The United States courts interpret standard terms in favour of the weaker party; F. Kessler, 'Contracts of Adhesion' in 43 *Col. L.R.* (1943) 629.

5 L. L. Anderson, 'The Disputes Article in Government Contracts' in 44 *Mich. L.R.* (1945) 211. 6 32 Stat. 326 (1902). 7 Art. 9.

in toto private law rules to determine whether any sum is a penalty or liquidated damages.[1] Well might Williston state that 'performance of government contracts and breach of government contracts are governed by the same rules as are applicable between private parties'.[2] In view of this judicial attitude, a recent Supreme Court decision is all the more interesting.[3] A contract for the supply of dried eggs provided for the payment of a sum by way of liquidated damages if the contractor failed to provide inspection facilities even though he delivered without delay. Only by a five to four majority did the Supreme Court hold that the rules of private law were to apply so as to declare the sum a penalty. In a powerful dissent, Frankfurter J. argued that private law rules were inapplicable to government contracts where these rules were contrary to the overriding interests of the State.[4]

The Walsh-Healey Act,[5] the Davis-Bacon Act[6] and the Eight Hour Law[7] compel government contractors to observe fair labour practices. The Miller Act[8] makes it compulsory for contractors to furnish bonds in accordance with its provisions.

For other conditions, as in England, one must turn to the standard forms of contract. Until 1926 each Department had its own standard forms, but in that year the President approved a series of uniform forms of contract for works construction, supply, small supply purchases, and coal purchases, which were drafted by an Interdepartmental Board of Contracts and Adjustments.[9] The use of these forms is obligatory throughout the government service. They give the Government approximately the same protection as the English ones. What is not clear is on what principles the dividing line between statutory terms and standard terms has been drawn. It is not explained by constitutional requirements, and seems purely arbitrary.

8. MEANS OF SETTLING DISPUTES

Disputes in England are usually settled by arbitration in accordance with the standard terms.[10] Government Departments were authorised by the Treasury to make termination settlements on war contracts, but where

---

1 *Wise* v. *Wise* (1919), 249 U.S. 361; *Maryland Dredging and Contracting Co.* v. *U.S.* (1916), 241 U.S. 184; *Pacific Hardware & Steel Co.* v. *U.S.* (1913), 48 Ct. Cl. 399.
2 Vol. IX at 297.   3 *Priebe & Son* v. *U.S.* (1948), 332 U.S. 407.
4 Cf. Note, 'Adaptation of Private Contract Principles to Government Contracts' in 27 *Indiana L.J.* (1952) 279 and cases cited.
5 41 U.S.C. s. 35.   6 40 U.S.C. s. 276a.
7 40 U.S.C. s. 324.   8 40 U.S.C. s. 270a.
9 McGuire, *Matters of Procedure under Government Contracts, passim*; Sears, *Cases and Materials on Administrative Law*, 690 et seq.; Bennett, *loc. cit.*, Appendix.
10 E.g. cl. 61, form CCC/Wks/1.

large sums were involved Treasury sanction was required.[1] In France the *Conseil d'Etat* and the *Conseil de Préfecture* exercise jurisdiction.

The procedure in the United States differs from both the above procedures and is much more complex.[2] A dispute on the facts arising out of a contract must be brought before the contracting officer, from whom there is an appeal to the head of the Department. His decision on matters of fact is final, except that the Court of Claims can set aside his decision if he acts arbitrarily or if his decision is so grossly erroneous as to imply bad faith.[3] Questions of law arising out of these facts are settled by the General Accounting Office.[4] Typical matters decided by the Department will be the value of extra work done, and disputes about specifications. Many problems relating to withdrawal of bids and modification of contracts will be ones of mixed law and fact the legal portion of which is referable to the claims department of the General Accounting Office. Questions of interpretation will also be dealt with by that office. Within one year the contractor can demand a review of this decision by the Comptroller-General, the head of that office.[5] Even if the latter decides against the contractor he may still recommend that Congress compensate him by private Act.[6]

If the contractor has exhausted these administrative remedies he may take a dispute on a point of law to the courts by suing the United States in the Court of Claims. If a sum of not more than $10,000 is claimed the United States District Courts have concurrent jurisdiction. The Comptroller-General has not always followed the earlier decisions of the courts; sometimes he has been embarrassed by conflicting decisions of the Court of Claims and the District Court.

It is difficult to assess the merits of the three widely different methods of settling disputes arising out of government contracts. Obviously, the matter must be looked at within the framework of the constitutional law of each country. Moreover, to reach a conclusion involves a consideration of the value of arbitration. Perhaps the provision for arbitration contained in British government contracts is a concession to businessmen, whose preference for it rather than for slow and expensive litigation is well known.

1 See *First Report of the Committee of Public Accounts*, 1945–6, pp. 48–9.

2 L. M. Cherne, *op. cit.* ch. v.

3 *Bein v. U.S.* (1944), 101 Ct. Cl. 144; Williston, *op. cit.* IX, 431.

4 See Willoughby, *The Legal Status and Functions of the General Accounting Office of the National Government*; R. M. Foster, 'General Accounting Office and Government Claims' in 16 J.B.A.D.C. (1949) 275. For war-time contracts, a similar procedure was evolved: see the Contract Settlement Act, 1944, 58 Stat. 651.

5 Hotchkiss, *The Judicial Work of the Comptroller of the Treasury*, ch. II; Mansfield, *The Comptroller-General, passim.*

6 This has, however, occurred only three times between 1928 and 1941; Cherne, *op. cit.* col. 15923.

9. RELIEF

All three systems recognise the special position of the State, by never ordering the specific performance by it of a contract. In France this rests on the *contrat administratif*, in the United States on judicial decision,[1] and in England on section 21 (1) of the Crown Proceedings Act.

10. REFORM OF THE ENGLISH LAW OF GOVERNMENT CONTRACT

The English reliance on standard terms has hindered the development of a separate branch of government contract law. Yet at the same time there is a separate body of principles in practice, though not law in the strict sense. Is it desirable that there should be wide discrepancies between the law as found in statute and judicial decision, and the law as it functions in reality? The argument in favour of the present arrangement would be two-fold. First, that there is no justification for a separate series of rules for government contracts because the Government must not be accorded privileges. But this is to shut one's eyes to the facts. What is the difference from the viewpoint of a company whose business it is to execute government work between rules with legal effect, and conditions with which they must always comply or else lose all government contracts? Secondly, it can be argued that the present system is flexible; it permits a ready alteration of terms in the light of experience or altered business practice. The main objection to the present system is that there is no certainty; the lawyer advising his client cannot base his advice on the usual sources—if his advice is to depend on the particular terms in government contracts, and on arbitrations the findings of which are not reported, he can neither know the answer to his client's problems nor have easy access to the materials with which to furnish a confident answer. It is also untidy and a stumbling block to the development of legal principles for the law to be found in extra-legal sources, and for the recognised lawmakers to play no part in shaping it. Flexibility is necessary only in part of the field. The rules relating to agency, appropriations, advertisement, bidding, supervision, direction, power to amend with consequent amendment of contract price, labour practices and rescission are, it is submitted, already rigid. It is at least arguable that the ready access to and symmetry of the law relating to government contracts are more important factors than that flexibility afforded by the present arrangements. If that is so, reform of the law along the lines now to be suggested may be worthy of consideration.

---

1 *U.S.* v. *Jones* (1889), 131 U.S. 1.

There are, perhaps, three classes of terms. First, the ones just discussed, which should be given statutory sanction in a Government Contracts Act. Secondly, terms less immutable, but which are regularly inserted in certain classes of contract. To standardise these without making them inflexible and yet to be fair to the contractors, it is suggested that the Act authorise their embodiment in delegated legislation, in the drafting of which it would be compulsory to consult the trade interests affected. Any amendments would be made in the same manner. There would then be flexibility, and at the same time the terms would be accessible in the published statutory instruments. Any further special terms peculiar to the contract would be added to it by agreement. It may be contended that on some occasions the government would want to deviate from the statutory instrument. That could be allowed in one of two ways. Either an administrative tribunal with representatives of the Government and trade interests as members could permit if it found it just and reasonable,[1] or a Minister might certify, in a reasoned document laid before Parliament, that it was necessary in the public interest.

This treatment of rigid, standard and special terms would put the law on an appropriate juristic basis. It would be as certain and accessible as reasonably possible, would protect the interests of the contractor and yet at the same time leave to the State overriding powers in an emergency or other special circumstance.

II. STATE-CONSUMER RELATIONSHIPS

The arrangements made to supply the public with such essentials as water, electricity, gas, telephone services and transport may take various forms, but the interest of the State in the service is always recognised.[2] If private enterprise supplies the service, then the State regulates the charges and conditions under which it is administered. This may take the form of a concession from the State, in which event there is a relationship between State and concessionary both contractual and regulatory.[3] Alternatively, private enterprise might administer the service, controlled by an administrative commission which fixes tariffs and conditions subject to judicial review. Transportation[4] and radio[5] are controlled in this manner in the

---

1 Cf. the law of carriage; Kahn-Freund, *The Law of Carriage by Inland Transport*, ch. VIII.

2 *Ex rel. Cayuga Corp.* v. *Public Service Commission* (1919), 226 N.Y. 527 at 532 (*per* Cardozo J.).

3 Duguit, *Traité*, III, 446 *et seq.*

4 Interstate Commerce Act, 49 U.S.C. and Supplement.

5 Communications Act, 1934, 47 U.S.C. Supp. 301.

United States. Very often in England local authorities have supplied services direct, for example, water, and until recently, gas and electricity. There has been a recent tendency for State corporations to take over the direct supply of these services both in France and Britain. In both countries this has been done with gas,[1] electricity,[2] coal,[3] some forms of transport,[4] and in France alone with banking and insurance,[5] and in England alone with air transport.[6] Sometimes the State itself supplies the service, for example, the British telephone service. The same legal problems are posed, whenever the Administration, whether State, public corporation or local authority, is supplying the consumer direct. In each case, too, there is an obligation to serve the public generally and by way of corollary a compulsion in the content of the contract.[7]

Characteristic of the legal arrangements made are the provisions of the Gas Act, 1948.[8] Section 56 provides that gas shall be supplied on the conditions set out in the third schedule to the Act. This schedule is a code of forty-seven clauses dealing (*inter alia*) with the following matters affecting the consumer. The appropriate area board 'shall, upon being required to do so by the owner or occupier of any premises situated within the Board's area of supply and within twenty-five yards from any main of the Board through which the Board are for the time being distributing gas, give and continue to give a supply of gas to those premises'. Detailed provision is made for the laying of pipes, for charging on a meter, recovery of charges, the right to cut off supply in case of default, liability for escape of gas, and rights of entry and inspection. The supply of other services, for example, water, also regarded by the State as a public function, is provided on a similar basis. In each case the consumer enters into no formal contract with the supplier.

An important service maintained in Britain by the State itself is the telephone service. Statutory instruments[9] made under the Telegraph Act 1951 prescribe the call charges, the conditions under which the service

1 Gas Act, 1948, 10 & 11 Geo. VI, c. 67; law 46–628 of 8 April 1946.
2 Electricity Act, 1947, 10 & 11 Geo. VI, c. 54; law 46–628 of 8 April 1946.
3 Coal Industry Nationalisation Act, 1946, 9 & 10 Geo. VI, c. 59; law 46–1072 of 17 May 1946.
4 Transport Act, 1947, 10 & 11 Geo. VI, c. 49.
5 For details of French nationalisation schemes, see Julliot de la Morandière et Byé, *Les Nationalisations en France.*
6 Civil Aviation Act, 1946, 9 & 10 Geo. VI, c. 70; laws 46–628 of 8 April 1946 and 46–835 of 25 April 1946.
7 T. A. Lenhoff, 'Scope of Compulsory Contracts Proper' in 43 *Col. L.R.* (1943) 586 at 597.
8 See Stemp & Wing, *The Gas Act*, 1948.
9 Telephone Regulations 1951 S.I. 2075.

shall be discontinued, and the immunity of the Postmaster-General for any loss or injury which may be incurred or sustained in connection with telephonic service.

These situations differ from ordinary contracts because of the element of compulsion which they contain. A contract may be compulsory in one of two senses;[1] either because one or both parties is under a compulsion to make it, or because once a contract is made its terms are in part or wholly not the subject of agreement but created by law. The supplier is usually under a compulsion to perform these public services if the consumer requests; the latter is free in theory to make the request or not, but once the service is undertaken the statutory provisions have compulsive force.

In order to ascertain the rights and liabilities arising from these relationships one must first decide whether the relationships are contractual. The duty to enter into business relations with another is older than contract itself. In *Lane* v. *Cotton*[2] it is shown that in the sixteenth-century public carriers, innkeepers and farriers were deemed to be exercising a public calling, and that an action for breach of their duties was an action on the case. With the growth of contract, difficulties of classification have arisen. In English law one may still sue in tort even though there is a contract between the parties, if that duty the breach of which is complained of arises independently of the contract.[3] An action in tort lies against a bailee failing to take due care both in England[4] and the United States.[5] Nor is there any doubt that an action on the case lies for non-performance of a duty, as where an innkeeper refuses to accommodate travellers.[6] Carriers, innkeepers and others exercising public callings have a duty to perform that service, and breach of the duty is a tort. There may also be a contract for breach of which an action will lie. Similarly, the refusal of English public bodies to supply is a breach of statutory duty[7] and may be a tort.[8] There is a similar cause of action in the United States.[9] Are these also cases where there may be both a liability in tort and contract?

1 Cf. M. Radin, 'Contract Obligation and the Human Will' in 43 *Col. L.R.* (1943) 575 at 578.
2 (1701), 1 Ld Ray. 746.
3 E.g. *Jarvis* v. *Moy Davies, Smith Vandervell & Co.*, [1936] 1 K.B. 399; cf. Winfield, *Province of the Law of Tort*, 40; *Jackson* v. *Mayfair Window Cleaning Co. Ltd.*, [1952] 1 All E.R. 215
4 *Turner* v. *Stallibrass*, [1898] 1 Q.B. 56.
5 Prosser, *Handbook of the Law of Torts*, 203.
6 *Constantine* v. *Imperial Hotels Ltd.*, [1944] K.B. 693; even though no special damage is proved.
7 *Clegg Parkinson & Co.* v. *Earby Gas Co.*, [1896] 1 Q.B. 592.
8 Salmond, *op. cit.* 505 *et seq.*
9 *Restatement*, Torts, S. 763.

The difficult problem is the nature of the relationship after the request of the consumer for the service is complied with. If the provisions of the Gas Code are broken does the action lie in contract or for breach of statutory duty? Has the consumer entered into a contract on those terms contained in the Code? Is the telephone agreement a misnomer, because there is no contract at all? Is the request of the consumer merely the act which brings the parties into relationship with one another? Or is there a contract of which the compulsory terms are not part, because they are duties imposed irrespectively of the fact that a contract exists?

Beyond the usual contract-tort distinctions, county court jurisdiction, punitive damages and the like,[1] this raises two points of particular importance for public authorities. An action for breach of statutory duty does not lie merely because a breach of duty is proved; there must also be a statutory intention to give a civil remedy to those aggrieved by the breach.[2] If there is no contract the consumer may find himself remediless[3] because the courts find that the duty is one owed to the public in general. So in the United States it has been held that there is no cause of action for failure to provide transportation facilities unless contractual relations have been entered into.[4] Secondly, the appropriate method of compelling performance of a public duty is mandamus, whereas the method of preventing a contractor from refusing to perform his contract may be an order for specific performance or sometimes an injunction. Mandamus is not a completely satisfactory remedy, because its scope in the field of administrative law is still uncertain—in particular whether a duty must be owed to him seeking it, or whether his special interest in the performance of a general duty will suffice.[5] In the United States it has been held that injunction does not lie before the contractual relationship commences.[6] It is doubtful whether mandamus is available if there is a contract.[7]

In *Read* v. *Croydon Corporation*[8] the court of first instance had to determine whether the duty of the corporation as a supplier of water to a rate-payer who was already being supplied by it was contractual or statutory.

1 Clerk & Lindsell, *op. cit.* 4.
2 For a decision that no action lay against the Petroleum Board for failure to supply petrol to a retailer, see *Eric Gnapp Ltd.* v. *Petroleum Board*, [1949] 1 All E.R. 980.
3 Sometimes, a separate action under *Donoghue* v. *Stevenson* may lie; e.g. *Barnes* v. *Irwell Valley Water Board*, [1939] 1 K.B. 21.
4 *Little Rock & Fort Smith Rly.* v. *Conatser* (1896), 61 Ark. 560.
5 See p. 139 *infra*.
6 *Cox* v. *Malden & Melrose Gaslight Co.* (1908), 199 Mass. 324.
7 *Loraine* v. *Pittsburgh J.E. and E.R.R.* (1903), 205 Pa. 132; *State ex rel. Marion* v. *Marion Light & H. Co.* (1910), 174 Ind. 622; *Horton* v. *Interstate T. & T.* (1932), 202 N.C. 610. Cf. *State ex rel. Anderson* v. *Brand* (1938), 13 N.E. 2nd 955.
8 [1938] 4 All E.R. 631.

Stable J. ruled that there was not a contract 'although rights and obligations may be created thereunder similar to, or identical with, rights which
may be created by contract'.[1] He had the support of many *dicta*,[2] including
one uttered in the House of Lords.[3] There are other *dicta* to the effect that
the relationship is contractual.[4] An interesting case on telephone agree-
ments is *Postmaster-General* v. *Wadsworth*.[5] A subscriber claimed that he
had been overcharged. The Postmaster-General relied on a regulation
which provided that the production of a certified account of the sum
owing shall be conclusive evidence of both the amount and the liability,
and the subscriber denied that the reference in his agreement was sufficiently
specific to incorporate this regulation into it. Slesser L.J., in finding for the
Postmaster-General, held that even if the subscriber had not contracted
subject to the regulations he would have been bound by them. It does not
follow that this case is authority for the proposition that those regulations
were not part of the contract. It may be that it decided that they were part
of it by necessary implication,[6] just as the statutory provisions about leases
contained in the Law of Property Act, 1925,[7] the Landlord and Tenant
Act, 1927,[8] and the Leasehold Property (Repairs) Act, 1938,[9] are incorporated in appropriate leases.

English courts then have not yet decided whether there is a contract
between statutory undertaker and consumer. It is possible that the
contradictions in the cases might rest on the wording of the respective
statutes, although this does not seem likely, for the essentials of each case
are similar. For the reasons now adduced it is suggested that the relationship is contractual. There is no relation between them until the consumer
applies to the undertaker. When the latter is satisfied that the customer is
entitled to the service, and commences to supply him, it is suggested that
a contract is made. Whether there is also a formal written agreement as
there used to be for telephones, or not as in the case of gas, does not affect

1 At 648.
2 E.g. *Clegg Parkinson Co.* v. *Earby Gas Co.*, [1896] 1 Q.B. 592 at 595 (*per* Wright J.).
3 *Milnes* v. *Mayor of Huddersfield* (1886), 11 App. Cas. 511 at 523 (*per* Earl of
Selbourne); cf. Halsbury, XXXIII, 451 n.r.
4 E.g. *Edmundson* v. *Mayor of Longton* (1902), 19 T.L.R. 15 at 16 (*per* Lord Alverstone C.J.); *Countess of Rothes* v. *Kirkcaldy & Dysart Waterworks Commissioners* (1882),
7 App. Cas. 694 at 707 (*per* Lord Watson); *Barnes* v. *Irwell Valley Water Board*, [1939]
1 K.B. 21 at 44 (C.A.) (*per* Slesser L.J.); *Griffiths* v. *Smith*, [1941] A.C. 170 at 208
(*per* Lord Porter).
5 [1939], 4 All E.R.
6 In May 1949 the Postmaster-General announced in the House of Commons that
he was dropping a scheme to raise telephone rentals because it would be necessary to
enter into separate new contracts with all subscribers (Hansard, 5 s. vol. 465, col. 958).
7 15 & 16 Geo. V, c. 20.   8 17 & 18 Geo. V, c. 36.
9 1 & 2 Geo. VI, c. 34.

the juridical nature of the relation—there is an offer and acceptance whether with or without some terms additional to those laid down by statutory authority. There may be that consent which is of the essence of contract, even though a party is induced by pressures outside himself.[1] The point surely is whether that external pressure is lawful, or whether it amounts to duress. The circumstances under discussion differ from ordinary contracts in that the statute can apply only if the relation is of such a nature as to make it applicable; it must be that category of relation, and its establishment is as to one party voluntary. So dominated by the notion of status is the English law of contract that it is content with the slightest degree of consent. A common carrier who is bound to carry certain goods at the behest of a member of the public can enter into a contract with him. It is submitted that a public body supplying essential services may do the same. That compulsory terms are imposed by statute is irrelevant. Compulsory contracts only seem paradoxical because freedom of contract has been exalted as a value. Freedom is, of course, indispensable, but contract is a means only. That they must be linked is not proved, and it seems that it is socially desirable that the law should take into account those interferences with economic liberty imposed for the common good and mould them within the framework of its existing principles. Then, there is nothing objectionable in holding that these relationships are contractual. The compulsory statutory terms are part of the relevant contract. This obviates the need for a litigant to surmount the obstacles of an action for breach of statutory duty, and is also consistent with the main body of the law of contract.

The same problem has attracted the attention of French jurists. There is not unanimity, but in a recent and thorough investigation one writer,[2] arguing by analogy to *le contrat d'adhésion*, contends that supply of gas on conditions prescribed by law is not a unilateral arrangement, but is contractual because there is an element of free consent. He points out that all contracts do not require the same degree of consent, and that it is enough if there is the bare minimum which is found in these supplier-consumer public contracts. Waline agrees and points out that the usual criteria will determine whether the contract is administrative.[3] Any illegal act of the enterprise may be annulled by the *Conseil d'Etat* as an *excès de pouvoir*, and a failure to act may amount to a *faute de service* for which damages may be recoverable in the *Conseil d'Etat*.

It is maintained that the present state-consumer relationships are effected

---

1 Cf. E. W. Patterson, 'Compulsory Contracts in the Crystal Ball' in 43 *Col. L.R.* (1943) 731 *et seq.*; M. Radin, *op. cit.*

2 Péquignot, *op. cit.* 67 *et seq.*   3 417. See p. 83 *supra.*

in a satisfactory manner, except that there is need for further consultation of interested parties in the framing of the conditions of supply. It would only remain for the courts to recognise the existence of a contract between supplier and consumer, and thus afford the consumer the usual remedies for breach of contract.

12. THE CIVIL SERVICE

In the nineteenth century it was proper to regard the law of the Civil Service as a matter of internal administration. The text-books were entitled 'The Law of Officers'[1] and they examined from a common-law angle the liabilities, rights and duties of officers. Since then, the law of external administration has acquired a new significance with the vast increase in State functions.[2] There is a new science of public administration in which the law and the administration of the Civil Service must be geared in harmony. Henceforth, the Civil Service must be judged by its effectiveness as a means to the end of government.

Much thought has been given to the role of the Civil Service, and it may be summed up, perhaps, in Friedrich's phrase, as 'responsible bureaucracy'.[3] It is generally agreed that this bureaucracy must be professional, based on a career-service system. Beyond the need for competitive examination, classification and the like, it is thought that the civil servant should be secure against removal or discrimination for arbitrary reasons.[4] Here, the law must play its part, for it can give him this security either by upholding contracts which make him dismissible only for cause, or by setting up under statute a system of administrative bodies to enforce with due procedural safeguards administrative responsibility. If the law does neither of these, it is not making its contribution to the creation of an efficient bureaucracy.

In the light of these observations, the English law will now be examined. It has developed in so peculiar a fashion that it is impossible to appreciate it without first considering the law relating to the armed forces.

Dickson v. *Combermere*[5] established a principle which has since been consistently followed. There, a lieutenant-colonel in the British army sued a former Secretary of State for War for wrongful dismissal. Finding for the defendant, Cockburn C.J. said:[6] 'The Sovereign has the power of

1 E.g. Meachem, *A Treatise on the Law of Public Offices and Officers*.
2 Hart, *op. cit.* ch. IV.
3 C. J. Friedrich (and others), *Problems of the American Civil Service*, 'Responsible Government Service under the American Constitution', 1–74.
4 Cf. Commission of Inquiry on Public Service Personnel, 'Better Government Personnel' (New York, 1935), 6.
5 (1863), 3 F. & F. 527.   6 At 585.

dismissing any officer. He receives his commission from his Sovereign and holds it at his pleasure, and it is the will of the Sovereign to withdraw it.' He pointed out that the Sovereign is the first in military command under the Constitution, with prerogative control of the armed forces. The nature of this prerogative control was confirmed, and the principle of *Dickson* v. *Combermere* approved, by the Court of Appeal in *China Navigation Co. Ltd.* v. *Attorney-General.*[1] There is a long series of cases confirming that no member of the armed forces can bring an action setting up that he has been wrongfully dismissed in breach of contract; the Sovereign may dismiss him at his pleasure.[2]

That this prerogative control has even wider implications was shown in *Leaman* v. *Rex*[3] which decided that a soldier could not claim by petition of right for arrears of pay accrued to the date of his dismissal.[4] The House of Lords has also expressed the opinion (*obiter*) that a contract purporting to engage a military servant for a fixed period cannot be enforced.[5]

A civil servant also is ordinarily dismissible at pleasure.[6] That prompts the question whether the Crown can contract with him on any other terms, and whether it is liable for arrears of his pay. Some writers say unequivocally that there can be no contractual relation between the Crown and its civil servants.[7] One finds this difficult to reconcile with *Fisher* v. *Steward*[8] which held that a surveyor of taxes, although unable to sue for unlawful dismissal, could be sued on a counterclaim by the Crown for the enforcement of his promise to return his commission of appointment on the cessation of his appointment. The authorities must be examined to see what is the legal basis for the rule that a civil servant is dismissible at pleasure.

It is submitted that there is always a contract between the Crown and a civil servant, in which a term is implied that the Crown may dismiss at

1 (1932), 48 T.L.R. 375 at 378 (*per* Scrutton L.J.).
2 *De Dohsé* v. *Reg.* (1886), 3 T.L.R. 114 (H.L.); *Mitchell* v. *Reg.* (1896), 1 Q.B. 121 n.; *In re Tufnell* (1876), 3 Ch. D. 164; *Owners of S.S. Raphael* v. *Brandy*, [1911] A.C. 413; *Grant* v. *Secretary of State for India in Council* (1877), 2 C.P.D. 445. The High Court of Australia has denied that there is a contractual relationship between the State and a member of the armed forces; *Commonwealth* v. *Quince* (1944), 68 C.L.R. 227. See also E. R. Keedy, 'A Petition of Right: *Archer-Slee* v. *Rex* in 87 *U. of Pa. L.R.* (1938) 895.
3 [1920] 3 K.B. 663, followed in *Cooke* v. *Rex*, [1929] Ex. C.R. 20.
4 Cf. D. W. Logan, 'A Civil Servant and His Pay' in 61 *L.Q.R.* (1945) 240 at 260.
5 *De Dohsé* v. *Reg.* at 115 (*per* Lord Halsbury L.C.); nor in a declarator action in Scotland; *Griffin* v. *Lord Advocate*, [1950] S.C. 448.
6 *Slingsby's Case* (1680), 3 Swanst. 178; *Hill* v. *Reg.* (1854), 8 Moo. P.C. 138; *In re the Governor-General & Executive Council of New South Wales* (1858). 11 Moo. P.C. 288; *Shenton* v. *Smith*, [1895] A.C. 229.
7 E.g. Ridges, *Constitutional Law of England*, 198 n. 81.
8 (1920), 36 T.L.R. 395.

will. Confusion has arisen because writers and sometimes judges have applied to civil servants precedents concerning military servants. It has been shown that the latter rest on the peculiar prerogative control of the armed forces; there is no corresponding prerogative control of civil servants.[1] Lord Hobhouse summed up the matter neatly in *Shenton* v. *Smith*:[2] '...unless in special cases where it is otherwise provided, servants of the Crown hold their office during the pleasure of the Crown; not by virtue of any special prerogative of the Crown, but because such are the terms of their engagement....'[3]

Many statutes such as the Exchequer and Audit Departments Act, 1866,[4] and the Import Duties Act, 1932,[5] incorporate special conditions for certain civil servants in the courts.[6] In *Dunn* v. *Reg.*[7] the court decided that the Crown could dismiss at pleasure a civil servant whom it had appointed for a fixed term. Many have treated this case as authority for the proposition that no contractual variation of the right of the Crown to dismiss at will is valid if not ordered by statute. With respect, Glanville Williams[8] seems right in saying that the case is not a binding authority for that, because the appointing officer was acting outside the scope of his authority, and because one may appoint a man for a fixed term and still dismiss him at pleasure—that merely means that his appointment will cease in any event after that period. Nevertheless, an *obiter dictum* of the Court of Appeal in *Hales* v. *Rex*[9] and a decision of a court of first instance[10] hold that a person employed on a contract for a fixed period subject to dismissal for misconduct can be dismissed at will.

Since then, there have been opposing *dicta*, of which that of Lord Atkin in *Reilly* v. *Rex*[11] is the most important. The plaintiff had been appointed for a fixed period subject to dismissal for cause. During that period his office was abolished by statute. Because that made the contract void for subsequent impossibility, he could not sue for breach of contract. Lord Atkin said:

If the terms of the appointment definitely prescribe a term and expressly provide for a power to determine 'for cause' it appears necessarily to follow that any implication of a power to dismiss at pleasure is excluded.

1 [1895] A.C. 229 at 234–5.
2 Cf. Halsbury, *op. cit.* VI, 488; Emden, *op. cit.* 21.
3 Most Departments, of course, have a statutory basis for the employment of staffs. See, for example, s. 3 (2), Minister of Town and Country Planning Act, 1943.
4 29 & 30 Vic. c. 39.   5 22 & 23 Geo. V, c. 8.
6 *Gould* v. *Stuart*, [1896] A.C. 575; *Browne* v. *Commissioner for Railways* (1936), 36 S.R. (N.S.W.) 21; *R. Venkata Rao* v. *Secretary of State for India in Council*, [1937] A.C. 248 at 258 (*per* Lord Roche).   7 [1896] 1 Q.B. 116.
8 At 64.   9 (1918), 34 T.L.R. 589 at 589 (*per* Pickford L.J.).
10 *Denning* v. *Secretary of State for India in Council*, (1920) 37 T.L.R. 138; cf. *Finn* v. *R.*, [1933] N.Z.L.R. 1018.   11 [1934] A.C. 176 at 179.

Tucker J. (as he then was) ignored this *dictum* in *Rodwell* v. *Thomas* in 1944, saying:[1]

> The authorities show, not only that *prima facie* an established civil servant can be dismissed at pleasure, but that the court will disregard any term of his contract expressly providing for employment for a specified time or that his employment can only be terminated in specified ways. The court regards such a provision in a contract as a clog on the right of the Crown to dismiss at pleasure at any time.

Yet since then another judge has said:[2]

> ...in regard to contracts of service, the Crown is bound by its express promises as much as any subject. The cases where it has been held entitled to dismiss at pleasure are based on an implied term which cannot, of course, exist where there is an express term dealing with the matter.

Although there have been no decisions on the point in England since *Reilly* v. *Rex* there have been two in Canada. In *McLean* v. *Vancouver Harbour Commissioners*[3] the *dictum* was followed in holding that a civil servant whose contract provided that he could not be dismissed for illness was not dismissible at will. In *Genois* v. *Rex*[4] a civil servant engaged for a fixed period was dismissed during that period. Turning down his claim for wrongful dismissal, the court held that, following *Reilly* v. *Rex*, had there been a provision for dismissal for cause there would have been a cause of action, but that an employment for a period did not rebut the presumption that he was dismissible at pleasure.

It is open for the courts to declare the law as follows: that there is an implied term in the contract of civil servants that the Crown may dismiss them at will, that the implied term may be expressly or impliedly excluded, that a contract providing for dismissal for cause will exclude it, but that employment for a fixed term will not itself be inconsistent with the implied term.[5] The Crown Proceedings Act makes no changes, because actions for breach of contract can be brought only where a petition of right was previously available.

In a recent New Zealand case[6] a civil servant sued the Crown for breach of contract because it had transferred him to another Department for security reasons against his wishes. The Public Service Code which applied to him provided for dismissal on three months notice. The court dismissed

1 [1944] K.B. 596 at 602.
2 *Robertson* v. *Minister of Pensions*, [1949] 1 K.B. 227 at 231 (*per* Denning J.).
3 [1936] 3 W.W.R. 657.   4 [1937] Ex. C.R. 176.
5 *Ctra.* Keir & Lawson, *op. cit.*, 509.
6 *Deynzer* v. *Campbell*, [1950] N.Z.L.R. 790; cf. *Nicol* v. *Lawrie*, 1950 (3) S.A. 151, A.D.

the suit for different reasons: Gresson J. held that on the authority of *Reilly* v. *Rex* and *Robertson* v. *Minister of Pensions* the Crown here had no power to dismiss at pleasure, but that it had an implied right of transfer; other members of the Court held, in reliance on *Dunn* v. *Reg.* and the *Amphitrite case*, that the statutory provision did not prevent the Crown from either dismissing or transferring a civil servant when the public interest demanded it.

The most interesting recent case is a Scottish one, *Cameron* v. *Lord Advocate*.[1] The plaintiff accepted an offer of civil employment by the Crown in Nigeria, but on his arrival there the contract was repudiated. Lord Mackay said that the cases on the armed forces were irrelevant because the duty to serve arises independently of contract. Although agreeing with a general principle along the lines of the *Amphitrite* judgment, that the Crown cannot by contract be prevented from acting for the public welfare, he denied that the doctrine applied to contracts of employment of this type. He explained the *Dunn Case* on the basis that the civil servant had no authority to make a contract of employment, approved the *dicta* of Lords Hobhouse and Atkin previously cited, and, denying that exceptions were limited to statutory ones, concluded: 'For that breach of contract I know of no law that immunises the Government and its responsible officials from paying damages.'

Even though the Crown should not assert the right to dismiss any servant at will, it can and does attain the same end in practice by very rarely contracting that a servant may be dismissed for cause. There seems no justification for this. Public policy does not demand it;[2] contract could provide expressly for dismissal for cause and on notice. In any event any employer has a right at common law to dismiss for misconduct. Indeed, the Crown practice is contrary to public policy because it tends to dissuade the best personnel from entering the service, it is calculated to deceive employees about their rights, and it deprives them of that sense of security essential for the best performance of their duties. So long as it is the practice of the Crown to rely on the implied term and even to maintain that it is absolute, the best method of changing this may be to abolish by statute the implied term.

It is sometimes contended that the Crown is a model employer. It is not easy to prove this contention statistically if the aggrieved employee

1 [1952] S.C. 165.
2 J. D. B. Mitchell, 'Limitations on the Contractual Liability of Public Authorities' in 13 *Mod. L.R.* (1950) 318, 455, suggests that there may be a general rule, based on public policy, that the State cannot be prevented by contract from performing its essential functions, but he denies that public policy would extend that rule to the proposition that civil servants are necessarily dismissible at pleasure.

cannot pursue any civil remedy. To this it may be rejoined that the Crown has a fair system of administration which ensures that no one is dismissed or has his promotion retarded without full consideration of his case by the head of the Department or some other responsible supervising officer. But this protection is illusory in England. In many countries that system succeeds in securing the rights of a servant and yet maintaining administrative discipline. In those countries the servant has a legal right to a fair hearing, and in default of that may have the administrative decision quashed by the ordinary courts. The British civil servant enjoys no such protection. The procedure is extra-legal, and he has no right to challenge it in the courts; if he is dismissed without being given an opportunity of being heard, the courts are powerless. That the civil servant may in fact be treated fairly is no answer; in that case there is all the more reason why the Crown should not oppose a judicial review.

The further point may be made that the civil servant has all the benefits of Whitleyism, whereby the National Council on which he is adequately represented settles the terms and conditions of his employment. The value of this can be gauged from the decision in *Rodwell* v. *Thomas*[1] that terms embodied in a resolution of the Council are not part of the contract of a civil servant. The conclusion is inescapable that the legal protection of the civil servant's security of tenure in England is inadequate.

It is the opinion of many text-book writers[2] on constitutional law that the civil servant cannot sue for money earned for services rendered, but there is little reliable authority for this opinion. The only English decision seems to be *Lucas* v. *Lucas and High Commissioner for India*.[3] It was there decided that the pay of a civil servant could not be attached because there was no enforceable debt in the hands of the Crown. This followed the Scottish decision, *Mulvenna* v. *Admiralty*.[4] Yet the Scottish court purported to rely on *Leaman* v. *Rex*[5] and did not heed the important distinction between civil and military servants. The *Lucas* decision can also be justified on the ground that the rule of court controlling garnishee procedure did not then bind the Crown. Moreover, there are several English and Commonwealth decisions holding that a civil servant can sue for arrears of pay, none of which was cited. They include *Bushe* v. *Reg.*,[6] *Sutton* v. *Attorney-General*[7] and *Carey* v. *Commonwealth*.[8] Nor is there any policy

1 [1944] K.B. 596.
2 E.g. Anson, *Constitution*, II, pt. II, 335–6; Mustoe, *op. cit.* 41.
3 [1943] P. 68.
4 [1926] S.C. 842; disapproved in *Cameron* v. *Lord Advocate, supra.*
5 [1920] 3 K.B. 663.   6 *The Times* newspaper, 29 May 1869.
7 (1923), 39 T.L.R. 295.
8 (1921), 30 C.L.R. 132; cf. *Bertrand* v. *Rex*, [1949] V.L.R. 49.

justification for the alleged rule. If the civil servant has performed his work, surely he should be paid for it; it is a separate question whether the Crown may dismiss him or reduce his salary. The *Lucas Case* neither need nor ought to be followed. It is, however, certain that the Superannuation Acts, 1834[1] to 1919, providing for civil service pensions, prevent a claimant from suing for them.[2] There seems no good reason for this, and the proposed reforms of the Tomlin Commission[3] should be implemented.

An employee is often prejudiced by a statute abolishing his office, or making him redundant. It has been shown that in England his contract is then void. Many other countries recognise his right to sue the State, not for breach of contract, but for damages for liability based on risk. The inadequacy of English common law is often recognised by statutes expressly compensating him for loss of office.[4]

A useful comparison with the law of the civil service in the United States is made difficult because rules of the constitution impinge on the topic.[5] A distinction is drawn between officers and employees, but the courts have not fixed the criteria of the distinction.[6] One distinction is that whereas employees usually have a contract of service which they can enforce in the courts, an officer is said to have no contractual relationship with the United States. This only means that he has not the benefit of that article of the constitution[7] which declares void any act of Congress interfering with an existing contract.[8] A further constitutional complication is that the President can always dismiss executive officers.[9] Nevertheless an officer can sue for accrued salary,[10] and for a pension payment which has become due under a statute,[11] although he may not complain if a statute alters the terms of pensions.[12] One writer has said that the principle of the law is to deny the civil servant in the United States common-law rights only where public policy inexorably demands it.[13]

The United States does not grant the civil servant a remedy in contract alone. Statutes commonly prescribe procedures regulating administrative

1 Particularly s. 30, s. 9 of the Superannuation Act, 1887, s. 4. Superannuation Act, 1909.

2 *Cooper* v. *Reg.* (1880), 14 Ch.D. 311; *Considine* v. *McInerney*, [1916] 2 A.C. 162; *Nixon* v. *Attorney-General*, [1931] A.C. 184.

3 Cmd. 3909 of 1931 at 216; cf. Fabian Publications, *The Reform of the Higher Civil Service* at 32.

4 E.g. s. 60 Gas Act, 1948. 5 See Field, *Civil Service*, passim.

6 *Groves* v. *Barden* (1915), 169 N.C. 8. 7 Art. I, s. 10.

8 *Butler* v. *Pennsylvania* (1850), 10 How. 402.

9 *Myers* v. *U.S.* (1926), 272 U.S. 52.

10 *Fisk* v. *Jefferson Police Jury* (1885), 116 U.S. 131; *O'Leary* v. *U.S.* (1933), 77 Ct. Cl. 635. An enlisted man can sue for his pay; *In re Grimley* (1890), 137 U.S. 147.

11 *Roddy* v. *Valentine* (1935), 197 N.E. 260.

12 *U.S.* v. *Teller* (1882), 107 U.S. 64. 13 Hart, *op. cit.* 22.

proposals. The United States has frankly recognised a dilemma: either the removing officer has such a broad discretion that, as in the British Civil Service, there is nothing to prevent arbitrary conduct, or the extent of judicial review is so great that he and not the civil servant may virtually be on trial.[1] This is primarily a problem for the lawmakers, and the courts can only give effect to the legislative will. Where a statute provided that officers 'may be removed by the board for cause' it was held that a removal effected without giving to the officer notice and an opportunity to be heard was invalid, a far-sighted decision considerably in advance of English law.[2] If, however, the statute is subjective in form, for example, 'for such cause as they may deem sufficient', then the courts will not review.[3] Also, the Supreme Court has affirmed by an evenly divided vote the majority judgment of the lower court that a civil servant could not claim that she had been denied due process in a loyalty order proceeding because she had no legally protectible interest to which the due process could apply.[4] When a statute provides for a hearing, the courts will quash any decision reached without notice and fair hearing.[5] Not merely must the employee have the opportunity to give an explanation but he also must have access to all evidence on which the State relies, and time and opportunity to refute it.[6] Both Congress and the courts seem more zealous in protecting the civil servant than their English counterparts.

Some French public servants are subject to *contrat administratif* by special arrangement, for example, propaganda officers.[7] Others, like the employees of concessions, are subject to the private law of contract, but the large majority is subject to neither but to statutory regulation.[8] It is this last group that must now be considered.

Hauriou[9] explains that the elements of a civil contract are absent; no formal contract is made; there is no offer and acceptance[10] since an individual becomes a civil servant by the unilateral act of nomination; the rights and duties can be modified without consent. The relationship is *réglementaire* and not contractual.

1 White, *Introduction to the Study of Public Administration*, ch. 15.
2 *Ham* v. *Board of Boston Police* (1886), 142 Mass. 190.
3 *Lacy* v. *Young* (1921), 240 Mass. 118.
4 *Bailey* v. *Richardson* (1951), 71 S. Ct. 669.
5 *Sharkey* v. *Thurston* (1935), 268 N.Y. 123.
6 *McCarthy* v. *Emerson* (1909), 202 Mass. 352.
7 Décret of 6 July 1942.
8 G. Jèze, 'Le Contrat Administratif de Louage de Services Personnels' in 43 R.D.P. (1926) 5; and see art. 5 of the law of 19 Oct. 1946.
9 Hauriou, *op. cit.* 590 *et seq.*
10 Probably the French civil law of subjective assent assists this conclusion; cf. Cohen, *Des Contrats par Correspondance en Droit Français, en Droit Anglais et en Droit Anglo-Américain, passim.*

The right to salary, pension and promotion is given by law. Duguit points out[1] that it is not in return for consideration furnished, but to secure the proper functioning of the service. Yet, once the salary or pension has accrued, the servant is able to recover it by action in the *Conseil d'Etat*[2] (*le droit acquis*). Although he has no right to future salary (*le droit éventuel*) because it may be changed by unilateral act, the *Conseil d'Etat en pleine juridiction* will compensate him on the principle of risk. In the same way, he may be compensated if his office is abolished by law.[3]

Disciplinary control is also according to law. The law recognises a graded series of punishments ranging from reprimand to dismissal. Disciplinary bodies are set up to investigate alleged breaches of discipline. A servant aggrieved by their decision can ask the *Conseil d'Etat* to nullify it[4] for *excès de pouvoir*, either because of a defect in form[5] or because it was not according to law, or because of abuse of power. A civil servant has a statutory right to inspect all documents and reports on which the Administration relies when contemplating disciplinary measures against him.[6]

The advantages of the French system over the English are obvious. The civil servant is assured of a fair hearing. Although the right of the State to change his conditions at will is recognised, he may sometimes obtain damages if his position is altered to his detriment by statute, and his right to accrued salary and pension is inviolable.

Belgium, too, although in many aspects, and particularly that of recruitment, based on the British Civil Service system, has statutory procedures controlling discipline, which guarantee to the civil servant compliance with the rules of natural justice.[7]

1 *Traité*, 106.   2 *Lafage*, Sirey, 1913, 3, 1.
3 *Villenave*, Sirey, 1904, 3, 12.   4 Hauriou, *op. cit.* 615 *et seq.*
5 *Zickel*, 21 April 1893; *Carré*, 23 Feb. 1906 (*Conseil d'Etat*).
6 22 April 1905, art. 65.
7 P. M. Gaudemet, 'Le Statut des Agents de l'Etat en Belgique' in 66 *R.D.P.* (1949) 326.

Chapter IV

EXPROPRIATION, QUASI-CONTRACT AND TRUSTS

I. EXPROPRIATION

A. *England*

It is important to consider to what extent a petition of right lay for expropriation by the Crown, because the cause of action under section 1 of the Crown Proceedings Act (where petition of right formerly lay) is wider than the new cause of action in tort authorised by section 2.

In Roman law, actions relating to disputed titles to property were actions *in rem*, and were not founded on alleged wrongdoing.[1] Modern Continental civil codes embody the same principle, and so does the English real action. The petition of right was developed about the same time as the real action, and it is not therefore surprising that the petition was available for the recovery of land; indeed Holdsworth argued that 'in the Middle Ages a petition would lie for any cause of complaint which would have supported a real action against a subject'.[2] Many Year Book cases illustrate the use of the petition for the recovery of land,[3] and even in respect of interferences with easements.[4]

The most important English case on expropriation of land by the Crown is *Attorney-General* v. *De Keyser's Royal Hotel Ltd.*[5] During the War of 1914–18 a London hotel was requisitioned without any agreement on the compensation to be paid. The claim of the suppliants for compensation was resisted by the Crown on the plea that they were at most entitled to an *ex gratia* payment. The suppliants first pleaded that possession was taken by the Crown in circumstances from which an agreement to pay compensation could be implied. The House of Lords rejected this plea because the Crown had entered upon the property under a claim of right which was necessarily incompatible with an agreement to pay. The Crown contended that it had occupied the property by prerogative right, and that in such circumstances there was no liability to pay compensation. Legislation,[6] under which expropriation in an emergency was permitted on payment of compensation, had been passed. The House of Lords held that this

---

1 Cf. *Mémoires de l'Académie*, Rapport de E. Freund, 31.
2 H.E.L. IX, 43.
3 *Rex* v. *William Hoove*, Y.B. 34 Hen. VI, pl. 18; Brooke, *Peticion et Monstrans de Droit*; Staunford, *op. cit.* 72 a.
4 *Clifton's Case*, Y.B. 22 Ed. III, pl. 12.   5 [1920] A.C. 508.
6 Defence Act, 1842, 5 & 6 Vict. c. 94, s. 19.

legislation must be presumed to have displaced the prerogative power to expropriate, and that the compensation payable under the statute could be recovered from the Crown by petition of right. It was not decided whether the Crown was liable to pay compensation when expropriating under prerogative powers.

Viscount Dunedin[1] also held that if the suppliant had asserted that the Crown had no right to expropriate, his action could not lie because his consequent action in trespass would be barred by the rule that the King can do no wrong. For a long time actions for the recovery of land have been brought not by a real action but by an action of ejectment. This action sounding in tort, the question arose whether it, like trespass, could not be brought by petition of right. Holdsworth[2] and Glanville Williams[3] think that a petition of right was available either for restitution or compensation for a taking of land, whereas Robertson thought it available for restitution only.[4]

Since the *De Keyser Case*, petition of right has been allowed when goods have been wrongfully detained,[5] and there are *dicta* that compensation in lieu of restitution can then be given.[6] On the other hand, nineteenth-century cases declared that it did not lie for trespass to land,[7] although it would lie for ejectment.[8] There is an *obiter dictum* that a lawful interference not amounting to dispossession of land cannot be complained of by petition of right.[9]

Perhaps, if the action were for the recovery of property which the Crown had wrongfully taken for its own use, or damages in lieu thereof, a petition of right for detinue or ejectment would have lain. On the other hand, for trespass, nuisance or conversion not amounting to a dispossession but only wrongful interference, the petition would not have been available,[10] although an action may now lie under section 2 of the Crown Proceedings Act. Compensation for a lawful taking may be recovered under section 1, wherever a statute authorises compensation. Whether compensation is recoverable for a taking by virtue of the prerogative is unsettled. Probably an action would lie under section 1 if an agreement

---

1 At 523.
2 *H.E.L.* IX, 41.
3 At 16.
4 At 335–6.
5 *Bucknall* v. *Rex* (1930), 46 T.L.R. 449; cf. *Feather* v. *Reg.* (1865), 6 B. & S. 257 at 294 (*per* Cockburn L.J.); *Tobin* v. *Reg.* (1864), 16 C.B.N.S. 310 at 358 (*per* Erle C.J.).
6 *Feather* v. *Reg.* (1865), 6 B. & S. 257 at 294 (*per* Cockburn L.J.); *Buckland* v. *Rex*, [1933] 1 K.B. 329 at 343–4 (*per* McCardie J.).
7 *Raleigh* v. *Goschen*, [1898] 1 Ch. 73 at 79 (*per* Romer J.).
8 *In re Gosman* (1880), 15 Ch. D. 67.
9 *France, Fenwick & Co., Ltd.* v. *Rex*, [1927] 1 K.B. 458 at 467 (*per* Wright J.).
10 See Sir Arnold McNair, Note in 43 *L.Q.R.* (1927) 9.

to pay compensation could be implied from a taking or interference by the Crown.

Of course, expropriation is usually carried out under the authority of statutes which prescribe the payment of compensation. Formerly, diverse unrelated statutes, each with a different procedure, sanctioned this, but great advances towards uniformity have been made recently. The Acquisition of Land (Authorisation Procedure) Act, 1946,[1] and the Town and Country Planning Act, 1947,[2] now furnish a uniform code for ordinary and emergency compulsory purchases. The procedure is the same whether it is the Crown or some other body which is acquiring the land. The Lands Tribunal Act, 1949,[3] has made further improvements, by setting up a Lands Tribunal to determine all compensation questions formerly dealt with under the Acquisition of Land (Assessment of Compensation) Act, 1919.[4] The tribunal, composed of a legal chairman and other members who are either lawyers or land valuers, makes a final decision subject to the right to state a case on a point of law to the Court of Appeal. Besides the statutes authorising compulsory purchase to which the Act is to apply, there is power to add any further cases involving value of land where to do so is desirable for uniformity of decision or to make economic use of land valuers. In introducing the Bill in the House of Commons, the Attorney-General[5] explained that it was designed to strike a balance between the legal and valuation elements involved in these issues, particularly those relating to development values under the Town and Country Planning Act, 1947.

B. *United States*

The United States constitution enacts:[6] 'No person shall be...deprived of life, liberty or property, without due process of law; nor shall private property be taken for public use, without justification.' The Tucker Act gives to the Court of Claims jurisdiction over claims founded on the constitution and over contracts express or implied. Although it might appear that whenever there was a taking there would be a right of action, the courts, influenced by the former tortious immunity, have until recently declared that only when an implied promise to pay can be spelt out of the circumstances is there an action against the United States.[7] If, for example,

1 9 & 10 Geo. VI, c. 49.
2 10 & 11 Geo. VI, c. 51, s. 37, pt. III.
3 12 & 13 Geo. VI, c. 42.   4 9 & 10 Geo. V, c. 57.
5 Hansard, vol. 462, 5 s., col. 42 *et seq.*
6 See Note, 'The Fifth Amendment and the Tucker Act' in 32 *Yale L.J.* (1922) 725.
7 *U.S.* v. *Great Falls Manufacturing Co.* (1884), 112 U.S. 665; L. L. Anderson, 'Tort and Implied Contract Liability of the Federal Government' in 30 *Minn. L.R.* (1946) 133 at 135.

the United States appropriated property under a mistaken claim of right which manifested an affirmative governmental intention not to pay, it would not be actionable under the Tucker Act. Doubt has been cast on this by a recent decision of the Supreme Court that 'we need not decide whether repeated trespasses might give rise to an implied contract...if there is a taking, the claim is therefore founded upon the Constitution and within the jurisdiction of the Court of Claims to hear and determine'.[1] Whether the taking is under a common-law or statutory power there is liability. Taking under requisition or with an admission of the ownership of the plaintiff, unaccompanied by any refusal to pay, will be construed as a promise to pay compensation.[2]

In the United States too, it is important to know whether there is a liability apart from the newly devised action in tort because the scope of the action under the Tucker Act is in many respects wider than that under the Federal Tort Claims Act.[3]

An action under the Tucker Act will lie only if there is a taking. An agent must have actual authority from the Government. If the property is put to some active use there is little difficulty in proving a taking. On the other hand, an occasional trespass or the causing of mere consequential damage will be insufficient. Substantial interference with use and enjoyment, although not amounting to dispossession, is enough. The repeated firing of guns over land,[4] or the frequent landing and taking off of aircraft,[5] have each been held to be a taking. That restrictions on billposter advertising should not be a taking seems consistent with principle, but it is more surprising that the destruction of property to prevent the spreading of a fire is also not a taking.[6]

C. *France*[7]

In France, the inviolability of private property, and the right to compensation of those deprived of it by State necessity are recognised in the Declaration of Rights of Man of 1789.[8]

1 *U.S.* v. *Causby* (1946), 66 S.C. 1062 at 1068 (*per* Douglas J.).
2 *Langford* v. *U.S.* (1879), 101 U.S. 341; *Tempel* v. *U.S.* (1918), 248 U.S. 121; Shealey, *op. cit.* 66.
3 See particularly s. 421 (a); cf. H. Street, 'Tort Liability of the State: The Federal Tort Claims Act and the Crown Proceedings Act' in 47 *Mich. L.R.* (1949) 341 at 353 n. 63.
4 *Portsmouth Harbor Land & Hotel Co.* v. *U.S.* (1922), 260 U.S. 327.
5 *U.S.* v. *Causby.*
6 *Pennsylvania Coal Co.* v. *Mahon* (1922), 260 U.S. 393 at 415; *Bowditch* v. *Boston* (1879), 101 U.S. 16 at 18.
7 Croquez, *Le Code de l'Expropriation*; Baudry, *L'Expropriation pour Cause d'Utilité Publique*.
8 Cf. art. 545, Civil Code.

France has built up a systematic body of rules governing expropriation of land. A public authority desiring to expropriate land for any purpose must comply with a general statutory procedure.[1] It must prove the authority of law or decree for the acquisition and that it is being acquired for *un objet d'utilité publique*.[2] A formal declaration of the expropriation is necessary. The expropriation, which is normally made by the Administration, is subject to challenge before the *Conseil d'Etat* for *excès de pouvoir* on the usual grounds.[3] There must be a transfer of the property to the Administration.[4] There is always a right to an indemnity, which, failing agreement, is fixed by a tribunal. This tribunal, *la commission arbitrale*, which in 1935 replaced the jury system, consists of a presiding magistrate, two civil servants, a notary and one representative from a panel of property owners locally nominated[5] but not interested in the subject-matter. From its decision there is an appeal to a civil court. There is a further right of appeal to the *Cour de Cassation* but only for *incompétence, excès de pouvoir* or *vice de forme*.

There is an expropriation only when there is dispossession: permanent damage is not essential. For an interference not amounting to expropriation, caused by the execution of public works, the remedy is an action for damages in the *Conseil de Préfecture* with a right of appeal to the *Conseil d'Etat en pleine juridiction*.

For an indirect expropriation, one which consists of an encroachment in the course of the execution of public works, and which has not been sanctioned in advance by the expropriation procedure above, for example, an encroachment by telegraph lines or road widening, an application to the civil court for indemnity may be made.

It seems inconsistent with the French theory of separation of powers to vest so much of the control of expropriation in civil courts. The inability of these courts to order the removal of unauthorised encroachments by the public works Administration is one result of this deplored by so many French jurists.[6]

D. *Conclusion*

The development in Anglo-American countries has been bedevilled by the former tortious immunity of the State. It has led to strained interpretations of contracts, particularly in the United States. A good opportunity to systematise the law was missed when the Federal Tort Claims Act and

1 Décret-loi, 8 Aug. 1935.
2 Intention to destroy or resell will not be valid reasons, Hauriou, *op. cit.* 730.
3 Baudry, *op. cit.* 22.　　　　　　　4 *Ubi supra*, ch. III.
5 *Ubi supra*, p. 73.　　　　　　　6 E.g. Berthélemy, *op. cit.* 620.

the Crown Proceedings Act were passed. The French distinction between dispossession and other interferences has much to commend it. In framing general principles of compensation to be worked out by a tribunal, England is proceeding along sound lines; the jurisdiction of the tribunal should clearly extend to awarding compensation for prerogative expropriations. That the sum fixed by the tribunal is recoverable by action is important. It is thought that it is unnecessary for France to have separate procedures for indirect expropriation. Where there is an interference not amounting to dispossession, this should be a tort subject to the same rules as other governmental torts. The liability under statute and in tort should be mutually exclusive. There should be no cases like *U.S.* v. *Causby* where a liability in nuisance and one under the Tucker Act might co-exist.

2. QUASI-CONTRACT

A. *England*

The petition of right was always freely available for the recovery of property. Therefore, a liability in quasi-contract to restore property or money of the subject received from the Crown could be enforced by petition of right.[1] This proposition, approved in the *Bankers' Case* (1700),[2] does not seem to have been seriously disputed by the Crown since 1848.[3] It also enabled money due under a statute to be recovered by a petition of right.[4] In a recent case,[5] whether the Crown was bound to repay money paid even by mistake of law was considered. The court said that the Crown, as the fountain of justice, and having regard to the possible effects on the attitude of tax-payers, should not generally withhold money so paid. This seems merely an exhortation and without legal effect, in view of an express decision,[6] approved in this case, that the Crown is not bound to repay money paid by mistake of law.

One possible exception to the above rule must be considered. Sometimes, quasi-contracts arise out of facts which constitute a tort, but the plaintiff desires to obtain restitution by quasi-contract instead of suing for damages in tort. Before 1947, of course, the Crown was not suable in tort, and there was some doubt whether the remedy in quasi-contract was not in these circumstances also barred. The only relevant *dicta*, all *obiter*, are

---

1 Glanville Williams, *op. cit.* 14.   2 14 St. Tr. 1.
3 *Baron de Bode* v. *Reg.* (1848), 13 Q.B. 364. The plea of the Crown failed; cf. Robertson, *op. cit.* 337.
4 *Dickson* v. *Reg.* (1885), 12 L.T. 405 (excise duty); *Malkin* v. *Rex*, [1906] 2 K.B. 886 (licensing compensation); *Stern* v. *Reg.*, [1896] 1 Q.B. 211 (death duties); *Constantinesco* v. *Rex* (1926), 42 T.L.R. 383 (income tax).
5 *Sebel Products* v. *Commissioners of Customs and Excise*, [1949] Ch. 409.
6 *William Whiteley Ltd.* v. *Rex* (1909), 101 L.T. 741.

inconclusive.[1] If the only objection to the action were that there could be no tort to waive,[2] then the action would lie. Indeed, in view of the ruling of the House of Lords in *United Australia Ltd.* v. *Barclays Bank Ltd.*[3] that in this type of action in quasi-contract there is no waiver but only an election between alternative remedies, there was a liability even before 1948. If, on the other hand, the rule had been that a liability in tort was not to be enforced by a circuitous method, nothing in the Crown Proceedings Act has altered it. The better view, however, is that there never has been such a restriction on the liability of the Crown in quasi-contract. The question is not merely of academic interest now that the Crown is suable in tort, for there may still in certain cases be advantages in proceeding by quasi-contract.[4]

Many contend that petition of right was available only in a defined and exhaustive list of circumstances, and the Court of Appeal has recently supported this.[5] This list would include claims for the recovery of property and money in the hands of the Crown. Yet these are not the only instances which, in the case of private citizens at least, might give rise to an action in quasi-contract. For example, if the plaintiff pays money which the defendant owes, he may recover it by an action in quasi-contract. Glanville Williams[6] argues that this gap is filled by section 4 (1) of the Act which provides that 'the law relating to indemnity and contribution shall be enforceable by or against the Crown'. With respect, this seems wrong, because section 4 (1) applies 'where the Crown is subject to any liability by virtue of this Act'. The sole relevant section in the Act is section 1, which only makes an action available where a petition of right formerly lay. Section 4 (1), it is submitted, is designed to provide for an entirely different contingency. For example, a landlord is suing his tenant for breach of covenant, and the tenant desires to bring in the Crown, his assignee, on a third party notice to compel the Crown to indemnify him; section 4 (1) authorises that, just as section 4 (2), by making Part II of the Law Reform (Married Women and Tortfeasors) Act, 1935,[7] bind the Crown, subjects the Crown to the rules of contribution and indemnity affecting joint tortfeasors. Even if Glanville Williams'

---

1 *Brocklebank Ltd.* v. *Rex*, [1925] 1 K.B. 52 at 68 (*per* Scrutton L.J.); *Marshal Shipping Co.* v. *Board of Trade*, [1923] 2 K.B. 343 at 356 (*per* Atkin L.J.); *Bristol Channel Steamers Ltd.* v. *Rex* (1923), 40 T.L.R. 550 at 551 (*per* Bailache J.).

2 This was the argument for the Crown in the *Brocklebank Case*, at 67.

3 [1941] A.C. 1 at 19 (*per* Viscount Simon).

4 See *Bavins Jnr & Sims* v. *L. & S. W. Bank, Ltd.*, [1900] 1 Q.B. 270; cf. A. L. Corbin, 'Waiver of Tort and Suit in Assumpsit' in 19 *Yale L.J.* (1910) 221.

5 *Anglo-Saxon Petroleum Co.* v. *Lords Commissioners of the Admiralty*, [1947] K.B. 794 at 801-2 (*per* Scott L.J.).

6 14.   7 25 & 26 Geo. V, c. 30.

argument were sound, there would still be residuary cases of quasi-contract for which the Crown is not liable. For example, if the plaintiff preserves the belongings of the defendant from impending harm, an action in quasi-contract neither sounds in tort nor seeks the recovery of property received by the defendant.

It is submitted that petition of right was never limited to the cases specified above, but, as Viscount Dunedin said in the House of Lords, it was available whenever 'in consequence of what has been legally done any resulting obligation emerges'.[1] If that is so, then there are now no restrictions on the liability of the Crown in quasi-contract.

B. *United States*

The Tucker Act makes the United States suable in contract express or implied. It may be sued for a *quantum meruit* on an implied contract.[2] The courts have consistently held that implied contract means a contract where agreement may be inferred, and not a contract implied in law: the United States is not liable under the Tucker Act for quasi-contract.[3] To this there is one important exception; money paid to the United States by mistake of law, as well as of fact, is recoverable.[4] The explanation of this anomaly is that 'the United States is required to be honest with its citizens just as much as its citizens are required to exercise common honesty with their Government'.[5] Although the frequent judicial references to the desirability of not giving a tort-tainted remedy have led some writers[6] to the conclusion that quasi-contractual liability is denied only when there is also a tort, this is not borne out by the cases, and does not command general support from jurists.[7]

The Federal Tort Claims Act creates no new liability in quasi-contract. In some respects it is more serious in the United States than in England that actions against the Administration in quasi-contract are restricted. For instance, in some States damages for use and occupation of land cannot

---

1 *Attorney-General* v. *De Keyser's Royal Hotel Ltd.*, [1920] A.C. 508 at 530.

2 *Clark* v. *U.S.* (1877), 5 Otto, 539 (U.S.).

3 *U.S.* v. *Minnesota Mutual Investment Co.* (1926), 271 U.S. 212.

4 Williston, *op. cit.* IX, 296 n. This forthright declaration of legal liability contrasts strongly with that faint-hearted exhortation of English judges where verbiage conceals the innate weakness of the law, found not only in the *Sebel Products Case*, p. 125 *supra*, but also in the law relating to disclosure of state documents. If the Crown 'should' pay back money, and if it 'ought' to produce documents, why not declare the law to that effect?

5 *Kirkendall* v. *U.S.* (1941), 90 Ct. Cl. 606 at 616 (*per* Whaley C.J.).

6 J. A. Crane, 'Jurisdiction of the Court of Claims' in 34 *Har. L.R.* (1920) 161 at 173.

7 Williston, *op. cit.* IX, 296; Anderson, *op. cit.* 138.

be recovered in an action of trespass where the land has not been damaged, although in an action in quasi-contract the court will award damages for the unjust enrichment.[1]

C. *France*

In France the broad basis of liability for *faute de service* and *risque*[2] will include most of those factual situations which in the Anglo-American system are within the scope of quasi-contract. In the residuary circumstances which would nevertheless fall within the civil principle of *enrichissement sans cause* the *Conseil d'Etat* will award damages; for example, where taxes have been unlawfully levied, or where a concessionnaire has incurred expenses in carrying on a service after the concession has ended.[3]

No issue of principle justifies these gaps in Anglo-American law. They are due rather to the failure of the common law to assimilate this new hybrid concept of quasi-contract. Reforming the law by extending private law to the State, the legislators, too, have thought their task done if they added to the existing liability of the State in contract a liability in tort. There is some excuse for the United States because their statute was avowedly not comprehensive; it was a tort claims act. Since the English statute purported to range over the whole field of governmental civil liability, the failure to provide more explicitly for quasi-contract is more reprehensible, but seems to be due to ill-considered drafting, not to deliberate omission.

3. TRUSTS

That the Crown can be a trustee has been generally recognised by writers for at least a hundred years.[4] Lord Atkin confirmed it in the House of Lords.[5] The United States can also be a trustee.[6] Hanbury thinks this rule of law unsatisfactory 'for many reasons'.[7] However, he states only one reason: that it would conflict with the principle that the executive freedom of the Crown should not be fettered. In the light of the observations[8] earlier herein on the *Amphitrite Case*,[9] the only one supporting the alleged principle, this reason can hardly be regarded as convincing.

1 *Raven Red Ash Coal Co.* v. *Ball* (1946), 185 Va. 534; cf. *Cohen* v. *City of New York* (1940), 283 N.Y. 112; *Michigan Central Railway* v. *State* (1927), 85 Ind. App. 557.
2 Indeed, Hauriou, *op. cit.* 336 suggests that unjust enrichment is the basis of all liability of the French administration for damages.
3 Waline, *op. cit.*, bk. IV, tit. I, ch. II.
4 Chitty, *Prerogatives of the Crown*, 378; Spence, *Equitable Jurisdiction*, II, 32; Lewin, *Trusts*, 25.
5 *Civilian War Claimants Association* v. *Rex*, [1932] A.C. 14 at 27.
6 *Restatement*, Trusts, S. 95.   7 Hanbury, *Equity*, 316.
8 P. 98 *supra*.   9 [1921] 3 K.B. 500.

Elsewhere, the same writer has stated that it is almost 'impossible to fix a trust inferentially on the Crown'.[1] Perhaps closest to this view is the Canadian case, *Chipman* v. *Rex*.[2] Rejecting the claim by the plaintiff that the Crown, having sold his land, was therefore a trustee for the purchase monies, Angers J. said:[3] 'I do not think that the Crown can be placed in the position of a trustee by implication; the Crown can only be constituted a trustee by the express provisions of an Act of Parliament or a contract to which the Crown is a party.'[4]

It is submitted that the English cases do not support these wide propositions. In the first of them cited by Hanbury an attempt was made to hold the Crown liable as trustee of *bona vacantia* where next of kin of the deceased had later been traced.[5] Whether a trust could be inferred was not even argued, the case being decided solely on the point that the claim was statute-barred. The only other cases relied on by him arose out of claims by citizens to moneys received by the Crown under treaties.[6] Treaties are 'acts of State', rights claimed under which are outside the jurisdiction of municipal courts. The claimants of reparation moneys paid under the Versailles treaties failed not because the Crown could not be a trustee by implication, but because the treaties were acts of State. The same rule applies in the United States at common law,[7] but legislative changes have been made there to ensure that the citizen has a remedy once Congress has appropriated funds.[8] On the other hand, an Australian decision[9] has held the Crown to be an implied trustee so as to fix an assignee of the Crown with notice of the rights of a beneficiary. Although the occasions on which the Crown may be a trustee are few,[10] there seems little authority for the view that the Crown cannot be an implied or constructive trustee.

The general right to equitable relief against the Crown was proclaimed by the courts in 1668.[11] By the early nineteenth century it was recognised

1 Hanbury, *Essays in Equity*, 88.   2 [1934] Ex. C.R. 152.
3 At 159.
4 Cf. *Hereford Ry. Co.* v. *Reg.* (1894), 24 S.C.R. 1; *Western Dominion Coal Mines Ltd.* v. *Rex*, [1946] 4 D.L.R. 270.
5 *In re Mason*, [1928] Ch. 385.
6 *Civilian War Claimants Association* v. *Rex*, [1932] A.C. 14; cf. *Administrator of German Property* v. *Knoop*, [1933] Ch. 439; *Rustomjee* v. *Reg.*, [1876] 2 Q.B. 69. See G. W. Keeton, 'The Crown as Agent' in 77 L.J. *News.* (1934), 268.
7 *Z. & F. Assets Realization Corp.* v. *Hull* (1940), 114 F. 2nd 464.
8 Mandamus, injunction and receivership lie to compel the Secretary to the Treasury to pay those entitled; *Mellon* v. *Orinoco Iron Co.* (1924), 266 U.S. 121; *Doerschuck* v. *Mellon* (1931), 55 F. 2nd 741 at 754 (*per* Groner A.J.).
9 *Blackwood* v. *London Chartered Bank of Australia* (1870), 9 S.C.R. (N.S.W.) Eq. 101; cf. *Welden* v. *Smith*, [1924] A.C. 484.
10 Cf. *Civil Air Transport Inc.* v. *Central Air Transport Corp.*, [1952] 2 All E.R. 733 at 744.
11 *Pawlett* v. *Attorney-General* (1668), Hardres 465.

that the Court of Chancery could administer this relief only on a petition of right[1] whereas the Court of Exchequer could give it on a bill filed against the Attorney-General.[2] Since at least the Judicature Act,[3] other branches of the High Court have had the right to grant relief in equity against the Crown. The only doubt has been when a petition of right was necessary. Since the Court of Exchequer had the power to grant relief even where the Crown's rights were directly affected it would seem that a petition of right would have been unnecessary even in such a case, for example, an action for breach of trust, but there is powerful contrary opinion.[4] Some authoritative text-books[5] have denied that trusts are enforceable against the Crown. A Canadian case has held them to be enforceable only with statutory authority.[6] These views seem plainly wrong: at the most they may be taken as a recognition of the fact that judgments against the Crown are not in the last resort enforceable.[7] There seems at least no difficulty in making a declaration that the Crown is a trustee of certain monies.[8] The Crown Proceedings Act further makes the Crown liable under section 1 where formerly a petition of right lay, but it does not specifically deal with trusts. It may be necessary to know when a petition of right was formerly necessary. There seems no reason to think that breaches of trust as such could ever be regarded as torts so as to make section 2 operative.[9]

A suitor against the United States seems to be in a much worse position. A breach of trust is not actionable as such.[10] The problem of whether a breach of trust comes within the tort liability of the Federal Tort Claims Act has been canvassed;[11] it certainly does not come within the Tucker Act. The distinction between tort and breach of trust seems of such long standing and so clear-cut as to make it unlikely that the courts will declare a breach of trust actionable under the 1946 Act. The United States citizen appears remediless.

1 *Clayton* v. *Attorney-General* (1834), Coop. T. Cott. 97; *Taylor* v. *Attorney-General* (1837), 8 Sim. 413.

2 *Deare* v. *Attorney-General* (1835), 1 Y. & C. (Ex.) 197 at 208.

3 For the effect of the statute of 1842 transferring Exchequer jurisdiction to the Court of Chancery, see p. 132 *infra*.

4 *Esquimalt & Nanaimo Rly. Co.* v. *Wilson*, [1920] A.C. 358 at 367–8 (*per* Lord Buckmaster).

5 E.g. Lewin, *op. cit.* 25.   6 *Henry* v. *Rex*, [1905] Ex. C.R. 417.

7 P. 182 *infra*.   8 *Miller* v. *Rex*, [1950] 1 D.L.R. 513.

9 See Winfield, *Province*, ch. VI; s. 3 of the Crown Proceedings Act (N.Z.) expressly makes the Crown liable for breach of trust.

10 Perry, *Trusts and Trustees*, S. 40, 41; *Restatement*, Trusts, S. 95.

11 H. G. Aron, 'Federal Tort Claims Act', in 33 *A.B.A.J.* (1947) 226 at 228.

Chapter V

REMEDIES AGAINST THE STATE

In this chapter it will be considered to what extent relief obtainable against a private citizen is not available against the Administration.[1]

1. DECLARATORY JUDGMENTS[2]

A litigant does not always desire to coerce his opponent.[3] Often, all that is required by both parties is a determination of what the law is in order that their future conduct shall be within the law. England evolved the declaratory judgment to meet this need. It is of particular utility in the adjudication of conflicting claims of the Administration and the citizen.[4] The legal limits of the powers of officials can thereby be determined; usually, further sanction will be unnecessary to secure their compliance with the law. Moreover, it often avoids the use of the rather unwieldy prerogative orders. The development of this remedy, particularly against the Administration, will now be sketched.

A. England

Since 1668 equitable relief against the Crown might be given in the form of a declaration, even though the courts could not give effect to the judgment.[5] If a cause of action existed, then a Bill could be brought in the Court of Exchequer against the Attorney-General without using a petition of right.[6] The Court of Chancery could not give declaratory relief except as incidental to other relief,[7] but in the 1830's the practice grew up of granting a petition of right that the Attorney-General be joined as defendant in an action in the Court of Chancery for a declaration.[8]

---

1 Section 21 (1) of the Crown Proceedings Act provides that except as therein mentioned, the court has the same power to give relief against the Crown as against a subject.

2 The most comprehensive comparative study of the subject is in Borchard, *Declaratory Judgments*.

3 Cf. W. I. Jennings, 'Declaratory Judgments against Public Authorities in England', in 41 *Yale L.J.* (1932) 407 at 416.

4 Cf. E. M. Borchard, 'Declaratory Judgments in Administrative Law' in 11 *N.Y.U.L.Q.R.* (1933) 139.

5 *Pawlett* v. *Attorney-General* (1668), Hardres 465; *Casberd* v. *Attorney-General* (1819), 6 Price 411; *Hodge* v. *Attorney-General* (1839), 3 Y. & C. Ex. 342.

6 *H.E.L.* IX, 31–2.

7 *Elliotson* v. *Knowles* (1842), 11 L.J. Ch. N.S. 399.

8 E.g., *Clayton* v. *Attorney-General* (1834), Coop. t. Cott. 97.

Although the equitable jurisdiction of the Court of Exchequer was transferred to the Court of Chancery in 1842,[1] since the jurisdiction to make
declaratory judgments was on the Revenue side[2] of the Court of Exchequer
no transfer of that was effected by that statute. There seems to be no action
for a declaration against the Attorney-General between that date and 1911.
Meanwhile, order 25, r. 5 of the Rules of the Supreme Court provided:

> No action or proceeding shall be open to objection on the ground that
> a merely declaratory judgment or order is sought thereby, and the court
> may make binding declarations of right whether any consequential relief
> is or could be claimed, or not.

In *Dyson* v. *Attorney-General*[3] the plaintiff claimed a declaration that
notices issued by the Commissioners of Inland Revenue under the
Finance (1909–10) Act, 1910, were invalid. Relying on the precedents in
the Court of Exchequer, the Court of Appeal held that these proceedings
against the Attorney-General without recourse to a petition of right were
lawfully instituted, and the declaration under order 25 was made.

A decision reached shortly afterwards underlined the importance of
this order. In *Guaranty Trust Co. of New York* v. *Hannay & Co.*[4] it was held
that no consequential relief need be claimed, and that there need not be
a cause of action providing there was not merely a hypothetical dispute;
a declaration might be given, for instance, where injury was merely
threatened.

It has been mentioned that a declaratory judgment could be given on
a petition of right, and that has occurred in cases in this century, too.[5]
The disadvantage was that the *fiat* had to be obtained. Allen[6] asserts that
the *fiat* was required for the declaratory action against the Crown, but the
precedents on which he relies are not declaratory actions at all, but relator
actions[7] where, of course, it is beyond dispute that the Attorney-General
can only be joined at the instance of a private individual if he consents.
There can be no doubt that the *fiat* was not required for a declaratory
action.

Because a *fiat* was necessary for a petition of right it was important to
decide whether a declaratory action against the Attorney-General could

1 5 Vict. c. 5.
2 33 Hen. VIII, c. 39, and see *Attorney-General* v. *Halling* (1846), 15 M. & W. 687.
3 [1911] 1 K.B. 410; [1912] 1 Ch. 158. See. p. 134 *infra* for further comment on
this case.
4 [1915] 2 K.B. 536.
5 E.g. *P. & O. Steam Navigation Co.* v. *Rex*, [1901] 2 K.B. 686. And see s. 7,
Petitions of Right Act, 1860.
6 *Law and Orders*, 63; cf. Minutes of Evidence, Report of Committee on Ministers'
Powers, Cmd. 4060 (1932), 76, Q. 1041.
7 Cf. G. Sawer, 'Law and Orders', in 3 *Res Judicatae* (1947) 80.

always be instituted in lieu of a petition of right. Could it lie for breach of contract by the Crown in anticipation of what would ordinarily be eventually determined by petition of right? Could there never be a declaratory judgment if the rights of the Crown were directly affected? Certainly there were cases in the Court of Exchequer where declarations directly affecting the rights of the Crown were granted,[1] but there seem to be none in the Court of Chancery. The issue is complicated by the fact that *Dyson's Case* proceeds on the unsound historical premise that these precedents applied in the Chancery as well as the Exchequer.[2] A few Commonwealth cases have held that a declaratory action lies for interpretation of a contract;[3] some have left it open;[4] but the large majority of reported decisions holds that if the rights of the Crown are directly affected then the required declaratory judgment can be obtained only on a petition of right.[5] Yet if the Exchequer jurisdiction was not transferred by the Act of 1842 (and the fact that the *Clayton Case* procedure continued after 1842 supports that supposition), these cases seem difficult to justify. Nor will a declaratory judgment be granted, if the question is purely hypothetical. In *In re Barnato deceased*[6] trustees took out a summons to determine what death duties would be payable in the event of a particular beneficiary dying within five years from the date of a proposed advancement of trust funds. Because the rights of the Crown could arise only if the contingency happened, and because the proposed advancement would not affect the rights of the Crown, an application to have the Commissioners of Inland Revenue joined as defendants for the purpose of the declaratory judgment sought was refused.

Section 23 (2) (*b*) of the Crown Proceedings Act provides that 'civil proceedings against the Crown' shall include proceedings for the obtaining of any relief against the Attorney-General. Therefore, a declaratory action is now brought in accordance with the general provisions of section 17 (3). With the abolition of the *fiat*, too, there is no longer any doubt that

1 E.g. *Hodge* v. *Attorney-General* (1839), 3 Y. & C. Ex. 342.
2 Cf. *H.E.L.* ix, 322; Hanbury, *Essays*, 122; Clode, *Petition of Right*, 141–53.
3 *The Qu'Appelle Long Lake & Saskatchewan Railroad & Steamboat Co.* v. *Rex* (1901), 7 Ex. R. 105; *Leyden* v. *Attorney-General*, [1926] Ir. R. 334.
4 *Electrical Development Co. of Ontario* v. *Attorney-General and Hydro-Electric Power Commission of Ontario*, [1919] A.C. 687.
5 *Esquimalt & Nanaimo Rly. Co.* v. *Wilson*, [1920] A.C. 358; *Bombay & Persia Steam Navigation Co. Ltd.* v. *Maclay*, [1920] 3 K.B. 402 at 408; *McDougall* v. *Attorney-General*, [1925] N.Z.L.R. 104; *Attorney-General for Ontario* v. *McLean Gold Mines Ltd.*, [1927] A.C. 185; *Lovibond* v. *Grand Trunk Rly.*, [1936] 3 D.L.R. 449 (P.C.); *Royal Trust Co.* v. *Attorney-General for Alberta*, [1936] 4 D.L.R. 98; *Greenlees* v. *Attorney-General (Canada)*, [1945] 2 D.L.R. 641; *ctra. Gruen Watch Co.* v. *Attorney-General for Canada*, [1950] 4 D.L.R. 156 at 176 (per McRuer C.J.).
6 [1949] Ch. 258.

a declaratory judgment is available against the Crown. The procedures on the former petition of right and the former action for a declaration against the Attorney-General are now the same.

In the *Dyson Case* it was not considered whether or not order 25 applied to the Crown in accordance with the principle that statutes do not bind the Crown unless so stated, either expressly or impliedly. This is a serious omission which seems to have escaped notice.[1] It has been held that *Dyson's Case* is inapplicable[2] in New Zealand because the New Zealand statute governing declaratory judgments does not bind the Crown. Furthermore, other rules of court made under the same authority as order 25 have been held not to bind the Crown.[3] The gap has now been filled, since order 1 A of the Rules of the Supreme Court (Crown Proceedings), 1947,[4] provides expressly that the Rules of the Supreme Court shall with certain specific exceptions apply to all civil proceedings against the Crown. Another gap remains: a declaratory judgment is available only in the High Court.

The declaratory judgment is a discretionary remedy: in deciding whether to grant it against the Crown the Courts will consider whether the judgment can be effective at the time that it is made.[5]

B. *United States*

Not for a long time did the United States allow a declaratory judgment, even in private law. Influenced by the *Hannay Case* in which one party was American, and encouraged by the writings of E. M. Borchard, Congress passed the Declaratory Judgment Act of 1934. Based on the English practice, this Act allowed a declaratory judgment at the discretion of the court 'in cases of actual controversy'.

A declaratory judgment is available against the United States[6] only in cases falling within the purview of the Tucker Act.[7] It is not available to compel the comptroller to return moneys,[8] nor where the Court of

1 The reasoning of the judges in *Dyson's Case* cannot be justified: Order 25, together with the Petitions of Right Act, 1860, was the successor to the *Clayton Case* type of procedure, and that Order has not been made to bind the Crown; the use of the declaratory judgment can be defended only on the assumption that the former jurisdiction of the Court of Exchequer, as transferred by the Judicature Act, was being invoked.

2 *McDougall* v. *Rex*, [1925] N.Z.L.R. 104.

3 Robertson, *op. cit.* 611, and unreported cases cited by him there.

4 S.R. & O. 1947, no. 2530/L. 33, 1947.

5 *Gruen Watch Co.* v. *A. G. Canada*, [1950] 4 D.L.R. 156.

6 It is, however, often made available by statute against individual officers of the Government, e.g. Nationality Act, 1940, 54 Stat. 1171 authorises actions against heads of Departments for declarations of nationality.

7 Borchard, *Declaratory Judgments*, 373.   8 *Palbicke* v. *Lee* (1937), 126 Fla. 765.

Claims has not jurisdiction under the Tucker Act.[1] In *Yeskel* v. *U.S.*[2] the contractor with the defendant did not perform his contract whereupon the defendant demanded payment from the surety of the contractor, refusing to sue the contractor: a declaratory judgment of the position of the three parties was refused on the ground that the Declaratory Judgment Act could not be invoked against the United States when the statute relied on as taking away governmental immunity applied only to money claims. It does not seem therefore that the waiver of immunity contained in the Federal Tort Claims Act is enough to allow declaratory actions.[3] A declaratory action does not lie against a State suable only by consent.[4] The procedural details of the action against the United States are the same as those of actions against subjects. The matter is free from any historical confusion, because the declaratory action there is the creature of statute.

C. *France*

France has no special declaratory action but the *Conseil d'Etat* and the *Conseils de Préfecture* have the right to declare any administrative act void for *excès de pouvoir*.[5] This wide remedy must be applied for within two months. The applicant must show that he has some personal interest, moral or material, in the action of which he complains. This *contentieux d'annulation* is exercised for any of the following reasons; *l'incompétence*, *le vice de forme*, *le détournement de pouvoir* and *violation de la règle de droit*. There can be no doubt that an effective judicial control of the Administration is exercised by this means.

2. MANDAMUS

One American writer[6] has defined mandamus as 'a command issuing from a common-law court of competent jurisdiction, in the name of the State or sovereign, directed to some State or corporation, officer or inferior court, requiring the performance of a particular duty therein specified, which duty results from the official station of the party to whom the writ is directed, or from operation of law'. In origin mandamus was a prerogative writ issued by the King, as the fountain of justice, from the King's Bench to provide a remedy at the discretion of the court where no

---

1 *Lynn* v. *U.S.* (1939), 110 Fed. 2nd 586.
2 (1940), 31 F. Supp. 956; cf. *Atlantic Meat Co.* v. *R.F.C.* (1948), 166 F. 2nd 51.
3 Cf. Note, 'Developments in the Law—Declaratory Judgments 1941-9' in 62 *Harv. L.R.* (1948-9), 787 at 824-5.
4 *Purity Oats* v. *Lee* (1928), 125 Kan. 558.
5 The literature on this is voluminous, but among recent publications in England may be mentioned M. Hersant, 'Esquisse de Recours Contentieux contre l'Abus de Pouvoir Administratif' in *Law Society, op. cit.* 110; Treves, 'Administrative Discretion and Judicial Control' in 10 *M.L.R.* (1947) 276; Sieghart, *Government by Decree*, ch. v.
6 High, *Extraordinary Legal Remedies*, 4.

other remedy was available. Except that the United States treats it as an ordinary action between parties, whereas in England it is still a prerogative order, the English and American rules of mandamus are fundamentally the same. It has been pointed out that the great advantage of mandamus over other prerogative orders is that it is not limited to the control of judicial or quasi-judicial powers, but also covers administrative acts.[1]

This last fact makes it important in connection with proceedings against the Crown, but before its availability there is considered, it is best to summarise the general rules governing its use.

The most important rests on a distinction between a peremptory duty and a discretion. Mandamus lies to command the performance of a duty, whether arising at common law or by statute,[2] but not to control the exercise of a discretion. So, before the passing of the Crown Proceedings Act, an order of mandamus would lie to compel the Attorney-General to consider an application for a *fiat* to a petition of right but not to question his refusal to grant it.[3] A complication is the frequent blending of duties and discretions. To decide whether mandamus lies, one must disregard the general functions of the body[4] and consider whether in respect of that specific matter sought to be enforced there is 'the smallest fragment of valid discretion anywhere'.[5]

The role of mandamus is the more important because the courts readily find that a discretion has been exhausted and only a duty remains. For instance, in a Canadian case,[6] an official was authorised to issue building permits 'when he is of opinion that the work proposed to be done is in accordance with the provisions of this and all other bye-laws'. Mandamus was applied for by the plaintiffs to compel the grant of a permit. Because there was no evidence that the by-laws had not been complied with, and the official rested his refusal only on the orders of his superiors, it was held that the discretion was exhausted and that mandamus would lie to compel him to grant the permit. Further, it has long been recognised that mandamus will lie if a discretion has been abused.[7] In the United States,[8] and sometimes in the Commonwealth,[9] it lies where a discretion has been

1 E. C. S. Wade, 'The Courts and the Administrative Process' in 63 *L.Q.R.* (1947) 164 at 170.   2 Jennings, *Principles of Local Government Law*, 299.
3 *Ex parte Newton* (1855), 4 E. & B. 869.   4 Hart, *op. cit.* 441.
5 Lucas, *The Primordial Functions of Government and the Legal Status of Sovereignty*, 86.
6 *The Murray Co. Ltd.* v. *District of Burnaby*, [1946] 2 D.L.R. 541.
7 Tapping, *Mandamus*, 14: '...although there may be a discretionary power, yet if it be exercised with manifest injustice, the Court...is not precluded from commanding its due exercise.'
8 *Van de Vegt* v. *Board of Commissioners* (1936), 98 Colo. 161; F. H. Sherwood, 'Mandamus to Review Administrative Action' in 45 *Mich. L.R.* (1946) 123.
9 *R. ex rel. Lee* v. *Workmen's Compensation Board*, [1942] 2 W.W.R. 129 C.A. Br. Col.

exercised without substantial evidence on which to justify it, or where the reviewing court considers that a statute has been misinterpreted.[1] The grant of mandamus is always discretionary, even though there is a *prima facie* case.[2] The court considers whether there is some other adequate remedy, whether its order will be nugatory, whether it is consistent with public policy to make it, and whether the plaintiff has come into court with clean hands.

Mandamus has never been available against the Crown, presumably on the argument that the King could not be subject to the jurisdiction of his own courts.[3] Nor does it lie against the President of the United States or State governors.[4] Far more controversial is the question whether it lies against servants of the Crown. In *Reg.* v. *Secretary of State for War*[5] an attempt was made to compel the Secretary of State to carry out the terms of a Royal Warrant regulating soldiers' pay. The Court of Appeal refused the application, Charles J. saying:[6] 'It is also beyond question that a mandamus cannot be directed to the Crown or to any servant of the Crown simply acting in his capacity of servant.' Again in *Reg.* v. *Lords Commissioners of the Treasury*[7] mandamus was applied for to effect the repayment by the Treasury of bills paid by a county treasurer in respect of prosecutions at assizes. The statute in question had appropriated money for general purposes. Mandamus was refused because the function of the Treasury was to advise the Crown whether a minute authorising payment ought to be issued, it being the function of the Crown, of course, through its agents, to issue the minute. No duty to the public was owed by the Treasury officials.

These decisions have been widely misunderstood. Firstly, it is incorrect to state that mandamus does not lie against servants of the Crown.[8] In *Reg.* v. *Commissioners for Special Purposes of the Income Tax*,[9] where the Commissioners had certified certain taxes to be overpaid, mandamus lay to compel them to carry out the statutory duty to order repayment. It is submitted that two questions must be asked: Was it a duty or a discretion?

---

1 *Work* v. *U.S. ex rel. Rives* (1925), 267 U.S. 175; Gellhorn, *Administrative Law*, 928, for other authorities; cf. Mansfield, *op. cit.* 111.

2 Robinson, *Public Authorities and Legal Liability*, 225 et seq. and authorities cited; Gellhorn, *Administrative Law*, 912 et seq.

3 *Reg.* v. *Powell* (1841), 1 Q.B. 352 at 361; cf. Robertson, 111; Griffits, *Guide to Crown Office Practice*, 160–1.

4 *Denby* v. *Berry* (1922), 279 F. 317, rvsd. on other grounds (1923), 263 U.S. 29.

5 [1891] 2 D.B. 326.

6 334.

7 (1872), 7 Q.B. 387; cf. *Rex* v. *Commissioners of Customs* (1836), 5 A. & E. 380.

8 *Board of Education* v. *Rice*, [1911] A.C. 179.

9 (1888), 21 Q.B. 313.

If the former, was the duty directly imposed on the servant of the Crown? If so, then mandamus would lie against him.

A study of the Commonwealth cases is helpful here. In the Australian case, *ex parte Krefft*,[1] it was held that payment could not be enforced against an official if the duty to pay were imposed on the Crown, which had merely delegated the function to him. The Canadian courts have seized on an admission by counsel for the Crown in *Reg. v. Lords Commissioners of the Treasury*[2] that 'where the legislature has constituted the Lords of the Treasury agents to do a particular act, in that case a mandamus might lie against them as mere individuals designated to do that act'. For instance, in *Minister of Finance of British Columbia v. Rex*,[3] the court distinguished between 'a Minister acting as a servant of the Crown and acting as a mere agent of the Legislature to do a particular act' and, although refusing the writ on other grounds, conceded its availability against a Minister designated by the Legislature to pay compensation out of a land registration fund. The United States, too, recognises that mandamus lies in such a case. In *McAdoo v. Ormes* Van Orsdel J. said:[4]

...where money has been appropriated by Congress...the officials of the Treasury Department are charged with the ministerial duty of making payment upon demand of the person in whose favour the appropriation has been made, and they may be compelled to make payment by mandamus....

The second error[5] is to state that mandamus does not lie against an inferior officer. The view seems to depend on *dicta* of two of the four judges in *Rex v. Jeyes*.[6] This case was explained two years later by Coleridge J.[7] The issue is not the inferiority of the officer but whether any duty is imposed directly on him. If the duty is imposed on his superior then mandamus will lie, if at all, against that superior only. For example, in a Canadian case,[8] where a judge had not heard an application for a grant of letters of administration, it was held that mandamus would lie against the judge but not against the clerk of the court who could only issue the grant when directed to do so by the judge.

---

1 (1876), 14 S.C.R. (N.S.W.) 446; cf. *In re Sooka Nand Verma* (1905), 7 W.A.L.R. 225. 2 At 389–90 (*per* Jessel, Solicitor-General).

3 [1935] 3 D.L.R. 316; cf. *Rex ex rel. Lee v. Workmen's Compensation Board*, [1942] 2 W.W.R. 129.

4 (1918), 47 App. (D.C.) 364 at 367; cf. *McCarl v. Willy* (1925), 5 F. 2nd 964; *Louisiana v. Jumel* (1882), 107 U.S. 711; *Louisiana v. McAdoo* (1913), 234 U.S. 627. See also W. H. Mack, 'Compulsory Process to the Comptroller-General' in 3 *Geo. Wash. L.R.* (1934) 97.

5 E.g. Mustoe, *op. cit.* 99; Emden, *op. cit.* 78.

6 (1835), 3 A. & E. 416.

7 *Rex v. Payn* (1837), 6 A. & E. 392 at 401.

8 *Re Macdonald*, [1930] 2 D.L.R. 177.

Professor Wade states that the applicant for mandamus must show 'that the duty is owed to himself and not merely to the public at large' and, in the next sentence, adds that 'the nature of many of the public services today is such that the idea of duty to the Crown is out of date'.[1] It is suggested, with respect, that it is doubtful whether a duty to the individual applicant need be proved. That would mean that mandamus would lie only where an action in tort for breach of statutory duty would lie.

Certainly, some *dicta*, such as the following of Lord Esher, might seem at first sight to support Wade's argument:[2] '...a mandamus would not lie against the Crown, and...it will not lie against the Secretary of State because in his capacity as such he is only responsible to the Crown and has no legal duty imposed upon him towards the subject.' The confusion seems to arise from the cases denying mandamus because no duty is imposed directly on the agent. Then, there is the usual duty of the servant to his master, the Crown, and that is insufficient to cause mandamus to lie. But Lord Esher was not using 'subject' in contrast with 'the public'; he was using it to mean the public in contrast with the Crown. His opinion is clarified in another case where he said:[3] '...where officials [have] a public duty to perform, and [have] refused to perform it, mandamus will lie on the application of a person interested to compel them to do so.'

There seems to be no case which has been decided on the basis that the applicant for mandamus must prove a duty owed to him. *Obiter dicta* in two cases[4] (one unreported), and a dissenting judgment in a third[5] have indicated that the applicant must have a right to enforce the performance of the duty. The general view of the judges is that the applicant must show some special interest in the subject-matter.[6] The vicar of a parish has been held to have sufficient interest to secure a mandamus ordering the licensing justices to hear an application for the transfer of a licence according to law.[7] Clearly, no legal duty was owed to him.

It is submitted that the use of concepts like 'right' and 'duty' confuses the issue. What in fact the court does is to consider whether the interest which the applicant asserts is one which needs protection. Thereby the

1 E. C. S. Wade, 63 *L.Q.R.* 164, *op. cit.* 170.
2 *Reg.* v. *Secretary of State for War*, [1891] 2 Q.B. 326 at 339.
3 *Reg.* v. *Commissioners for Special Purposes of the Income Tax*, [1888] 21 Q.B. 313 at 317.
4 *Reg.* v. *Lewisham Union*, [1897] 1 Q.B. 498 at 501 (*per* Bruce J.); and a *dictum* of Channell J. cited by Avory J. in the case next cited.
5 *Rex* v. *Manchester Corporation*, [1911] 1 K.B. 560 at 564 (*per* Avory J.).
6 *Ibid.* at 563 (*per* Alverstone C. J.) and at 564 (*per* Pickford J.); *Reg.* v. *Leicester Guardians*, [1899] 2 Q.B. 632.
7 *Reg.* v. *Cotham*, [1898] 1 Q.B. 802.

general interest in public rights and liberties can be reconciled with the need to prevent vexatious litigation.

In the United States, no more than a public duty is required. The weight of authority favours the ruling that when the interest is public, no special interest has to be proved.[1] Any member of an affected class may sue. Decisions in a few States[2] suggesting that a special interest must be proved to support an application for mandamus to enforce a public duty have been much criticised.[3] And even in these states, the courts will go far in finding a special interest.[4]

It remains to consider the effect of the Crown Proceedings Act on the above rules. Section 38 (2) provides in effect that the Act shall not affect 'proceedings on the Crown side of the King's Bench Division'. Mandamus, therefore, still does not apply to the Crown. Section 21 (2) provides:

The court shall not in any civil proceedings grant any injunction or make any order against an officer of the Crown if the effect of granting the injunction or making the order would be to give any relief against the Crown which could not have been obtained in proceedings against the Crown.

This forbids an action for mandamus against a Crown servant acting as an agent of the Crown. Section 30 (5) of the Act provides that the court, in considering whether to grant mandamus, shall not take into account any further remedy provided by the Act. Nor is the availability of mandamus in the United States affected by the Federal Tort Claims Act.

3. INJUNCTION

Whether at common law an injunction would be granted in England against a Department or a civil servant acting as such is doubtful. The text-book writers disagree,[5] and the cases holding that it could be granted are of slight authority.[6] Canada[7] and New Zealand[8] refuse the relief. On

1 *County Commissioners of Pike County* v. *People ex rel. Metz* (1849), 11, 111, 202.
2 E.g. *People ex rel. Drake* v. *Regents of the University of Michigan* (1856), 4 Mich. 98; *Dupre* v. *Doris* (1942), 26 A. 2nd 623.
3 F. J. Goodnow, 'Interest in Mandamus Cases' in 8 *Pol. Sc. Q.* (1893), 48; Note, 'Mandamus—Right of Individual to Enforce a Public Right' in 43 *Col. L.R.* (1943), 124.
4 E.g. *Kern* v. *City Commissioners of Newton* (1938), 147 Kan. 471 where a negro obtained mandamus to compel the municipality to admit negroes to its swimming pool.
5 Lucas, *op. cit.* 90; Morgan, *op. cit.* xlii; Mustoe, *op. cit.* 108; and Allen, *Law and Orders*, 63 think it available; cf. Emden, *op. cit.* 66; *ctra.* Robertson, *op. cit.* 21.
6 *Rankin* v. *Huskisson* (1830), 4 Sim. 13; *Ellis* v. *Grey* (1833), 6 Sim. 214.
7 *Attorney-General for Ontario* v. *Toronto Junction Recreation Club* (1904), 8 Ont. L.R. 440.
8 *Timaru Harbour Board* v. *New Zealand Railway Commissioners* (1895), 13 N.Z.L.R. 425.

the other hand, it has been freely awarded against Government Departments in Australia.[1]

One very important issue is whether an unauthorised trespass by an officer of the Crown can be restrained even though he purports to act in execution of his duties. The United States will not grant an injunction against its officers while they are acting within the scope of their authority.[2] On the other hand, if their act is *ultra vires*, injunction will lie.[3] If the most recent English decision is to be relied on, injunction against an official at common law is not granted 'when a wrong (has) been done which purported to be an exercise of a statutory authority'.[4] Nor will injunction against a Minister be granted in Canada to restrain the *ultra vires* acquisition of land.[5]

The Crown Proceedings Act empowers courts to give the same relief against the Crown as against a citizen except that a declaratory judgment is to replace an injunction or an order for specific performance.[6] By section 21 (2), 'the court shall not in any civil proceedings grant any injunction or make any order against an officer of the Crown if the effect of granting the injunction or making the order would be to give any relief against the Crown which could not have been obtained in proceedings against the Crown'. The effect of this is to displace the cases cited above which declared that injunctions were available against servants acting in their official capacity.[7] It seems that not even a declaratory judgment of injunction could be awarded against the United States.

The inability of the French civil courts to control *voies de fait* and indirect expropriations of the public works Administration has been

---

1 *Attorney-General* v. *Williams*, [1913] S.R. (N.S.W.) 295; *Randwick Municipal Council* v. *Nott*. (1940), 14 L.G.R. 222; *Sharp* v. *Board of Land and Works* (1947), 5 Argus L.R. (Current Notes) 81.

2 *Larson* v. *Domestic & Foreign Commerce Corp.* (1949), 337 U.S. 682.

3 'And in case of an injury threatened by his illegal action, the officer cannot claim immunity from injunctive process' (*per* Hughes J. in *Philadelphia Co.* v. *Stimson* (1911), 223 U.S. 605 at 620); followed in *Toledo P. & W.R.R.* v. *Stover* (1945), 60 F. Supp. 587; and see *Work* v. *Louisiana* (1925), 269 U.S. 250.

4 *Hutton* v. *Secretary of State for War* (1926), 43 T.L.R. 106 at 107 (*per* Tomlin J.) followed in *Bird* v. *Auckland District Land Registrar*, [1952] N.Z.L.R. 463; but *ctra.* *C.P.R. Co.* v. *A. G. Saskatchewan*, [1951] 3 D.L.R. 362 holding that an injunction would lie against a Minister to prevent him enforcing an unconstitutional Act, but *quaere* whether as an officer or as an individual.

5 *Melbourne* v. *McQuesten*, [1940] O.W.N. 311.   6 S. 21 (1).

7 In *Underhill* v. *Ministry of Food*, [1950] 1 All E.R. 591 an interlocutory declaratory judgment in lieu of an interlocutory injunction was refused on the ground that s. 21 applied only to final injunctions. If this case is rightly decided, then surely the section does not *prevent* such an injunction being given, but revives the old common-law uncertainty. Could not a declaratory action lie in any event without invoking this section?

mentioned previously.[1] In any event, the *astreinte*, the French substitute for injunction, is not so effective a contrivance.[2] French administrative tribunals, too, can only provide relief by a mandate, which, though not so named, 'is indistinguishable from the *astreinte*'.[3]

It is submitted that the ends of justice would be served by making injunctions available against government servants. To withhold them against a servant even where his act is plainly illegal, if he merely purports to be acting on behalf of the Crown, is particularly objectionable. The Treasury Solicitor says that this immunity is essential because the Crown might in an emergency want to override the law, leaving it to Parliament to decide whether to ratify *ex post facto*, and that it would be prevented from so doing by interlocutory injunction.[4] This ignores the prerogative rights of the Crown in an emergency which are untouched by the Act. Moreover, it takes no account of the fact that injunction is a discretionary remedy. It is yet another example of the unwillingness of the Executive to trust the Judiciary. English law compares unfavourably both with Australia and the United States in this regard.

1 See p. 124 *supra*.
2 For an account in English of this remedy, see J. Brodeur, 'The Injunction in French Jurisprudence' in 14 *Tulane L.R.* (1940) 211.
3 *Ibid.* 217 n. 31.
4 Sir Thomas Barnes, 'The Crown Proceedings Act 1947', in 26 *C.B.R.* (1948) 387 at 395.

Chapter VI

SUBSTANTIVE LIMITATIONS ON THE LIABILITY
OF THE STATE

I. STATUTES[1]

A. *The Effect of Statutes upon the Liabilities of the State at Common Law*

Only by tracing the origins of the common-law rules on this topic is it possible to appreciate the present law. In the sixteenth century the general principles of statutory interpretation were that the determining factor was the intention of the Legislature,[2] and that, where possible, vested rights should be respected.[3]

In the same period can be traced the establishment of the distinctions between the fundamental rights of the Crown and the rights of the subject, the working out of the prerogative.[4] The courts determined that the King had certain rights in the sphere of justice and administration which constituted his prerogative and were to be free from interference. On the other hand, that the subject also had rights equally fundamental, the rights to property and protection of his person, was recognised by the courts. This 'antithesis between the supreme authority of the king and the sanctity of private right'[5] is exemplified by the attitude of the courts to the dispensing power of the King. He might dispense with a statute restricting his choice of officials because it was a right of his office, part of his prerogative and not affecting the proprietary rights of his subjects.[6] This may be contrasted with the ruling of Illingworth C.B.:[7]

...a law which belongs to a special person, whether this be common law or special law, such as the Statute of Additions, of which every man shall have advantage, so that it affects every subject of the king, this the king cannot of common right defeat.

The earliest judicial utterance on the effect of statutes on the Crown seems to be in 1457 by Ashton J. who stated:[8] '...quant un remedy soit

1 This section is a revised summary of my article, 'The Effect of Statutes upon the Rights and Liabilities of the Crown' in 7 *U.T.L.J.* (1948) 357.
2 *Heydon's Case* (1584), 3 Co. Rep. 7a.
3 *Elme's Case* (1571), 3 Dyer 373a.
4 Chrimes, *English Constitutional Ideas in the Fifteenth Century*, 43.
5 McIlwaine, *The Growth of Political Thought in the West*, 370.
6 Y.B. 2 Hen. VII, ff. 6–7.   7 Y.B. 5 Ed. IV, ff. 33–4.
8 Y.B. 35 Hen. VI, f. 62.

fait pur un statute ce ne serra entendu en contre le roy s'il ne soit pas expressement reherse.' This, and a series of similar statements which followed closely upon it,[1] are couched in such wide terms that the inference might be drawn that the rule was that statutes bound the King only when he was expressly named, and that no distinction was made between his prerogative and other rights.

A consideration of the leading case, *Willion* v. *Berkley*,[2] however, reveals the falsity of such an inference. The issue was whether the provisions of the Statute of Westminster, *De Donis Conditionalibus*, bound the King so as to prevent him from alienating, to the detriment of those entirled in reversion, or their issue, property given to them in tail. It was held that in view of the object of the statute and the mischief it sought to remedy the intention must be presumed to be that the King was bound. Similarly, it was held that the King, though not named, was bound by the Statute of Merton[3] made against usury in doubling the rent in the case of an heir who defaulted in payment[4] and by the Statute of Merton[5] which ordained that suit to the lord might be done by attorney.[6]

By 1561 it was established that the Crown was bound by a statute which was intended to bind it. Where the statute affected the rights of the subject rather than the Crown, the courts would readily read into the statute an intention to bind the Crown. On the other hand, there was a strong presumption that a general statute would not affect the prerogative rights of the King unless he were named in it.

It has been said in at least one modern case[7] that the true reason for this presumption is that '*prima facie* the law made by the Crown, with the assent of Lords and Commons, is made for subjects and not for the Crown'. The authority cited for this statement is the following sentence in *Willion* v. *Berkley*:[8] 'And because it is not an act without the King's assent, it is to be intended that when the King gives his assent, he does not mean to prejudice himself or to bar himself of his liberty and privilege, but he assents that it shall be a law among his subjects.' On this two comments must be made: that the quotation is from the argument of counsel on the losing side, and that it refers both to 'intent' and to the King's 'liberty and privilege'. If the rule is expressed as at the commence-

1 Y.B. 2 Hen. VII, f. 20 (*per* Mordaunt Sjt.); (1498) Keilwey 35 (*per* Fineux C.J. and Brian C.J.); Fitzherbert, *Nouvelle Natura Brevium*, fly-leaf; Brooke, Parlement et Statutes, no. 6; cf. Thorne, *Discourse upon Exposicion and Understandinge of Statutes*, 110.
2 (1561), Plowden 223.   3 20 Hen. III, c. 5.
4 Y.B. 35 Hen. VI, f. 61.   5 20 Hen. III, c. 10.
6 Cf. Fitzherbert, *op. cit.* tit. Parlement et Statutes, no. 30.
7 *Attorney-General* v. *Donaldson* (1842), 10 M. & W. 117 at 124 (*per* Alderson B.).
8 *Ubi supra*.

ment of this paragraph, there is a risk of it being construed as extending to circumstances not affecting the King's interests. The cases up to and including *Willion* v. *Berkley* furnish no precedent for that.

In the course of his argument that the Crown was intended to be and was therefore bound by statutes protecting the interests of individuals, counsel in *Willion* v. *Berkley* said:[1] 'So in general statutes made for the safety of inheritances, or for the public good, the expositors of them have constructed them according to the course of the common law, viz. that they shall include the king, notwithstanding he is not named', and a little later suggested that statutes for 'the public utility of the realm' should bind the King.[2] These expressions are too wide to harmonise with the general principles set out above, for they would encroach on that sphere of administration and policy which, it has been suggested, was the preserve of the Crown.[3]

Next came three cases at the beginning of the seventeenth century, all reported, and two of them judged, by Coke. These have been largely relied on in modern decisions and text-books. In the *Case of the Ecclesiastical Persons* (1601) it was said that 'in divers cases the King is bound by act of Parliament although he be not named in it, nor bound by express words: and therefore all statutes which are made to suppress wrong, or to take away fraud, or to prevent the decay of religion, shall bind the King'.[4] The case cannot, however, be accepted as authoritative because it was heard only in Parliament on consideration of a Bill for the confirmation of conveyances made by subjects to the Queen. In the *Case of a Fine levied by the King*[5] it was said that 'a General Act shall not bind him, unless he be expressly named, unless it be in special cases'.[6] This was not a judicial decision, but only a consultation given by Popham C.J. and Coke as Attorney-General.[7]

The third case is the *Magdalen College Case*,[8] which contained the following statements by Coke:

...the King shall not be exempted by construction of law out of the general words of Acts made to suppress wrong, because he is the fountain of justice and common right, and the King being God's lieutenant cannot do a wrong....And though a right was remediless, yet the act which

1 *Ibid.* at 236.   2 *Ibid.* at 237.
3 Cf. P. Birdsall, 'Non Obstante' in *Essays in History and Political Theory in Honour of Charles Howard McIlwain*, 55–60.
4 5 Co. Rep. 14a at 14b.   5 (1605), 7 Co. Rep. 32a at 32b.
6 Although this is no judicial precedent, Jenkin's version of it at 307: 'Roy n'est lie per ascun statute si il ne soit expressement nosme' is now generally accepted as a maxim of English law. See, for example, Broom, *Legal Maxims*, 38.
7 See Note in 43 L.Q.R. (1927) 157.   8 (1615), 11 Co. Rep. 66b.

provides a necessary and profitable remedy for the preservation of it, and
to suppress wrong shall bind the King.[1] . . . That where the King has any
prerogative, estate, right, title or interest, that by the general words of an
Act he shall not be barred of them. . . . But in the case at Bar, the King is
not excluded of any estate, right, title, interest or prerogative, that he
had before the Act in the said house.[2]

In this case the Master, Fellows and Scholars of Magdalen College attempted
to evade the mortmain laws by conveying property to the Queen for
purposes other than those of the Crown. It would seem that the *ratio
decidendi* of the case is that the Act prohibited the transfer, and that the
statements made by Coke about statutes were *obiter*.[3] Yet they have been
quoted frequently in subsequent cases and text-books. Although Coke
was obviously relying on counsel's argument in *Willion* v. *Berkley* he
omitted the reference to public good made by counsel in that case. The
criticism has been made that the authorities 'are scarcely sufficient in
number or variety to justify us in adopting the very wide general propositions propounded by Lord Coke'.[4] However, in line with his classification, an Act for the consolidation of endowed rectories and vicarages,[5] an
Act requiring cases to be brought up by error,[6] the general provisions of
Magna Carta,[7] an Act against simony,[8] and the Statute of Marlbridge
that none may distrain his freeholders without the King's writ[9] have all
been held to bind the King, although he was not named therein. Another
writer complains that the *dicta* of Coke 'are surely opening a very uncertain latitude'.[10] It is agreed that it is not desirable to attempt a broad
classification, as Coke did, but at the same time his *dicta* are in substantial
accord with the theory that the King was bound by statutes the purpose
of which was to bind him, a purpose far more readily spelt out of statutes
not directly affecting his prerogative interests. Coke is emphasing in his
classification those circumstances not directly affecting the prerogatives
of the King.

In the two centuries after Coke, the rules which he had laid down were
faithfully copied by the text-books.[11] Both Bacon[12] and Chitty[13] stated

1 (1615), 11 Co. Rep. 66b, at 72a.   2 *Ibid.* at 74b–75a.
3 Cf. *Attorney-General* v. *Hancock*, [1940] K.B. 427 at 439–40 (*per* Wrottesley J.).
4 Hardcastle, *The Construction and Effect of Statutory Law*, 19.
5 *Rex* v. *Archbishop of Armagh* (1722), 1 Str. 516.
6 *Rex* v. *Wright* (1834), 1 A. & E. 434 (11 Geo. IV and 1 Will. IV, c. 70, s. 8).
7 Co. Inst. 77.   8 Coke on *Littleton*, 120 (31 Ed. I, c. 6).
9 52 Hen. III, c. 22.
10 Wooddeson, *Lectures on the Laws of England*, 1, 84.
11 E.g. Comyns, *Digest*, Parliament R. 8; Hawkins, *Pleas of the Crown*, bk. 11
ch. xlii s. 3; Viner, *Abridgement*, Statutes E. 10.
12 Bacon, *Abridgement*, Prerogative E. 5.   13 Chitty, *Prerogatives*, 382.

that statutes taking any 'prerogative, right, title or interest' from the King should not bind him unless he were expressly named, and that an Act of Parliament made for the public good bound him. Neither writer seemed to realise that there is no authority for the latter statement other than that of counsel in *Willion* v. *Berkley*. It follows from what has been written above that to state these two rules, both in fact based on non-binding precedents, as though they were fully accepted principles, and at the same time to omit all reference to the spirit and aim of the statutes, elements which were specifically considered in the leading cases, is calculated to mislead.

In the early nineteenth century the emphasis in the cases is still on the intention of the statute.[1] As the middle of the century approached, the courts tended to use the expression 'to that effect' instead of 'intention'. The origin of this seems to be in a judgment by Lord Kenyon in *Rex* v. *Cook*:[2] 'Generally speaking, in the construction of Acts of Parliament the King in his royal character is not included, unless there be words to that effect.'[3] This expression is ambiguous in that it is uncertain just how far the intention and purpose of a statute are to be considered, but at the same time it does not close the door on the consideration of these matters.

From 1870 onwards, there has been a steady drift away from the consideration of the policy of the statute. This drift is in line with the general trend towards the literal interpretation of statutes.[4] In consequence, the presumption that the King is not bound by them unless named therein seems almost irrebuttable. The steps by which this change has been brought about must now be marked out.

It is by the formulation of the rule that the King is bound by statutes only if bound expressly or by 'necessary implication' that the courts have whittled away the circumstances in which the Crown is subject to statutory liabilities. The expression 'necessary implication' seems first to have been used by Story J. in the American decision, *U.S.* v. *Hoar*:[5] 'Where the Government is not expressly or by necessary implication included, it ought to be clear from the nature of the mischief to be redressed, or the language used, that the Government itself was in contemplation of the Legislature, before a court of law would be authorised to put such

1 *Rex* v. *Allen* (1812), 15 East 332 at 340 (*per* Grose J.); *Rex* v. *Wright* (1834), 1 A. & E. 434 at 447 (*per* Tindal J.); *Moore* v. *Smith* (1859), 1 El. & El. 598 at 601 (*per* Hill J.).
2 (1790), 3 T.R. 519 at 521.
3 Cf. *Attorney-General* v. *Donaldson* (1842), 10 M. & W. 117 at 124 (*per* Alderson B.). *Ex p. Postmaster General. In re Bonham* (1879), 10 Ch. D. 595 at 601 (*per* Jessel M.R.).
4 A. J. Corry, 'Administrative Law and the Interpretation of Statutes' in 1 *U.T.L.J.* (1936) 286; *Scranton's Trustee* v. *Pearse*, [1922] 2 Ch. 87 at 123 (*per* Lord Sterndale M.R.). 5 (1821), 2 Mason 311.

a construction upon any statute.' Thus stated, the rule is unobjectionable. Then, ten years later in England, Dwarris stated in his text-book that a statute not naming the King can bind him only by necessary implication.[1] The omission of the second half of the rule as stated by Story J. alters the effect completely. Whether Dwarris did take the expression from this American judgment is not known; certainly it is not found in any of the authorities cited by Dwarris in support of his statements.[2] In 1845 Broom adopted the expression in the first edition of his text-book, acknowledging Dwarris as his authority.[3] The first English case to use this rule of the text-books seems to be a case at first instance in 1870.[4] Though the test was afterwards frequently used,[5] it was not until the case of *Gorton Local Board* v. *Prison Commissioners*,[6] heard in 1887 but not reported until 1904, that the courts indicated how narrowly 'necessary implication' was to be interpreted. The issue being whether government property was affected by local by-laws, Day J. said: 'In the absence of express words the Crown is not to be bound, nor is the Crown to be affected except by necessary implication. There are many cases in which such implication does necessarily arise, because otherwise the legislation would be unmeaning. That is what I understand by necessary implication.' Thenceforth, in almost every case this decision is cited with approval, the words 'necessary implication' used, and an ever diminishing regard paid to the purpose of the legislation.[7]

In the same period some Commonwealth decisions used the same test.[8] Yet, in general, the Commonwealth courts have not disregarded the intention of the statute. The judgment of Macdonald J.A. in *Attorney-General of British Columbia* v. *The Royal Bank of Canada and Island Amusement Company Limited*[9] is very interesting. The issue being whether

1 Dwarris, *General Treatise on Statutes*, II, 670.
2 Craies, *Statute Law*, 360 makes a similar error in citing *U.S.* v. *Hoar* as authority for the proposition that the United Kingdom and the United States have the same rules.
3 Broom, 31.
4 *Attorney-General* v. *Edmunds* (1870), 22 L.T. 667 at 667 (*per* Wills J.); *H.E.L.* x, 354 mistakenly cites *Crooke's Case* (1691), 1 Show. K.B. 208 for the proposition.
5 E.g. *In re Henley & Co.* (1878), 9 Ch. D. 469 at 482 (*per* Cotton L.J.); *Dixon* v. *Farren* (1886), 17 Q.B. 658 at 667 (*per* Wills J.).
6 [1904] 2 K.B. 165 at 167n.
7 E.g. *Hornsey U.D.C.* v. *Hennell*, [1902] 2 K.B. 73 at 80 (*per* Lord Alverstone C.J.); *Thomas* v. *Pritchard*, [1903] 1 K.B. 209 at 212 (*per* Lord Alverstone); *Cooper* v. *Hawkins*, [1904] 2 K.B. 164; *Stewart* v. *Thames Conservators*, [1908] 1 K.B. 893 at 901 (*per* Bray J.). In 1900 the Law Officers were of the opinion that if any sections of an act are expressed not to bind the Crown, then others do bind it unless excluded by implication (Treasury Minutes, 2492/00).
8 E.g. *Reg.* v. *Pouliot*, [1888] 2 Ex. C.R. 49 at 59 (*per* Burbidge J.): *Rex* v. *Rhodes*, [1934] 1 D.L.R. 251 at 255 (*per* Armour J.).
9 (1936), 51 B.C.R. 241 at 265.

the Crown was bound by company legislation requiring the return of funds to revived companies, he said:

> Where it is reasonably clear that the intention was that the Crown, as well as subjects, should for example pay a fee for certain services, viz., the use of registration facilities, or should assist in carrying out the purposes of an Act to make it workable (in this case restore the fund) it is not necessary that the Crown should be named. It is not depriving the Crown of any property or prerogative rights in the broad sense contemplated by the rule nor appreciably imposing obligations upon it. The purpose of the rule requiring the Crown to be named is to make the intention clear. When therefore it is not named in the sections of the Act under review one should look at the mischief to be remedied, the relief provided, coupled with the language employed, to ascertain whether or not the Crown, although not mentioned, was in fact within the contemplation of the Legislature.

The courts in Australia,[1] South Africa[2] and Scotland[3] have all paid specific attention to the purpose of the legislation.

In several recent cases English courts have followed the narrow view of the rule of 'necessary implication'.[4] Moreover, the Judicial Committee of the Privy Council has recently made a very restrictive interpretation,[5] which some Commonwealth courts have since found themselves compelled to follow.[6] In this case Lord du Parcq said:[7]

> It was contended on behalf of the respondents that whenever a statute is enacted 'for the public good' the Crown, though not expressly named, must be held to be bound by its provisions and that, as the Act in question was manifestly intended to secure the public welfare, it must bind the Crown.... The proposition...is supported by early authority, and is to be found in Bacon's Abridgement and other text-books, but in their

---

1 *Roberts* v. *Ahern* (1904), 1 C.L.R. 406 at 418 (*per* Griffith C.J.); *Minister for Works for Western Australia* v. *Gulson* (1944), 69 C.L.R. 338 at 347 (*per* Latham C.J.); cf. *Cain* v. *Doyle* (1946), 72 C.L.R. 409.

2 *Union Government* v. *Tonkin*, [1918] A.D. 533 at 540 (*per* Innes C.J.).

3 *Magistrates of Edinburgh* v. *Lord Advocate*, [1912] S.C. 1085 at 1090-1 (*per* Lord Dunedin); *Somerville* v. *Lord Advocate* (1893), 20 R. 1050 at 1065 (*per* Lord Kyllachy). Cf. *Encyclopaedia of the Laws of Scotland* (Edinburgh, 1928), v, 134.

4 *Attorney-General* v. *Hancock*, [1940] 1 K.B. 427 at 431 (*per* Wrottesley J.); *Rudler* v. *Franks*, [1947] K.B. 530; *Attorney-General* v. *Randall*, [1944] K.B. 709; *The Brabo*, [1947] 2 All E.R. 363 at 367 (*per* Scott L.J.). In *Territorial and Auxiliary Forces Association of the County of London* v. *Nichols*, [1949] 1 K.B. 35 at 37 the point was even conceded by counsel.

5 *Province of Bombay* v. *Municipal Corporation of the City of Bombay*, [1947] A.C. 58.

6 E.g. *Evans* v. *Schoeman*, [1949] A.D. 571 (South Africa); cf. *North Sydney Municipal Council* v. *Housing Commission* (1948), 48 S.R. (N.S.W.) 281.

7 At 62-3.

Lordships' opinion it cannot now be regarded as sound except in a strictly limited sense. Every statute must be supposed to be 'for the public good' at least in intention, and even when, as in the present case, it is apparent that one object of the legislature is to promote the welfare and convenience of a large body of the King's subjects by giving extensive powers to a local authority, it cannot be said, consistently with the decided cases, that the Crown is necessarily bound by the enactment.... If it can be affirmed that, at the time when the statute was passed and received the royal sanction, it was apparent from its terms that its beneficient purpose must be wholly frustrated unless the Crown were bound, then it may be inferred that the Crown has agreed to be bound.

The damage caused by writers such as Bacon becomes evident. They have set down a rule that statutes for the public good bind the Crown, a rule which has been shown not to be based on any reliable authority, and is not even mentioned by Coke. The courts reject the arguments of counsel supporting this rule, and at the same time limit even further the interpretation of 'necessary implication'.

Nor is this all. In furtherance of this tendency, the rule of 'necessary implication' is extended to all statutes regardless of whether the King's peculiar interests are affected. In a Scottish decision Viscount Dunedin, recognising that the intention to bind the Crown is readily found when those interests are not prejudiced, said:[1]

While I do not doubt that there are certain provisions by which the Crown never would be bound unless that were clearly expressed—such, for instance, as the provisions of a taxing statute...yet when you come to a set of provisions in a statute having for its object the benefit of the public generally, there is not an antecedent unlikelihood that the Crown will consent to be bound, and this, I think, would be so in the case of regulations which are meant to apply to all the land in a city, and where the Crown's property is not held *jure coronae*.

This view was uncompromisingly rejected by the Judicial Committee.[2] Thus, this arbitrary rule of 'necessary implication' is to apply to all statutes, whether the prerogative interests of the Crown are affected or not.[3] The distinction between these and other interests had some point in that it illustrated that clear words were required to prove that a statute was intended to interfere with prerogative rights, whereas it could more

1 *Magistrates of Edinburgh v. Lord Advocate*, [1912] S.C. 1085 at 1091.
2 At 64.
3 See *Attorney-General for New South Wales v. Curator of Intestate Estates*, [1907] A.C. 519 and *Minister for Works for Western Australia v. Gulson* (1944), 69 C.L.R. 338 at 343 for unsuccessful attempts by counsel to resist this tendency. Cf. Black, *Construction and Interpretation of the Laws*, 98.

easily be seen in other cases that it was the purpose of the legislature to bind the Crown. The courts which accepted the 'necessary implication' rule fifty years ago did at least sometimes pay lip-service to the idea that the intention must be looked at, but that no longer obtains to-day. Now, one text-book can sum up the law as follows:[1] 'The Crown is not bound by any statute unless expressly mentioned except where the Crown must have been intended to be bound by necessary implication, because otherwise the statute would be meaningless.' Two rays of hope can be discerned: the House of Lords has not pronounced authoritatively on the matter,[2] and Denning L.J. who is so refreshingly resuscitating the principles of *Heydon's Case*[3] has said:[4] 'It is, of course, a settled rule that the Crown is not bound by a statute unless there can be gathered from it an intention that the Crown should be bound. . . .'

Reference has been made to one United States decision of 1821[5] where the emphasis was on the intention of the statute. Since that time the United States has consistently regarded the purpose of the statute as the main criterion. In 1840 Barbour J. said in a Supreme Court decision that the 'Government is not to be construed to be embraced unless named, or what would be equivalent, unless the language is such as to show clearly that such was the intent of the act'.[6] In 1936 Stone J. (as he then was) said that 'the presumption is an aid to consistent construction of statutes of the enacting sovereign when their purpose is in doubt, but it does not require that the aim of a statute fairly to be inferred be disregarded, because not explicitly stated'.[7]

The issue arose in the important case, *U.S. v. Mineworkers of America*,[8] whether the Norris-La Guardia Act took away by implication the powers of the Government to enjoin. All the members of the Supreme Court were agreed that the legislative history and intent should be considered. The majority held that 'statutes which in general terms direct pre-existing rights or privileges' are presumed not to apply to the Government.[9] This

1 Broom, *op. cit.* 40.
2 It is submitted that the remarks of Viscount Dunedin, Lord Atkinson and Lord Parmoor in *Attorney-General* v. *De Keyser's Royal Hotel Limited*, [1920] A.C. 508 at 526, 538 and 576 respectively are inconclusive. As Lord Atkinson said (at 538), whether the test is 'necessary implication' or 'intention' in this case the result is reached that the Reform Act, 1842, binds the Crown.
3 *Seaford Court Estates Limited* v. *Asher*, [1949] 2 K.B. 481 at 499; [1950] A.C. 508.
4 *Tamlin* v. *Hannaford*, [1950] 1 K.B. 18 at 22; cf. the *Slatford Case*, [1952] 2 All E.R. 956. 5 See p. 147 *supra*.
6 *U.S.* v. *Knight* (1840), 14 Peters (U.S.) 301 at 315; cf. *Custer* v. *McCutcheon* (1930), 283 U.S. 514.
7 *U.S.* v. *California* (1936), 297 U.S. 175 at 186; cf. *U.S.* v. *Stevenson* (1909), 215 U.S. 190; *U.S.* v. *Rice* (1945), 327 U.S. 742 at 749.
8 (1946), 67 Sup. Ct. Rep. 677. 9 *Ibid.* 686.

view, as has been seen, has some historical foundation. Frankfurter J.,
however, said:[1] 'At best, this canon, like other generalities about statutory
construction, is not a rule of law. Whatever persuasion it may have in
construing a particular statute derives from the particular statute and the
terms of the enactment in its total environment.' It may perhaps be said
that in the United States the courts attempt to define the legislative
objectives and that the presumption that existing governmental privileges
have not been taken away by a statute is invoked only to resolve doubts.[2]
It is submitted that this is a much more satisfactory rule than the common-
law rule at present applied in the Commonwealth.

B. *The Effect of Legislation on the Common-Law Rules*

Canada, most of the Provinces of Canada, and New Zealand, but
not Australia, have introduced Interpretation Acts containing provisions
similar to the following:[3] 'No provision or enactment in any Act shall
affect, in any manner whatsoever, the rights of His Majesty, his heirs or
successors, unless it is expressly stated therein that His Majesty shall be
bound thereby.' Attempts have been made by the courts to lessen the
effects of such a clause by a strict construction of 'rights'. The Judicial
Committee of the Privy Council has observed that the word connotes
'the accrued rights of His Majesty, and does not cover mere possibilities
such as rights which, but for the alteration made in the general law by the
enactment under consideration, might have thereafter accrued to His
Majesty under some future contract'.[4] In New Zealand it has even been
suggested that the expression means 'his ancient prerogatives, those rights
which are incommunicable and are appropriated to him as essential to his
regal capacity'.[5] In the same case it was suggested 'that such Acts are not
binding on the Crown unless by reasonable intendment the Legislature
has shown an intention that the Crown shall be bound'.[6] None the less,
it seems that the words of such Acts are so clear that there is no room to
imply, in the light of the purposes of the Act, an intention that the Crown
shall be bound. The Judicial Committee of the Privy Council has reached
this conclusion,[7] and so have several Canadian cases.[8]

---

1 *Ibid.* 706.   2 Cf. H. A. Walkup, *op. cit.* 36 *Geo. L.R.* 542 at 550.
3 Interpretation Act, R.S.C. 1927, c. 1, s. 16.
4 *Dominion Building Corporation Limited* v. *Rex*, [1933] A.C. 533 at 549 (*per*
Lord Tomlin).
5 *McDougall* v. *Attorney-General*, [1925] N.Z.L.R. 104 at 118 (*per* Read J.).
6 *Ibid.* 115 (*per* Herdman J.); cf. *In re Buckingham*, [1922] N.Z.L.R. 771; *Andrew* v.
Rockell, [1934] N.Z.L.R. 1056 at 1057–8 (*per* Ostler J.).
7 *In re Silver Brothers Ltd.*, [1932] A.C. 514 at 523.
8 *Rex* v. *Rhodes*, [1934] 1 D.L.R. 251 at 255 (*per* Armour J.); *Attorney-General for
British Columbia* v. *Parker*, [1937] 4 D.L.R. 242 at 245 (*per* McPhillips J.A.); *Rankin*
v. *Rex*, [1940] Ex. C.R. 105.

Section 40 (2) of the Crown Proceedings Act provides: 'Except as therein otherwise expressly provided, nothing in this Act shall...(*f*) affect any rules of evidence or any presumption relating to the extent to which the Crown is bound by any Act of Parliament.' The Maritime Conventions Act, 1911,[1] Part II of the Law Reform (Married Women and Tortfeasors) Act, 1935,[2] and the Law Reform (Contributory Negligence) Act, 1945,[3] it is expressly provided by the Act, shall bind the Crown.

The question arises whether other Acts which would impose a liability in contract or tort upon a private person will also bind the Crown. It is clear that there can be no statutory liability on the Crown, though there may be liability in tort where the Act in question does not bind the Crown. For example, the liabilities imposed by the Housing Act, 1936, on the owners of dwelling-houses unfit for human habitation will not apply to the Crown.

More important is the question whether statutes affecting tortious liability, such as the Fatal Accidents Act,[4] the Dogs Acts,[5] and section 1 of the Law Reform (Miscellaneous Provisions) Act,[6] now apply to the Crown. It will be recalled that section 2 of the Crown Proceedings Act declares that 'subject to the provisions of this Act, the Crown shall be subject to all those liabilities in tort to which, if it were a private person of full age and capacity, it would be subject (*a*) in respect of torts committed by its servants or agents....'. Since a private person is bound by statutes amending the law of tort, it can be argued that the Crown, too, must for the purposes of this Act be bound by them. There is no room here for application of the rule that the later of two conflicting provisions in one statute is the operative one.[7] All depends on the meaning of 'express'. It could be asserted that the only express provisions subject to which the presumption mentioned in section 40 (2) of the Crown Proceedings Act applies are those express references to the Law Reform Acts and the Maritime Conventions Act. On the other hand, in a case on another statute where one section applied 'subject to the provisions of the Act' and a later section applied 'except as in this Act expressly provided' the court looked to the general purpose of the Act to solve the problem of interpretation.[8] It does seem that a court making a broad approach to the problem

---

1 1 & 2 Geo. V, c. 57, s. 4.
2 25 & 26 Geo. V, c. 30; the United States is liable to make contribution; *U.S.* v. *Yellow Cab Co.* (1951), 340 U.S. 543.
3 8 & 9 Geo. VI, c. 28.   4 9 & 10 Vict. c. 93.
5 6 Ed. VII, c. 32.   6 24 & 25 Geo. V, c. 41.
7 Maxwell, *Interpretation of Statutes*, 163–5 and cases there cited.
8 *Thames Conservators* v. *Smeed Dean & Co.*, [1897] 2 Q.B. 334 at 355 (*per* Chitty L.J.).

could find that the policy of the Act required that statutes creating and affecting liability in tort should bind the Crown, and hold that section 2 made express provision to that effect.[1] Even if the Courts should choose this latter alternative, the Crown will be liable under section 2 (2) for breach of statutory duty only where, independently of the section, the statute imposing the duty binds the Crown. Prior to the Act, rules of Court probably did not bind the Crown, but they have now been made generally applicable to the Crown by a statutory instrument made under the Act.[2]

C. *The Right of the State to the Benefit of Statutes*

It has been recognised since at least the fifteenth century that the King can avail himself of the provisions of an Act of Parliament by which he is not named.[3] The United States is entitled to the benefit of a statute if that is the object of the statute.[4] Although the rule is usually cited in absolute terms in England, it probably applies subject to a contrary intention, express or implied.[5]

In *Cayzer Irvine & Company Limited* v. *Board of Trade*[6] the Crown argued that it was entitled to the benefit of a statute, which, it had already been decided, did not bind it. The Court of Appeal left the matter undecided, but it is submitted that at common law it would depend on the intention of the statute.

A further difficult point is whether the Crown is entitled to the benefit of statutory rights freed from the restrictions imposed by the statute on those rights. In both 1487[7] and 1594[8] it was held that the Crown could not claim a right given by an Act except subject to the conditions on which that right was given. In *Crooke's Case*[9] the arguments of counsel that 'if they have any right the King can only have it by this Act of Parliament, and then they must have it as this Act gives it' was accepted by the court. A later Irish case[10] followed *Crooke's Case* and extended it by holding the Crown to be bound by an amending statute cutting down rights conferred by an earlier one.

---

1 Cf. Glanville Williams, *op. cit.* 55 *et seq.*; Bickford Smith, *op. cit.* 62. Cf. *Chorlton* v. *Lings* (1868), L.R. 4 C.P. 374 at 393 (*per* Byles J.): 'The word "expressly" often means no more than plainly, clearly, or the like.'

2 See p. 134 *supra*.

3 Y.B. 12 H. 7, f. 20 (*per* Mordaunt); Y.B. 13 H. 7, f. 7 (*per* Woode J.); *Case of a Fine Levied by the King* (1605), 7 Co. Rep. 32b.

4 *Commonwealth* v. *Boston & Maine Ry. Co.* (1849), 3 Cush. (Mass.) 25 at 45 (*per* Shaw J.).   5 Halsbury, *op. cit.* VI at 483.

6 [1927] 1 K.B. 269.   7 Y.B. 12 H. 7, f. 21 (*per* Frowycke).

8 *Reg.* v. *Buckberd* (1594), 1 Leonard 149.

9 (1691), 1 Show. K.B. 208.   10 *Reg.* v. *Cruise*, [1852] 2 Ir. Ch. R. 65.

There have been conflicting Canadian decisions on the point.[1] At least twice the above rule has been followed.[2] On the other hand, the Supreme Court of Canada has held[3] that the Crown in an action for loss of services could rely on negligence in not complying with highway legislation, although the action was commenced outside the limitation period fixed by the legislation. Yet the same court has decided that if the Crown relies on a statute in order to claim damages against a third party for damage to its vehicle caused by the combined negligence of its employee and that third party, its claim is limited to that proportion of the damage which the statute authorises it to claim.[4]

In 1947[5] the Court of Appeal considered whether the Crown as salvor could be sued when it was guilty of misconduct in the course of an unsuccessful salvage attempt. By statute, the Crown was given the same rights in respect of salvage services as a private person. Here no *res* had been salved, and the court held that the Crown was not liable for its misconduct although a private person would have been. It must not be thought, however, that this is contrary to *Crooke's Case*. The Court of Appeal merely decided that it could not read into the Act an intention to make the Crown liable where no salvage was effected. It is submitted that if the Crown had recovered the *res* and claimed salvage, any reduction in its value due to the misconduct of the Crown would have been taken into account in determining this claim.

The effect of the Crown Proceedings Act on the above rules must be considered. Section 31 (1) is as follows:

This Act shall not prejudice the right of the Crown to take advantage of the provisions of an Act of Parliament although not named therein; and it is hereby declared that in any civil proceedings against the Crown the provisions of any Act of Parliament which could, if the proceedings were between subjects, be relied upon by the defendant as a defence to the proceedings, whether in whole or in part, or otherwise, may, subject to any express provision to the contrary, be so relied upon by the Crown.

It seems that this Act makes only one change in the common-law rules laid down above. The Crown may plead a statutory defence even though

1 See D. M. Gordon, 'How Far Privative or Restrictive Enactment Binds the Crown?' In 18 *Can. B.R.* (1940), 751.

2 *Re Excelsior Electric Dairy Machinery Limited* (1923), 52 Ont. L.R. 225; *Attorney-General of British Columbia* v. *The Royal Bank of Canada and Island Amusement Co. Ltd.* (1936), 51 B.C.R. 241; [1937] S.C.R. 459.

3 *Rex* v. *Richardson & Adams*, [1948] 2 D.L.R. 305; followed in *Rex* v. *Wilfred Lightheart*, [1952] Ex. 12; see my Note, in 26 *Can. B.R.* (1948), 994; cf. *re Rex* v. *Rutherford* (1927), 60 L.R. 654.

4 *Toronto Transportation Commission* v. *Rex*, [1949] 3 D.L.R. 161.

5 *Anglo-Saxon Petroleum Co.* v. *Lords Commissioners of the Admiralty*, [1947] 2 K.B. 794.

it cannot be shown that that was intended by the Act, and even though that Act has already been held not to bind the Crown. The point left undecided by *Cayzer's Case* is now settled in favour of the Crown.

2. ESTOPPEL

There are *dicta* in seventeenth-century cases which text-books have since relied on as authoritative,[1] that the Crown is not bound by estoppel.[2] To evaluate them, not only the cases but also the general law of estoppel must be briefly considered.

Three types of estoppel were then known. Estoppel by record prevented parties to suits from denying judgments: this was supported by the maxims, *interest reipublicae ut sit finis litium* and *nemo debet bis vexari pro eadem causa.* Secondly, there was estoppel by deed, preventing a party to a deed denying the facts stated in it, an illustration of the importance of a seal in English law. Thirdly, there was estoppel *in pais*, arising out of acts establishing certain relations of parties. As Holdsworth has pointed out,[3] it was only in the nineteenth century, with the great cases of *Pickard* v. *Sears*[4] and *Freeman* v. *Cooke*,[5] that the current equitable aspect of estoppel was developed. This, of course, rests on the idea that a person who has deliberately misled another by his acts or statements cannot give evidence conflicting with them. Equitable estoppel, arising out of the former estoppel *in pais*, and now known often as estoppel by conduct or representation, is the most important type of estoppel to-day.

Although one monograph[6] inclines to the view that the Crown is not bound by estoppels by record, this is not supported by the cases. There is clear authority[7] that 'the Crown...can take advantage of, and is bound by, an estoppel *per rem judicatam*, as much as any of the King's subjects'.[8]

The *dicta* in support of the general proposition that estoppels do not bind the Crown were all in cases concerning estoppels by deed. The opinion is widely held to-day that these estoppels do not bind the Crown.[9] Lord Atkin has said that 'there is authority for the general proposition so far as estoppel by deed is concerned'.[10] The key to this rule is found in

---

1 E.g. Chitty, *Prerogatives of the Crowne*, 381.

2 *Sir Edward Coke's Case*, (1624) Godb. 289 at 299 (*per* Hobart L.C.J.); *Rex* v. *Delme*, (1714) 10 Mod. 200; *Sheffeild* v. *Ratcliffe* (1624), Hob. 334 at 339.

3 *H.E.L.* IX, 144 *et seq.*   4 (1837), 6 A. & E. 469.

5 (1848), 2 Ex. 654.   6 Everest & Strode, *Law of Estoppel*, 8.

7 See F. E. Farrer, 'A Prerogative Fallacy—"That the King is not bound by Estoppel"' in 49 *L.Q.R.* (1933) 511 and cases there cited.

8 Bower, *The Doctrine of Res Judicata*, 129.

9 Halsbury, *op. cit.* VI, 483; Bickford Smith, *op. cit.* 19.

10 *Attorney-General to the Prince of Wales* v. *Collom*, [1916] 2 K.B. 193 at 204.

Bacon's version of it.[1] '...the King cannot be estopped, for it cannot be presumed that the King would do any wrong to any person, and therefore being deceived in his grant, makes it absolutely void.' Perusal of the cases shows that all turns on whether the King was deceived in his grant.[2] A party to a grant from the King cannot allege that the King is estopped by his grant where he knew or ought to have known of facts materially affecting the title of the King to make the grant to him. Although some Canadian courts[3] have stated in general terms that estoppels by deed do not bind the Crown, there, too, it seems to apply only where the King is deceived in his grant.[4]

There is no trace of a decision holding that the King is not bound by equitable estoppel. In 1884 the Judicial Committee of the Privy Council held in *Plimmer* v. *Mayor of Wellington*[5] that the Crown, having requested the plaintiff to extend a wharf which he used, was estopped from denying an interest in the property when the plaintiff later claimed compensation upon its compulsory acquisition. Rather surprisingly, Robertson[6] in 1908 stated, in unqualified terms, that no estoppels bound the Crown. Lord Atkin, however, followed *Plimmer's Case* in 1916,[7] and in his judgment emphasised that this was an equitable estoppel. There is a steady stream of Canadian[8] and Australian[9] decisions confirming that estoppels of this type bind the Crown.[10]

Estoppels can only bind the Crown where the agent was acting within the scope of his ostensible authority.[11] The Crown cannot be estopped by a representation of its servant where the representation is *ultra vires* the Crown.[12] So, in *Minister of Agriculture and Fisheries* v. *Matthews*[13] the Minister could not be estopped from denying that he had granted an agricultural tenancy where he was empowered only to grant a licence. In

1 *Abridgement*, 852.
2 *Bozoun's Case* (1584), 4 Co. Rep. 34b; *Duke of Cumberland's Case* (1610), 8 Co. Rep. 166b.
 3 E.g. *Western Dominion Coal Mines* v. *Rex*, [1946] 4 D.L.R. 270 at 272.
4 *City of Vancouver* v. *Vancouver Lumber Co.*, [1911] A.C. 711 at 721 (P.C.).
5 (1884), 9 App. Cas. 699.   6 Robertson, *op. cit.* 576.
7 *Collom's Case, supra* at 204.
 8 *Queen Victoria Niagara Falls Park Commissioners* v. *International Railway Co.*, [1928] 4 D.L.R. 755; *Rex* v. *Canadian Pacific Ry. Co.*, [1930] Ex. C.R. 26.
 9 *Attorney-General* v. *Municipal Council of Sydney* (1919), 20 S.R. 46 (N.S.W.).
 10 *Territorial & Auxiliary Forces Association of the County of London* v. *Nichols*, [1949] 1 K.B. 35, the point was left undecided.
 11 *Leen* v. *President of the Executive Council*, [1928] Ir. R. 408; *Hollett* v. *Rex*, [1949] 4 D.L.R. 225.
 12 *Attorney-General* v. *Municipal Council of Sydney* (1919), 20 S.R. 46 (N.S.W.); *Gillies Bros. Ltd.* v. *Rex* (1947), 2 D.L.R. 769; cf. company law cases like *In re Companies Acts ex parte Watson* (1888), 21 Q.B. 301.
 13 [1950] 1 K.B. 148.

Robertson v. *Minister of Pensions*[1] an applicant for a military pension claimed that a letter from the Director of Personal Services at the War Office accepting that his disability was attributable to military service estopped the Minister of Pensions from denying that fact. Denning L.J. in *Falmouth Boat Construction Co.* v. *Howell*,[2] expressly relying on the principle that he had laid down in the *Robertson Case*,[3] said: 'whenever government officers, in their dealings with a subject, take on themselves to assume authority in a matter with which he is concerned, he is entitled to rely on their having the authority which they assume. He does not know, and cannot be expected to know, the limits of their authority, and he ought not to suffer if they exceed it.' The House of Lords overruled this *dictum* in so far as it applied to the *Falmouth Case*, Lord Simonds adding that 'the illegality of an act is the same whether or not the actor has been misled by an assumption of authority on the part of a government officer however high or low in the hierarchy'.[4] The problem remains: although the principle enunciated in *Robertson's Case* is wrong in law, can the decision nevertheless be supported on a narrower ground?

The issue in such cases may be essentially one of agency. If the promise is within the legal competence of the Crown either at common law or by statute, then the Crown is bound by a representation made within the scope of the ostensible authority of the agent. *Robertson's Case* may be supported on the footing that it was within the apparent authority of the Director of Personal Services to state that the plaintiff's disability was attributable to military service: on the other hand it does not follow that a representation made by any Department of the Crown will estop the Crown merely because the matter was *intra vires* the Crown—it would not, for example, it is suggested, be within the ostensible authority of the Board of Trade to write the letter written by the Director in the *Robertson Case*.[5]

Estoppel is a device of equity, and will not be upheld where to do so would be contrary to public policy.[6]

The United States is bound by estoppels by record.[7] The view of the authors of the *Corpus Juris*[8] that it is bound also by estoppels by deed has

1 [1949] 1 K.B. 227.
2 [1950] 2 K.B. 16 at 26.   3 At 233.
4 [1951] A.C. 837 at 845; cf. *Pickell Ltd.* v. *Pickford*, [1951] 2 D.L.R. 119.
5 See also J. D. B. Mitchell, 'The Assumption of Authority by Crown Servants' in 100 *Law Journal* (1950) 493.
6 *Surveyor-General (Cape)* v. *Estate de Villiers*, [1923] A.D. 588; *Western Vinegars Ltd.* v. *Minister of National Revenue*, [1938] Ex. C.R. 39.
7 *First National Bank* v. *U.S.* (1932), 2 F. Supp. 107; *Tait* v. *Western Maryland Rly.* (1933), 289 U.S. 620.
8 *Corpus Juris Secundum*, XXXI, § 49.

been adopted by the courts in some jurisdictions.[1] Equitable estoppels may also bind the United States. This is usually justified by the maxim that 'he who seeks equity must do equity'.[2] Yet it does seem that the courts will not readily hold the United States bound by estoppel. Clear proof that the agent had authority to bind the Government is required.[3] The unauthorised appropriation of Government land is not beyond Government challenge because taxes have been levied on the expropriators.[4] It may even be that estoppels by conduct are binding on the United States only in the exercise of its proprietary but not its governmental functions.[5]

In *Federal Crop Insurance Corporation* v. *Merrill*[6] an agent of the governmental corporation had accepted an insurance policy contrary to a regulation of the corporation. It was held that 'the sovereign is neither bound nor estopped by acts of its officers or agents in entering into...an agreement to do...what the law does not sanction or permit'.

3. LIMITATION OF ACTIONS

A. *Nullum Tempus Occurrit Regi*

The common-law rule was *Nullum tempus occurrit regi*.[7] Numerous statutory exceptions to this have been made, and these have been consolidated in the Limitation Act, 1939.[8] Special periods of limitation are provided for claims for land and taxes and other specific matters,[9] and in the remaining cases the ordinary periods of limitation apply to the Crown.[10]

B. *Laches*

In the seventeenth century it was established that the Crown could not be prejudiced by the laches of its officers, and this was confirmed by a series of cases in the next two centuries.[11] The applicability of laches to the

---

1 E.g. *City of Winster Haven* v. *State*, 170 So. 100.
2 E.g. *Iowa* v. *Carr* (1911), 191 Fed. 257 at 266.
3 *U.S.* v. *California* (1946), 332 U.S. 19 at 40 (*per* Black J.); cf. *Reed as Warden* v. *Seymour* (1877), 24 Minn. 273 at 280 (*per* Berry J.). Wigmore, *op. cit.* §1057; E. Spilman, 'Evidence and Admissions of Government Employees under the Act' in 33 *A.B.A.J.* (1947) 958.
4 *Utah Light & Power Co.* v. *U.S.* (1945), 230 Fed. 328 at 342 (*per* Van Valkenburgh J.).
5 *U.S.* v. *Brookfield Fisheries* (1938), 24 F. Supp. 712; neither here nor elsewhere does this distinction seem to be important in English law.
6 (1947), 332 U.S. 380.
7 Y.B. 20 Ed. I, f. 69; Co. Lit., 119a n. 1.   8 2 & 3 Geo. VI, c. 21.
9 See Preston and Newsom, *Limitation of Actions*, 77 *et seq.*
10 S. 30(1).
11 Co. Lit. 576; *Sheffeild* v. *Ratcliffe* (1624), Hob. 334 at 347; *Attorney-General* v. *Chitty* (1744), Park. 37 at 48; *Rex* v. *Renton* (1848), 2 Ex. 216 at 220.

Crown is not mentioned either in the Limitation Act or in the Crown Proceedings Act. It is therefore pertinent to inquire whether the rights of the Crown are still unaffected by laches. Certainly, the commentaries on the latter Act maintain that this is the position.[1]

Holdsworth has explained that there are the following justifications for the maxim *Nullum tempus occurrit regi*.[2] First, that no laches can be imputed to an impeccable King. Secondly, that 'he cannot so nearly look to his particular because he is intended to consider *ardua regni pro bono publico*'. Thirdly, that he ought not to suffer for the negligence of his officers. Fourthly, that statutes do not bind the Crown. May it not be said that the first and third arguments have lost their force since the Crown Proceedings Act, that the second should only benefit the King in his private capacity, and that the fourth is no longer applicable since the Crown is now bound by limitation statutes? Could not it be contended that *cessante ratione cessat lex*, laches can now be imputed to the Crown?

There are, however, further reasons to support such a contention. It will be recalled that Coke and other seventeenth-century authorities maintained that the King was never bound by estoppels, but that now it is certain that equitable estoppels bind the Crown.[3] There is a close resemblance between equitable estoppel and laches. Both rest on acquiescence in the violation of a legal right: the former while the violation is in progress, the latter after it is completed. Both are equitable principles. Since the cases establishing the inapplicability of laches to the Crown the maxim that he who seeks equity must do equity has influenced the judges in deciding that the Crown is bound by equitable estoppel. English courts do not appear to have dealt with the application of laches to the Crown in the last hundred years. There seems no reason why they should not apply the same equitable maxim and hold the Crown subject to the doctrine of laches.

Section 30 (1) of the Limitation Act 1939 provides that 'this Act shall apply to proceedings by or against the Crown in like manner as it applies to proceedings between subjects'. Section 2 (7) impliedly preserves the doctrine of laches by providing that the normal periods of limitation for contract, tort and other actions shall not apply to any claim for equitable relief.[4] It can be argued that this Act subjects the Crown to the doctrine of laches. Some indirect support can be found in the Crown Proceedings Act. It is thought necessary in section 30 (2) expressly to provide that nothing in the Act 'shall prejudice the right of the Crown to rely upon the law relating to the limitation of time for bringing proceedings against

1 Glanville Williams, *op. cit.* 110; Bickford Smith, *op. cit.* 19.
2 *H.E.L.* x, 355.   3 P. 157 *supra*.
4 Cf. Preston & Newsom, *op. cit.* 240–1.

public authorities'. *Expressio unius est exclusio alterius.* Perhaps, therefore, this statute impliedly recognises that laches does affect the Crown.

In early cases in the United States, too, it was held that the Government was not prejudiced by laches.[1] In this century the courts have sometimes said, relying on the maxim that he who seeks equity must do equity, that the Government is so affected.[2] As in the case of equitable estoppel, the courts will certainly not hold the Government bound by agents acting without authority,[3] and it must now be regarded as doubtful whether the United States is prejudiced by the laches of its officers.

C. *Statutory Provisions*

Section 21 of the Limitation Act, 1939, re-enacting with slight alteration the Public Authorities Protection Act, 1893, provides:

No action shall be brought against any person for any act done in pursuance, or execution, or intended execution of any Act of Parliament, or of any public duty or authority, or in respect of any neglect or default in the execution of any such Act, duty or authority, unless it is commenced before the expiration of one year from the date on which the cause of action occurred.[4]

Actions under the Federal Tort Claims Act must be brought within two years. The benefit of section 21 has been extended to the Crown expressly by section 30 (2) of the Crown Proceedings Act, whereas the Federal Tort Claims Act has specially provided that the United States must be sued within two years from the accrual of the cause of action.[5] The objects of these provisions for shorter limitation periods are to prevent the Government's having outstanding financial liabilities hanging over its head for an excessively long time, and to reduce the risk of fraudulent claims[6]

1 *U.S.* v. *Kirkpatrick* (1824), 9 Wheat. 720 at 735.
2 E.g. *Pittsburgh Railways* v. *Carrick Boro* (1918), 259 Pa. 333 at 339; but see *Guaranty Trust Co.* v. *U.S.* (1938), 304 U.S. 126.
3 *U.S.* v. *California* (1946), 332 U.S. 19 at 40 (*per* Black J.).
4 The proviso to s. 1 of the 1893 Act (not repealed) provides that 'this section shall not affect any proceedings by any Department of the Government against any local authority or official of a local authority'. And see *Attorney-General* v. *West Ham Corporation* (1910), 26 T.L.R. 683.
5 § 420 now § 2401 (*b*).
6 Cf. Cardozo J. in *Thomann* v. *Rochester* (1931), 256 N.Y. 165 at 170: 'A judgment against a municipal corporation must be paid out of the public purse. Raids by the unscrupulous will multiply apace if claims may be postponed till the injury is stale. The law does not condemn as arbitrary a classification of rights and remedies that is thus rooted in the public needs.... Prompt service of the notice would have made it possible for the defendant to investigate the loss and ascertain whether the claim had been swollen in disfigurement of truth. Scrutiny becomes futile with the lapse of the obscuring years.'

without at the same time unduly prejudicing the claimant in his action.[1]

The United States act furnishes no extension for disability of the plaintiff.[2] It is usual for statutes of limitation to extend the period by the duration of the infancy or insanity of the plaintiff. It may have been thought by the framers of the Act that if, for instance, a six-year-old child were the victim of negligent driving by a Government servant, the Government could not countenance the possibility of the action being brought at any time within the next sixteen years. It is agreed that to extend the period in that way would be unwise. Yet it is contended that there is much to be said for the British compromise. After providing generally for an extension of the period of infancy or lunacy, section 22 (*d*) of the Limitation Act enacts that in actions against public authorities the period of one year shall be extended only when at the time of the accrual of the action the plaintiff proves that 'the person under a disability was not, at the time when the right of action accrued to him, in the custody of a parent'.[3]

A difficult problem under the English act, affecting all public authorities, and perhaps the Government above all, is to what actions in tort and contract the Act applies. The words 'In pursuance, or execution, or intended execution of any Act of Parliament, or of any public duty or authority' have been difficult to interpret. In *Bradford Corporation* v. *Myers*,[4] a local authority empowered by statute to supply gas sold coke to a private individual. A servant of the local authority negligently damaged the premises of the purchaser while delivering it, and in the subsequent action the House of Lords held that the Act was no defence. It was held that the coke was not sold in the direct execution of the statute, although the sale was *intra vires*. There was also no duty to sell. The remaining point was whether there was public authority. Lord Buckmaster held this to mean

1 It is rather surprising that English courts have extended the protection of the Act to Crown servants sued in a private capacity; *The Danube II*, [1921] P. 183 (C.A.).

2 § 2401 (*a*) provides, however, that in actions against the United States other than for tort the period of six years shall be the norm, but that if the plaintiff has a disability or is beyond the seas there is a period of three years from the end of the disability in which to sue; cf. the Limitation Act, 1950, (N.Z.) whereby the period of one year can be extended to six years either by consent of the defendant, or where the plaintiff satisfies the court that there was reasonable mistake or that the defendant would not be prejudiced. s. 23.

3 The 1893 Act contained no extension for infants, and the Court of Appeal in *Jacobs* v. *London C.C.*, [1935] 1 K.B. 67 held that none could be implied. The Law Revision Committee set up by the Lord Chancellor in 1934, in their Fifth Interim Report on Statutes of Limitation (December 1936, Cmd. 5334), recommended the inclusion of the extension.

4 [1916] 1 A.C. 242.

'an authority exercised impartially with regard to all the public' and thought the circumstances of the case outside this definition.[1] Lord Shaw held that this was no public authority because the right here arose not from the exercise of a public function but from a private bargain.[2]

It seems from the later House of Lords decision, *Griffiths* v. *Smith*,[3] that the tendency is to construe *Bradford Corporation* v. *Myers* narrowly. There, the plaintiff was invited by the headmaster of a non-provided school which her child attended to visit an exhibition of the work of pupils. She was injured during the exhibition by a collapse of the floor of the premises. In holding that the Act applied, the House of Lords unanimously agreed that the act was done in direct execution of a statute. Moreover, Lord Porter held that it was in execution of a public duty, and made this important distinction:[4] '...a private contract even if entered into in pursuance of an Act of Parliament is not thereby protected but an act which is done in performance of a public duty is still done in the execution of a public duty though it is performed through the medium of a contract.' Viscount Maugham said:[5] 'It is sufficient to establish that the act was in substance done in the course of exercising for the benefit of the public an authority or a power conferred on the public authority not being a mere incidental power, such as a power to carry on a trade.'

It is this last point which is of particular importance here. The Crown is entering into an increasing range of contracts not directly authorised by statute. When are they made in pursuance of a public duty or authority? Bickford Smith[6] suggests that 'some of the more commercial activities of the Crown, in particular as an owner or charterer of shipping' may not be within the Act, but unfortunately does not mention a decision absolutely at variance with his suggestion. This case, *Western India Match Co.* v. *Lock*,[7] must now be examined. While a ship requisitioned by the Minister of War Transport was operating under charter to him, it was (allegedly) negligently unloaded by his representatives. In an action in tort against these representatives the latter pleaded the Limitation Act, and the preliminary point of law whether they could so plead was considered by Lord Goddard. Although Lord Goddard spent some time in justifying the view that a power and not necessarily a positive obligation need only be shown, the only point at issue was whether the duty or authority was public. Counsel for the plaintiffs relied on the *dicta* of Lord Shaw and Lord Porter already cited to support their contention that this carriage of

1 *Ibid.* 247.   2 *Ibid.* 263. 4.
3 [1941] A.C. 170.   4 *Ibid.* 208.
5 *Ibid.* 185.   6 37.
7 [1946] K.B. 601.

commercial freight was merely a private contract. The Attorney-General argued that all he need show was that the Minister acted in the public interest, and it is clear that Lord Goddard, in finding for the Crown, accepted this argument. In his judgment he made no references to the judgments of Lord Shaw and Lord Porter. He held that the Minister had the power, in the public interest, to deal with and allot cargoes to ships requisitioned by him.[1] The House of Lords in *Bradford Corporation* v. *Myers* nowhere said that it was enough to prove that the making of the contract was in the public interest; surely, it was in the public interest that waste products from the gas plant of the corporation should be sold. In *Turburville* v. *West Ham Corporation*[2] one of the issues was whether a claim for a war time salary increase made available under statutory authority to serving soldiers also was a cause of action within the Limitation Act. Lord Oaksey and Wynn Parry J. in the Court of Appeal thought that the test was whether the payments were made for the public benefit, and they relied on the *dicta* quoted above of Lord Maugham in *Griffiths* v. *Smith*. They held that the payment was for the benefit of individuals and not for the public benefit, although Lord Oaksey pointed out the difficulties when he said that 'it may have an indirect bearing upon the morale of employees who were not called up and upon other members of the public'.[3] In *Firestone Tire and Rubber Co. (S.S.) Ltd.* v. *Singapore Harbour Board*[4] the Judicial Committee of the Privy Council held that the defendants, while acting as warehousemen, were protected by an Act similar in wording to the Limitation Act. The *dicta* of Viscount Maugham were approved and followed, with the explanation that a trading function would only be outside the Act if it were a mere subsidiary power.

The Committee on Limitation of Actions under the chairmanship of Tucker L.J. reported in 1949 that the present exemptions for public authorities should be repealed.[5] It proposed that the limitation period for actions in respect of personal injuries should be two years with a right for the court in its discretion to extend the period to six years. For all other actions a public authority, including the Crown, should be subject to the same rules of limitation as the private citizen.

---

1 *Ibid.* 606–7.
3 At 217.
5 Cmd. 7740.

2 [1950] 2 K.B. 208.
4 [1952] A.C. 452.

4. CONCLUSION

These substantive limitations discussed in this chapter seem to have some common characteristics. They are elaborations of the general medieval rule 'that in all cases where the King's right and that of a subject conflicted, the King was preferred'.[1] Developed as part of the King's personal prerogative rights, they are inappropriate to the present public and executive concept of the Crown. Reform is called for on the general principle that no Crown immunities are tolerable unless their retention can be affirmatively proved to be necessary in the public interest.

Moreover, the right of the Crown to be treated differently from other administrative bodies is increasingly difficult to justify.[2] The judges can do much to alleviate the defects, but in limitation of actions, at least, parliamentary intervention is required.

1 *H.E.L. op. cit.*, vol. 10, 357.
2 Cf. Report of the Committee on the Limitation of Actions, paras. 6, 13 and 25.

Chapter VII

PROCEDURAL LIMITATIONS ON THE
LIABILITY OF THE STATE

I. DISCOVERY OF DOCUMENTS[1]

At common law there were two separate rules affecting the production of documents by the Crown. First, the Crown, by virtue of its prerogative,[2] could not be subject to an order for discovery or interrogatories.[3] Nor did the rules of the Supreme Court made under the Judicature Acts bind the Crown.[4] Secondly, whether the Crown was party to litigation or not, it could refuse the production of a document if its production would be contrary to the public interest.

The leading case on the second rule is *Duncan* v. *Cammell Laird & Company Limited*[5] in which Viscount Simon, then Lord Chancellor, delivered the only speech after consultation with, and with the concurrence of, six other law lords. In a civil action the defendants had refused to produce the plan of a submarine made by them, because the First Lord of the Admiralty filed an affidavit objecting on the ground that it would be contrary to the public interest to produce it. Without inspecting the document, the House of Lords held that the document should not be produced. With the decision itself it seems difficult to quarrel, but the wide principles laid down in the judgment have been criticised.[6] Viscount Simon said:[7]

The principle to be applied in every case is that documents otherwise relevant and liable to production must not be produced if the public interest requires that they should be withheld. This test may be found to be

---

1 This discussion also relates *mutatis mutandis* to interrogatories.

2 *Attorney-General* v. *Newcastle-upon-Tyne Corporation*, [1897] 2 Q.B. 384 at 395 (*per* Rigby J.).

3 *Thomas* v. *Reg.*, [1874] L.R. 10 Q.B. 44; *The Helvetia* (1879) W.N. 48; *Crombie* v. *Rex*, [1923] 2 D.L.R. 542; *Michigan Fruit Co.* v. *Rex*, [1937] O.W.N. 685.

4 *In re La Société les Affréteurs Réunis and the Shipping Controller*, [1921] 3 K.B. 1 at 20 (*per* Greer J.).

5 [1942] A.C. 624. This decision conflicts with the earlier Privy Council case, *Robinson* v. *State of South Australia (No. 2)*, [1931] A.C. 704; but for New Zealand see s. 27, Crown Proceedings Act, 1950, and *Carroll* v. *Osburn*, [1952] N.Z.L.R. 763.

6 E.g. Note in 58 L.Q.R. (1942) 436; R. Pound, Note in 56 *Harvard L.R.* (1942) 806; D. P. Jamieson, 'Proceedings By and Against the Crown in Canada' in 26 *Can. B.R.* (1948) 373 at 386.

7 *Ubi supra*, 636.

satisfied either (*a*) by having regard to the contents of the particular document, or (*b*) by the fact that the document belongs to a class which, on grounds of public interest, must as a class be withheld from production.

Under (*b*) Viscount Simon supported the non-disclosure of Government files, not because anything secret was contained in the file the production of which was sought, but 'on the ground that the candour and completeness of such communications might be prejudiced if they were ever liable to be disclosed in subsequent litigation'.[1]

Further, the House overruled earlier cases[2] holding that the judge could probe an objection to produce by looking at the document. The objection of a head of a Government Department is conclusive, if validly taken. Not merely is the judge unable to look at the document, but if any party is about to put in evidence such a document it is the duty of the judge to stop him and refer the matter to the appropriate Government Department.[3] It should be noted that the 'judgment of the House in the present case is limited to civil actions, and the practice, as applied in criminal trials where an individual's life or liberty may be at stake, is not necessarily the same'.[4]

Viscount Simon laid down the principles which should be followed by ministers in deciding whether to object to production:[5]

> It is not a sufficient ground that the documents are 'State documents' or 'official' or are marked 'confidential'. It would not be a good ground that, if they were produced, the consequences might involve the department or the Government in parliamentary discussion or in public criticism, or might necessitate the attendance as witnesses or otherwise of officials who have pressing duties elsewhere. Neither would it be a good ground that production might tend to expose a want of efficiency in the administration or tend to lay the department open to claims for compensation. In a word, it is not enough that the minister of the department does not want to have the documents produced. The minister, in deciding whether it is his duty to object, should bear these considerations in mind, for he ought not to take the responsibility of withholding production except in cases where the public interest would otherwise be damnified, for example, where disclosure would be injurious to national defence, or to good diplomatic relations, or where the practice of keeping a class of documents secret is necessary for the proper functioning of the public service.

---

1 *Ibid.* 635.
2 E.g. *Asiatic Petroleum Co. Ltd.* v. *Anglo-Persian Oil Co. Ltd.*, [1916] 1 K.B. 822; *Spigelmann* v. *Hocker* (1932), 50 T.L.R. 87; but *ctra. Beatson* v. *Skene* (1860), 5 H. & N. 838; *Hughes* v. *Vargas* (1893), 9 T.L.R. 471; *In re Joseph Hargreaves Ltd.*, [1900] 1 Ch. 347.
3 *Hennessy* v. *Wright* (1898), 21 Q.B. 509 at 519; *ctra.* C. S. Emden, 'Documents Privileged in Public Interest' in 39 L.Q.R. (1923) 476 at 481.
4 *Ubi supra*, 633-4.   5 *Ibid.* 642.

It is becoming a common judicial practice to suggest to the executive how it should exercise its discretions.[1] These judicial suggestions can usually be dismissed as mere exhortations having no legal effect whatever; it is said that this rather platitudinous statement of Viscount Simon is 'not binding as a matter of law'.[2] Perhaps this assertion is too sweeping.[3] It is true that one of the main weaknesses of English administrative law is that the effectiveness of judicial control is often in proportion to the extent to which the administrator has given reasons for his action: the courts will not look behind the administrative decision but will quash it if it is bad on its face, as it will be if reasons wrong in law are given for the action.[4] It is submitted that it would be consistent with the *dicta* of Viscount Simon to apply that rule here. His view that the affidavit is conclusive means that the court cannot go beyond it. Yet he requires the objection to be 'validly taken' and emphasises that 'the decision ruling out such documents is the decision of the Judge'. If this emphasis has any point at all, it surely must mean that if in the affidavit itself the reasons given for non-production are wrong in law because contrary to these principles, the judge can declare the objection invalid and order production of the document. There are *dicta* in Commonwealth decisions to support this view.[5] Moving even further in this direction is the judgment of Lord Birnam in a Scottish case.[6] Commenting on these *dicta* of Viscount Simon, he said:

... the Lord Chancellor stressed the importance of remembering 'that the decision ruling out such documents is the decision of the judge'. If, as was maintained in the present case, the Court is bound by the opinion of the chairman of the Board of Control, I fail to see that it would be important or indeed accurate to attribute the decision to the judge.

Of course, so long as the Administration does not justify its actions by reasons, not even this interpretation will afford much protection to the aggrieved subject.

1 E.g. *Sebel Products Ltd.* v. *Commissioners of Customs and Excise*, [1949] Ch. 409 at 413 (*per* Vaisey J.).   2 Glanville Williams, *op. cit.* 130 n. 15.

3 Cf. Keir and Lawson *op. cit.* 508 that the judgment of Viscount Simon is 'the best statement of the law' on the topic.

4 E.g. *Hanson* v. *Radcliffe U.D.C.*, [1922] 2 Ch. 490: *Rex* v. *Ludlow ex parte Barnsley Corporation*, [1947] K.B. 634 at 638–40 (*per* Goddard L.C.J.); *Rex* v. *Northumberland Compensation Appeal Tribunal ex parte Shaw*, [1951] 1 K.B. 711.

5 *Griffin* v. *South Australia* (1925), 36 C.L.R. 378 at 397 (*per* Rich J.): 'Exceptional cases may arise where the claim is obviously futile and the Minister has misconceived the case and taken a mistaken view as to what documents are relevant'; *Sachs* v. *Minister of Justice*, [1934] A.D. 11 at 27 (*per* Tindall J.): 'In the absence of proof that the Minister's statement is not genuine or that it is frivolous or vexatious, the Court is bound by it.'

6 *M'Rae* v. *M'Rae*, [1947] S.C. 173 at 175; *Carmichael* v. *Scottish Co-operative Wholesale Society Ltd.*, [1934] S.L.T. 158 at 159 (*per* Lord Wark).

As the protection given by this second rule is so wide, the Crown Proceedings Act, 1947, was able to give the subject involved in litigation with the Crown the right to obtain an order for discovery against the Crown.[1] However, the rule in *Duncan* v. *Cammell Laird* is expressly saved by a proviso. If the Crown is a party to the litigation it need not disclose the existence of a document which it considers injurious to the public interest, and it may withhold from production any document the existence of which has been disclosed, by making an objection in the usual manner.[2] There seems no method by which the Crown can require a litigant in proceedings to which it is not a party not to disclose a document. Nothing in the Act affects the right of the court to see whether the objection is validly made.

In England, these rules have not been often at issue in judicial reviews of administrative adjudications. This is because so often the Executive has used its influence to prevent matters which involve the consultation of State documents from being regarded as justifiable at all. For example, when the Minister of Housing and Local Government, or rather the unknown (to the law) official in his Department decides under housing legislation whether to make a compulsory purchase order after the holding of a local inquiry, one cannot doubt that files of various technical aspects of the problem as well as the inspector's report will be consulted. Had the decision to make the order been treated as a judicial one, then the English courts, like those of the United States, would have had to determine whether objections to production of these files could be sustained. So long as there is no hearing at all, and not even the *audi alteram partem* rule of natural justice can be invoked, the further question of refusal to disclose files cannot come before the courts. Lord Greene, indeed, has said that the production of files in this type of case is 'alien to our whole conception of Government in this country'.[3] This judicial abstention from control of the Administration is severely criticised by American commentators on the relations between law and the Executive in England.[4]

The rules on discovery of State documents in the United States are not so clear-cut as in England, but are probably more satisfactory.[5]

1 S. 28 (1).   2 S. 28 (2), o. 31, r. 30.
3 *B. Johnson & Co. (Builders) Ltd.* v. *Minister of Health*, [1947] 2 All E.R. 395 at 401.
4 Schwartz, *Law and the Executive in Britain*, *passim*.
5 Wigmore, *op. cit.* VIII, § 2378 *et seq.*; Moore, *Federal Practice*, II, 2642; J. D. O'Reilly, 'Discovery against the United States—A New Aspect of Sovereign Immunity?', in 26 *North Carolina L.R.* (1942) 1; J. A. Pike and H. G. Fischer, 'Discovery against Federal Administrative Agencies' in 56 *Har. L.R.* (1943) 1125; R. Haydock Jr., 'Some Evidentiary Problems Posed by Atomic Energy Security Requirements' in 61 *Har. L.R.* (1948) 468; Note, 'Government Privilege against Disclosure of Official Documents' in 58 *Yale L.J.* (1949) 993.

Each head of a department is authorised by statute to 'prescribe regulations not inconsistent with law for the government of his department, the conduct of its officers and clerks, the distribution and performance of its business, and the custody, use and preservation of the records, papers and property appertaining to it'.[1] Departments have framed regulations forbidding their subordinates to disclose any documents without consent of the Attorney-General.[2] Wigmore[3] thought that the regulations were *ultra vires* but they have been upheld by the courts.[4] Although the Court of Claims may 'call upon any of the departments for any information or papers it may deem necessary' the head of the Department may refuse 'when in his opinion, such compliance would be injurious to the public interest'.[5]

The American courts have developed a theory of waiver. They have held that if the Government is instituting criminal proceedings, the accused is entitled to production of the government files and documents.[6] It is felt that it would be prejudicial to deny him access to material which the Government has been able to use in preparing its case. Here the departmental prohibitions are overridden.[7] It seems from the following judgment of Learned Hand J. that the degree to which the documents are relevant to the accused is estimated by the court.[8] Ordering the production of the reports of officials withheld from prisoners accused of conspiracy, he said:[9]

However none of these cases involved the prosecution of a crime consisting of the very matters recorded in the suppressed documents, or of matters nearly enough akin to make relevant the matters recorded. That appears to us to be a critical distinction. While we must accept it as lawful for a department of the Government to suppress documents, even when they will help determine controversies between third persons, we cannot agree that this should include their suppression in a criminal proceeding, founded upon those very dealings to which the documents relate, and whose criminality they will, or may, tend to exculpate.

1 R.S. S. 161.
2 11 Fed. Reg. 177A–107, sub-para. E.S. 51, 71.
3 *Op. cit.* 790.
4 *Ex p. Sackett* (1935), 74 F. 2nd 922; *U.S. ex rel. Touhy* v. *Ragen* (1951), 340 U.S. 462.
5 U.S. J.C. Tit. 28 para. 272.
6 *U.S.* v. *Krulewitch* (1944), 145 F. 2nd 76; refusal to produce in criminal proceedings is a breach of the 6th amendment—*U.S.* v. *Coplon* (1950), 185 F. 2nd 629.
7 *U.S.* v. *Beekman* (1946), 155 F. 2nd 580 at 584 (per Frank J.); the Supreme Court left this open in *U.S. ex rel. Touhy* v. *Ragen* n. 4 *supra*; cf. *Bowman Dairy Co.* v. *U.S.* (1951), 71 S.C. 675.
8 Approved by Wigmore, *op. cit.* 1947 Supplement, 138.
9 *U.S.* v. *Andolschek* (1944), 142 F. 2nd 503.

The same right to production is given to an applicant for Habeas Corpus, statutory bar notwithstanding.[1]

Questions of discovery have become very important in American administrative law, and may become so in England if the setting up of the Monopolies and Restrictive Practices Commission should herald the use of the commission on the American model as an instrument of administrative control. The following are typical American problems. The Federal Trade Commission seeks an injunction against a corporation to restrain it from carrying on an unfair trade practice. The corporation wants access to the files of the agency, to learn in advance details of the particular transactions relied on, and to discover how much the agency knows. Secondly, on a Government contract there is a report by an inspector that the work is below specification, a copy of which the contractor, who complains of breach of contract, seeks. Of course, these problems may raise other issues in the law of discovery: that a party shall not be required to disclose material relevant solely to his own case, that 'fishing' is forbidden, or that the knowledge is already possessed by the applicant, but the plea of 'state secrets' will in itself not excuse a Department from disclosing information within its knowledge.[2] More controversial is the question whether or not files can also be demanded. The cases are conflicting,[3] and it may be that if the relevance of the files is proved, and if no other privilege prevents it, the Government must produce them.

None the less, if the court finds that the document is an international or military secret of state then it will always uphold an objection to production. It cannot be stated with certainty what are the limits of these privileged State secrets, but the tendency is to limit them to 'pending international negotiations or military precautions against foreign enemies'.[4] For example, in *Robinson* v. *U.S.*[5] the Treasury refused to produce the correspondence relating to a suit for breach of contract, and relied on an opinion of the Attorney-General[6] that the certificate of the head of the Department was conclusive. Ordering production the court said:[7]

The power given to a head of a department to comply with a call for information or papers is not an arbitrary power to be exercised at will and to make the law and principle in regard to these calls differ in the case of

1 *U.S.* v. *Watkins* (1946), 67 F. Supp. 556.
2 *Fleming* v. *Bernardi* (1941), 1 F.R.D. 624; cf. *U.S.* v. *Cotton Valley Operators Committee* (1949), 9 F.R.D. 719.
3 *Walling* v. *Comet Carriers Inc.* (1944), 3 F.R.D. 442; *U.S.* v. *General Motors Corp.* (1942), 2 F.R.D. 528; *Walling* v. *Twyffort Inc.* (1947), 158 F. 2nd 944; *Bowles* v. *Ackerman* (1945), 4 F.R.D. 260.
4 Wigmore, *op. cit.* 2378a.   5 (1915), 50 Ct. Cl. 159.
6 (1871), 130 Op. 539.   7 *Ubi supra*, 165.

one department from what it would be in that of another. It is a legal discretion to be exercised under the circumstances of a particular case.

At the same time, great weight will be given to the opinion of the departmental head.[1] In *Crosby* v. *Pacific Steamship Lines*[2] an agent sued for commission on the sale of ships to the British Ministry of War Transport. An official of that Ministry refused to produce letters which determined whether there had been an effective agency. Haney J., ordering the letters to be produced, said:[3] 'Finally, refusal would be justified only when the public interest would suffer by disclosure. Does this mean that Walsh (the British official) is the final authority on that point? All reason says that the question is one for the court to determine.'

The courts recently have gone to considerable lengths to hold that the Government is an interested party, thus bringing in the principle of waiver. In *Zimmerman* v. *Poindexter*[4] the plaintiff sued the ex-Governor of Hawaii for false imprisonment, and sought discovery from an Army officer of confidential reports made by the Federal Bureau of Investigation. Because of the federal element in the case, and because United States attorneys represented the defendant (although the United States had no pecuniary interest in the suit) the court held that this was not a private suit and ordered production of the reports.[5]

It is clear that the United States courts are far less willing than the English courts to support a plea of privilege, and do not share the unwillingness of the latter to look themselves at the documents.

The Memorandum to the Crown Proceedings Bill justified section 28 (2) as follows:[6] '...the object of this provision is to maintain that degree of secrecy which is essential to protect the interests of the community in regard to defence, foreign relations, and related matters.' It would be generally agreed that a provision which achieved that and no more would be unobjectionable. The sponsors of this bill could scarcely maintain that it covers this and no more. If that were the object of it, why did the Government refuse to adopt the suggestions made on the second reading in the House of Commons that 'public security' or 'public safety' or 'defence of the realm' be substituted for 'public interest'?[7] Objection was also made to the fact that departments would determine conclusively whether the matter was one of 'public interest'. The Government spokesmen were at some pains to assure Parliament that the power would

---

1 *Pollen* v. *Ford Instrument Co.* (1939), 26 F. Supp. 583.
2 (1943), 133 F. 2nd 470.
3 *Ibid.* 475.   4 (1947), 74 F. Supp. 933.
5 *Ibid.* 936.   6 At ii.
7 Hansard, 5s. vol. 439, col. 1727-8.

not be abused. For instance, the Attorney-General said:[1] 'If a Minister, having considered the matter personally, is not able to decide that it is essential that a document should be withheld, he will disclose it along with all the other documents relevant to the case.' The Attorney-General added that during the tenure of that Government no document had been withheld except on the personal judgment of the Minister concerned. The question arises whether it is wise to couch legislation in general terms in reliance on assurances by Government spokesmen that advantage will not be taken of that general language. The statements of intention by one set of Government spokesmen are not binding on a subsequent Government: surely there was a need for more restrictive drafting. Are we to believe that at present the Minister does consider each case separately, that no instructions of a general nature to refuse production have been given to officers in particular Departments, that, for example, a factory inspector always gets a personal decision from the Minister before refusing production of some information material to litigation concerning an industrial accident?[2]

'Public interest' can be a large umbrella for the most varied of activities. It is instructive to examine some of the cases in which the plea has been made by the Crown.

Many of them have been libel actions based on official reports. Typical is *Beatson* v. *Skene*,[3] a libel action arising from a quarrel between two army officers, in which the production of correspondence between the plaintiff and the War Office and of minutes of a military inquiry was refused. Pollock C.B. said:[4]

...it cannot be laid down that all public documents, including treaties with foreign powers, and all the correspondence that may precede or accompany them, and all communications to the heads of departments, are to be produced and made public whenever a suitor in a court of justice thinks that his case requires such production. It is manifest (we think) that there must be a limit to the duty or the power of compelling the production of papers which are connected with acts of State.

The irrelevance of most of this to the case in issue is obvious; and the court actually allowed secondary evidence of the facts. Another illuminating case is *West* v. *West*,[5] an action against a father-in-law whose slanderous conversations with the Lord Chamberlain about the plaintiff

---

1 *Ibid.* col. 1686.
2 In New Zealand (see 166 *supra* n. 5) it has been held that the Minister himself must object except in the rare case where it is only practicable for the Head of the Department to do so; *Hiroa Mariu* v. *Hutt Timber and Hardware Co.*, [1950] N.Z.L.R. 458.
3 (1860), 5 H. & N. 838.   4 *Ibid.* 852–3.   5 (1911), 27 T.L.R. 476.

had caused her no longer to be invited to Court balls. The refusal of the
Lord Chamberlain to disclose these important 'State secrets' was upheld
by the court. It would be fair to say that the usual consequence of the
upholding of State privileges in these actions has been to enable an individual, often a civil servant, to evade on technical grounds a liability in
tort.[1]

In several divorce suits the production of medical records of soldiers has
been requested. In *Anthony v. Anthony*,[2] for example, the issue was
whether the husband had contracted syphilis during military service. Both
parties wanted his military records to be produced, but the court took the
War Office view that the public interest was best served by not producing
them.[3] This refusal to produce medical records will be increasingly
important if the Ministry of Health refuse to produce the medical records
which doctors must supply to it under the National Health Service Act,
1946.[4]

A liquidator who had taken out a misfeasance summons against
directors was not allowed to have the balance sheets of the company when
they were in the hands of the Inland Revenue.[5] The refusal of the
Minister of Transport in an action for damages against a railway company
arising out of a railway accident to let a plaintiff have access to a report on
the accident sent by the defendants was upheld,[6] although his predecessor,
the Board of Trade, had never withheld them from litigants.[7] The protests
of the judge at the lack of assistance from the Local Government Board were
unavailing in an action for nuisance caused by a smallpox hospital, when
the report of the inspector of the board was withheld.[8] In a recent Australian
case,[9] it was material to a private suitor to establish at what time a telephone
call had been made to a police station. Relying on *Duncan v. Cammell Laird*,
it was held that the production of this State secret, the local police station
telephone book, was injurious to the public interest. It cannot be denied
that the law should not allow the production of documents if to do so
would endanger either public safety, or indeed the public interest. But is

1 *Home v. Bentinck* (1820), 2 B. & B. 130; *Wyatt v. Gore* (1816), Holt (H.P.) 299;
Bradley v. M'Intosh (1884), 5 Ont. R. 227.
2 (1919), 35 T.L.R. 559.
3 Cf. *King v. King*, [1944] Q.W.N. (Aust.) 25.
4 National Health Service (General Medical and Pharmaceutical Services) Regulations 1948 (S. 1. 1948, No. 506) as amended; and G. D. Nokes, 'Professional Privilege'
in 66 L.Q.R. (1950) 88.
5 *In re Joseph Hargreaves Ltd.*, [1900] 1 Ch. 347.
6 *Ankin v. L.N.E.R.*, [1930] 1 K.B. 527.
7 *Woolley v. North London Ry. Co.* (1869), 1 L.R. 4 C.P. 602.
8 *Attorney-General v. Nottingham Corporation*, [1904] 1 Ch. 673.
9 *Seeney v. Seeney*, [1945] Q.W.N. 20.

not the consideration of the public interest afforded by our present system a one-sided one? The executive and, one fears, the judicial attitude in England may be summed up in the words of Pollock C.B.:[1] '...the general public interest must be considered paramount to the individual interest of a suitor in a court of justice.' A more precise analysis of this 'public interest' is called for. There is a public interest in the general security and in public safety which clearly will justify the withholding of military secrets. As Pound has said,[2] this interest is 'paramount', and, therefore, documents relating to defence or international affairs ought to be withheld.

It could be argued, however, that the interest in political institutions buttresses the claimed privilege, even beyond the sphere of international and military affairs. Viscount Simon justifies the privileges attaching to documents as a class, not because of their contents, but because 'the candour and completeness of such communications might be prejudiced if they were ever liable to be disclosed'.[3] This argument might be less open to objection if the secrecy were indispensable for inducing freedom of official communication or efficacy in the transaction of official business and if the secret should have remained inviolable.[4] Yet even thus restricted it calls for comment. Is it proved that employees make reports less honestly if they think that there is the slightest possibility of some one other than their employers seeing them at some future time? And if the argument has substance, is it not also applicable to the employees of public authorities other than the Crown, in respect of whom there is no similar privilege?[5] Is it true that 'Government-servants are reluctant to put their observations into writing if they are likely to be produced in a court of law'?[6]

One might assume, from the approach of Viscount Simon and other English judges, that the public interest is a simple concept consisting of some one element, which, when opposed by some conflicting private interest, shall always be supreme, something *ab extra*, which 'operates from outside the law as a paramount censor of rules of law and legal rights'.[7] That English judges have in the past viewed public policy in the field of

1 *Beatson* v. *Skene* (1860), 5 H. & N. at 853.
2 R. Pound, 'A Survey of Social Interests' in 57 *Har. L.R.* (1943) 1 at 17; cf. *Dusfresne Construction Co. Ltd.* v. *Rex*, [1935] Ex. 77 at 85 (*per* Angers J.).
3 *Duncan's Case* at 635.   4 Wigmore, *op. cit.* §237a.
5 *Blackpool Corporation* v. *Locker*, [1948] 1 K.B. 349 at 380 (*per* Scott L.J.): 'Public interest is, from the point of view of English justice, a regrettable and sometimes dangerous form of privilege, though at times unavoidable.'
6 Sir Thomas Inskip, 'Proceedings by and against the Crown' in 4 *Camb. L.J.* (1930) 1 at 10.
7 Stone, *op. cit.* 494.

176 Governmental Liability

contract in this light is a commonplace.[1] Yet it is clear that in a given case there may be several public interests involved, often conflicting ones. Is there not a public interest in the preservation of free political institutions against the acts of arbitrary political authority? Moreover, the suggestion, implicit in Viscount Simon's speech, that there is an antipathy between public and private interests, is surely misleading. If the private interest is an interest in securing an adequate remedy for a tort whether committed by a civil servant or otherwise, then it is also the public interest that justice should be administered so that the innocent are compensated for the wrongs done to them by their fellows.

It is contended, therefore, that sometimes there may be an overriding public interest in the non-disclosure of public documents, that the extent of that interest varies from case to case, and it will normally appertain only to defence and diplomatic matters, that often there are conflicting public interests, and that a decision whether a document is to be produced should only be made after these conflicting interests have been weighed. The *dictum* of Viscount Simon himself that 'in criminal trials where an individual's life or liberty may be at stake, it is not necessarily the same' is some recognition of the soundness of this reasoning.[2]

It might be objected that many of these arguments have lost their force in view of the governmental assurances on the passing of the Crown Proceedings Act, and that the cases cited have been without exception pre-Act ones. Two recent newspaper reports of cases, one of which the writer has been able to verify, indicate that little change in governmental attitude is to be expected. In one,[3] a wife cross-petitioned against her husband for divorce on the ground that he had service medical treatment for venereal disease during military service abroad. The War Office refused the request of the husband, who indignantly denied the allegation, that it should produce his medical history sheet, on the ground that it was contrary to the public interest. Then the wife herself made inquiries, and was shown the very document which it was prejudicial to the public interest to produce to the court, and, satisfied that her charge was groundless, withdrew her cross-petition. In the other case,[4] an inquest was held on an ex-serviceman, who had dropped dead on a special drill course. A pathologist gave evidence that deceased's heart was twice its normal size, and that to take such a drill course was 'the worst thing he could have done in his condition'. At the coroner's request, an army officer attended the

1 Lord Wright, 'Public Policy' in *Legal Essays and Addresses*, 66–95; Stone, *op. cit.* ch. 20 *passim*.   2 See p. 167 *supra*.
3 *Evening News* newspaper (London), 25 July 1949.
4 *Manchester Guardian* newspaper, 18 Jan. 1950; 2 Feb. 1950; see also 6 December 1952 for another example.

inquest with the army medical sheet of deceased, but, acting on instructions from the War Office, refused to disclose the document, the protests of the Coroner notwithstanding.

The next question to be answered is who should determine this issue of public interest, the judge or the Minister? The various reasons why the House of Lords has held that it must be the Minister will now be examined. The *dicta* of Pollock C.B.[1] that a judge could only consider the matter in public and that this is a matter for private consideration only were quoted with apparent approval by Viscount Simon.[2] It is, of course, a sound principle that publicity assists impartial governmental administration. That there are desirable limits to the application of that principle should not, as here, be made the pretext for an increase in arbitrary action. An impartial judge as well as a Minister biased in favour of the Department can adjudicate in private, if necessary. Secondly, several government spokesmen on the Crown Proceedings Bill, and Viscount Simon in the *Duncan Case* have explained that the judge would, if he were to see the documents, communicate with one party to the exclusion of the other, 'and it is a first principle of justice that the judge should have no dealings on the matter in hand with one litigant save in the presence of and to the equal knowledge of the other'.[3] But will the other party consider himself thereby aggrieved if the only alternative is a conclusive determination by a political chief from whom there is no appeal?

Surely the crucial issue is, which is most competent to assess the public interest, the Executive or the Judiciary? Viscount Simon has no doubt that it is the Executive. It is, however, to be noted that this view seems to rest on the assumption that departmental interest and public interest are one. The emphasis is on 'detriment to the public service', 'exigencies of the public service'.[4] No attempt was made to balance competing interests. To concede that the Executive is the best judge of its own interests is not to agree that it can best weigh the several social interests involved in deciding whether evidence on a particular fact in a particular case should be given. Or, as an American writer, considering some legal problems of atomic energy, has said, the problem is one of balancing a 'court's historical "expertness" in protecting individual rights' with 'its "inexpertness" in the technical problems of atomic energy'.[5] The War Office at least in part recognises the problem by its statement that its policy is to disclose service records in serious criminal cases only.[6] Can this rule-of-thumb

---

1 *Beatson* v. *Skene, ubi supra*, 853.   2 *Ubi supra*, 639.
3 *Ibid.* 640–1.
4 *Ibid.* 640, citing with approval *Admiralty Commissioners* v. *Aberdeen Steam Trawling and Fishing Co. Ltd.*, [1909] S.C. 335 at 340.
5 Haydock, *op. cit.* 475.   6 See case cited 176, n. 3 *supra*.

test, which ignores the materiality of the evidence, and attaches so little importance to civil and non-serious criminal cases, be accepted as an adequate appreciation of social interests?

The Attorney-General on the second reading of the Crown Proceedings Bill argued that where 'policy' is concerned 'it is for Ministers and not for the courts to judge and the Ministers must discharge their responsibilities under the control of Parliament'.[1] Here, of course, is one of the fundamental problems of administrative law. It is a resuscitation of the view of the Committee on Ministers' Powers that decisions may involve three elements, law, fact and policy, and that where the third is involved, then it is for the Executive to decide.[2] This 'hoary'[3] distinction is still not abandoned by some. To replace the word 'policy' by 'discretion' clarifies the matter. Decisions by the courts can involve at any time law, fact and discretion in varying proportions. No one denies that a judge exercises discretion when deciding whether to grant a decree *nisi* to a petitioner for divorce who confesses his own adultery. What determines whether the court can handle a matter involving discretion is the degree of discretion involved. It may be so wide that it is exclusively a matter for the Executive. The word 'policy' must not be used as a blanket justifying the executive claim to a monopoly of discretionary decisions by reliance on the constitutional maxim of political responsibility. One can agree that it was for the Minister of Town and Country Planning to decide in his discretion whether Stevenage was to be a New Town, without at the same time agreeing that the Executive must decide whether documents are to be produced in litigation before the ordinary courts.

Viscount Simon further thought that the judges were unsuited to the task because they 'would need to learn the methods of the Department, and that would be perfectly impracticable'.[4] Implicit in this again is the view that it is the departmental interest that matters, but discounting that implication, it seems within the competence of a judge to learn the reasons which the Executive has to support its argument that a document should not be produced. Judges grapple with facts more technical than these. Nor does the assertion that matters of State are too confidential to be communicated to the judges seem a cogent reason for denying judicial competence. These documents are, after all, seen by many civil servants. Is a High Court judge to be trusted less with a serviceman's medical sheet than the lance-corporal in the orderly room, or the sick-quarters orderly?

1 Hansard, 5s. vol. 439, no. 135, col. 1691.
2 73.
3 Jennings, *op. cit.* in 10 *Public Administration* (1932) 333 at 345.
4 Hansard, vol. 146, col. 929.

It has also been pointed out that some judges themselves have thought that they could not decide these matters. Perhaps the observations of a member of the House of Commons are in point.[1] '...it is perfectly natural for judges to say: "This is an enormous responsibility. Why should it be pushed on to us? We have quite enough work to do as it is." I do not think judges are themselves the best people to decide whether they should undertake this duty....' There seems then no good reason why the judge should not decide whether the disclosure of the existence or contents of a document is injurious to the public interest. It remains to consider what legislative changes should be made to effect this reform. The French rule that only the *Conseil d'Etat*, and not the parties, can demand production of the evidence seems unsatisfactory. The provisions contained in the Model Code of Evidence drawn up by the American Law Institute [2] deserve more detailed study.

A distinction is there drawn between 'secret of State' and 'official information'. The former is defined as 'information not open or theretofore officially disclosed to the public concerning the military or naval organisation or plans of the United States, or a State or Territory, or concerning international relations'. 'Official information' means 'information not open or theretofore officially disclosed to the public relating to internal affairs of this State or of the United States acquired by a public official...in the course of his duty...'. Unless either the judge finds that it is not a 'secret of State', or the head of the Department none the less consents to its disclosure, a secret of State must not be disclosed, and a judge is empowered to prevent its disclosure even if both parties are willing. 'Official information' is not to be disclosed if the judge finds that it is 'official information' and if also its disclosure 'will be harmful to the interests of the Government of which the witness is an officer in its governmental capacity'.

This distinction between 'secret of State' and 'official information' is a sound one. It recognises that the paramount interest in security requires that secrets of State should be *ipso facto* free from disclosure at the discretion of the Executive. Not so satisfactory is the provision relating to 'official information'. It revives the governmental/proprietary distinction which has bedevilled administrative law in civil countries since the Romans developed *fiscus*, which jurists have been striving to eradicate from American Local Government law,[3] and from which England has been mercifully free. There would have been no need to include it had the rule

---

1 Hansard, vol. 439, col. 1712.
2 (Philadelphia, 1942), Rules 227 and 228.
3 P. 16 *supra*.

dealt with the interests of the public instead of those of the Government. What is called for is a balancing of the conflicting interests. Military and diplomatic secrets apart, there is no justification for the assumption that governmental interest overrides all others. Then the judge could decide whether the production of any official information was injurious to the public interest. The claim to non-disclosure could be made by affidavit, and if a party objected, the matter could be raised on an *ex parte* application.[1] The documents and a detailed statement of reasons for non-disclosure could be forwarded under seal to the judge who would decide in his private room whether the document should be produced. This procedure would seem not to imperil the public security in any way, and would at the same time prevent excessive interference with the administration of justice.

2. TRIAL AT BAR

At common law the Crown had the right, in any case in which it was interested, to demand a trial at bar before a Divisional Court of the King's Bench Division. It seems that this right, originally enjoyed by all subjects, is now the Crown's right alone, because statutes taking it away from subjects did not bind the Crown.[2] For the same reason the Crown had a right at common law, strengthened by the Crown Suits Act, 1865,[3] to choice of venue. These rights have been held to exist not merely when the Crown is a litigant but also 'if an executive officer of the Government...is charged with maladministration in his official capacity'.[4]

The Crown Proceedings Act[5] provides that nothing in the Act shall prejudice these rights. The justification for these privileges is said to be 'the administrative difficulties which Government departments would experience if they had to make their records available elsewhere than in London'.[6] Nevertheless, they are much criticised.[7] Perhaps the court may take into account the conduct of the Crown in these matters when awarding costs.[8]

3. COSTS

At common law the Crown received but did not pay costs. Since 1855 inroads have been made in that rule, culminating in the Administration of Justice (Miscellaneous Provisions) Act, 1933, which provided that the

---

1 Cf. E. F. Iwi, Letter to *The Times* newspaper, 19 Feb. 1947.
2 *Attorney-General* v. *Churchill* (1841), 8 M. & W. 171 at 193.
3 S. 46.
4 *Dixon* v. *Farrer* (1886), 17 Q.B. 658 at 661 (*per* Field J.); (1887) 18 Q.B. 43.
5 S. 19 (3); s. 40 (2).   6 Bickford Smith, *op. cit.* 41.
7 *E.g.* Glanville Williams, *op. cit.* 127.   8 S. 19 (2).

Crown should pay and receive costs like an ordinary subject.[1] On the other hand, the United States receives but does not pay costs under the Tucker Act. The Federal Tort Claims Act allows costs to the successful litigant, but serious limits are imposed on the amount allowed for attorneys' fees in these costs. Unless a statute expressly so provides the United States is not liable for costs.[2]

One point of difficulty with regard to costs arises under the Public Authorities Protection Act, 1893.[3] That Act provided that in certain circumstances plaintiffs suing public authorities under the Act should pay solicitor and client costs. Since the Crown is an authority under the Act, the question arises whether the general provisions of the 1933 Act that costs awarded to the Crown shall be based on the same rules as those governing the award of costs to the private individual may be held to have repealed *pro tanto* the 1893 statute.

4. INTEREST

The ordinary rules as to interest on judgment debts, or costs, and even on damages for the period before judgment, apply to the Crown.[4] In the United States interest before judgment is not given against the United States.[5]

5. COUNTERCLAIMS AND SET-OFF

It was doubtful whether at common law there was a right of set-off against the Crown.[6] The Act now allows a subject sued by the Crown those rights of set-off and counter-claim which he would enjoy against other subjects.[7] These rights are not exercisable if the proceeding or the set-off or counterclaim arises out of a claim to repayment in respect of taxes, duties or penalties. This exception may work harshly, for example, a citizen paying Schedule A tax in one district and making his Schedule E return in another is denied the right to counter-claim in respect of a repayment when sued for the recovery of tax.

The rights of counter-claim of those sued by the United States are seriously restricted. An affirmative money claim must be one over which the court could have exercised jurisdiction in an original suit.[8] Any

1 23 & 24 Geo. V, c. 36, s. 7; in practice the Crown does not regularly take costs.
2 § 2412 (a); *Ewing* v. *Gardner* (1951), 71 J.C. 684.
3 56 & 57 Vict. c. 61, s. 1.   4 S. 24.
5 § 2674.
6 See F. E. Farrer, 'Equitable Set-Off against the Crown' in 72 *Solicitors' Journal* (1928) 262.   7 S. 38 (2).
8 *U.S.* v. *Shaw* (1940), 309 U.S. 495.

counter-claim must arise out of the same transaction or be one over which
the court would have had original jurisdiction.[1] Therefore, a tort by the
United States can be the subject-matter of a counter-claim only when the
Government bases its case on the same cause of action and the amount of
the counter-claim is such that a judgment against the United States would
result.[2]

6. ENFORCEMENT OF JUDGMENT[3]

A. *Execution*

'...No execution can issue against the Crown. The petitioner remains
dependent upon a combination of good-will and the moral pressure he may
hope to secure from public opinion.'[4] The rule is the same in the United
States and the Commonwealth.[5] A direction by Congress to refer a case
already decided by the Court of Claims to a Commission for further facts
in order that Congress could decide whether to find the judgment
awarded against the United States has been held valid: there was held to be
a sharp distinction between a judgment and the decision whether to
discharge it.[6] The Crown Proceedings Act provides that the appropriate Department shall pay the sum stated on the certificate or judgment
awarded against the Crown. This statutory duty is not enforceable,
because section 2 (2) only makes the Crown liable for breach of 'a statutory duty which is binding also upon persons other than the Crown and
its officers'.

This immunity is said to be justified on several grounds. It is argued
that it would be inconsistent with sovereignty and the separation of
powers to permit execution.[7] The substantial objection is that interference
with public property would hamper the State in the performance of its
public duties. At the same time, it would not be impossible to allow it,
with the consent of the court, against specified property of an unimportant
character.[8] There is a precedent in France where the unsatisfied judgment

1 *U.S.* v. *U.S. Fidelity & Guaranty Co.* (1940), 309 U.S. 506.
2 For a criticism of this judicial attitude, see Note, 'Governmental Immunity from
Counterclaims', in 50 *Col. L.R.* (1950) 505.
3 For a detailed account, see H. Street, 'The Provision of Funds in Satisfaction of
Governmental Liabilities' in 8 *U.T.L.J.* (1949) 32.
4 H. J. Laski, 'The Responsibility of the State in England', in 32 *Har. L.R.* (1919)
447 at 455.
5 S. 32 Crown Suits Act, 1908 (New Zealand); ss. 64–6 Judiciary Acts, 1903–33
(Commonwealth of Australia); Crown Suits Act, 1947 (Western Australia). See
E. Freund, 'Private Claims against the State', in 8 *P.S.Q.* (1893) 625 at 639; C.
Martindale, 'The State and its Creditors', in 7 *Southern L.R.* (1882) 544 at 548.
6 *Pocono Pines Assembly Hotels Co.* v. *U.S.* (1930), 69 Ct. Cl. 91.
7 *Briggs* v. *Life Boats* (1865), 11 Allen (U.S.) 157 at 162–3.
8 Cf. Report of the Committee of the Canadian Bar Association on Provincial
Legislation and Law Reform, 1936.

creditor of certain administrative bodies can enforce execution and sale, the property chosen being that the sale of which is least prejudicial to the public interest.[1]

B. *Attachment*

The rules of court authorising garnishee proceedings have been thought inapplicable to the Crown because of the presumption that the Crown is not bound by legislation in which it is not named.[2] Section 25 (4) of the Crown Proceedings Act now prohibits in Great Britain the use of attachment as a means of enforcing a judgment against the Crown, although, subject to certain exceptions, the Act reverses the common-law rule[3] that monies in the hands of the Crown are not attachable.[4]

It is instructive to look at the system devised by Rumania during the 1920's.[5] By a law of 1925[6] the *Cour de Cassation* was empowered to direct a modified form of execution against the Government, when the latter did not comply, within a specified period, with a pecuniary judgment delivered against it. The judgment creditor was allowed to attach any funds due to the Government in the hands of a citizen or any rents owed by tenants of Government property. This interesting measure has met with approval from French jurists.[7]

C. *Process against Officials*

It will be recalled that mandamus is not an effective means of compelling the payment of money by officials.[8]

The State of New York has devised what is apparently an effective method of enforcing payment. The State budget annually provides in advance a lump sum for judgments against the State. After the comptroller has paid out the whole of this allotted sum, he purchases any further judgments, paying claimants, as an investment for the sinking fund of the State pursuant to law; and when a new appropriation is available, these

---

1 Fayolle, *La Force Exécutoire des Décisions de Justice à l'Encontre des Administrations Publiques*, 170 *et seq.*; Berthélemy, 'L'Obligation de Faire ou de ne pas Faire et son Exécution dans le Droit Public', in 29 *R.D.P.* (1912) at 513.
2 Robertson, *op. cit.* 611.
3 F. F. Knight, 'Attachment of Monies in the Hands of the Crown' in 3 *Aust. L.J.* (1930) 323 and cases there cited.
4 S. 27.
5 Negulesco, *Traité de Droit Administratif*, 349.
6 Art. 13 of 'La loi de contentieux administratif' of 23 Dec. 1925.
7 E.g. G. Tari, *Des Moyens d'assurer l'Exéxution des Jugements Rendus contre l'Administration* (Paris, 1933).
8 P. 138 *supra*.

sinking funds are reimbursed with interest as allowed by law when computing interest for judgments.[1] Moreover, mandamus is available against the comptroller if he does not so pay a claimant.[2] This scheme avoids the necessity of exercising judicial process against the State, and at the same time gives the subject a legal right to compel payment by the official.

France also affords the citizen a remedy against officers. A minister refusing without good cause to honour a judgment against the Government may be sued for his *faute personnelle* in the civil courts.[3] If he should refuse to execute when required to do so by the *Conseil d'Etat* he is further liable to civil proceedings.[4]

1 J. W. McDonald, 'Court of Claims: The Administration of a Tort Liability Law in New York' in 9 *L.C.P.* (1942) 262 at 279; s 20 (7), (8), Court of Claims Act, 1939; New York State Finance Law, s. 98 (4).
2 Opinions of Attorney-General (New York, 1916) at 70.
3 Appleton, *op. cit.* 335.
4 A. Defert, *L'Exécution des Jugements contre les Personnes Morales du Droit Administratif*, 241.

CONCLUSION

The preceding chapters show that the royal immunities, both substantive and procedural, originated in a feudal background as prerogatives personal to the King. With the growth of the State, the distinction between the King in his personal capacity, and the Crown as the governmental organ, was obscured by an imperfectly understood theory of a royal corporation sole.[1] Immunity was reinforced by theories of divine right of kings and of sovereignty. The settlers in the United States and the Commonwealth, heedless of the reasons for the functioning of these immunities, nevertheless carried the same immunities with them to their newly formed States along with the rest of the common law. The vast increase of administration in nineteenth-century England led to the division of administrative bodies into two classes, the one subject to common law and the other nestling under the umbrella of the Crown and virtually free from legal liability. Many European countries, with France in the van, deprived administrative bodies of the hard core of their immunities, and, imbued with civil law notions of a separation between private and public law, subjected all administrative organs to a uniform body of public law administered by administrative courts. The increasing interference by the State with the activities of the citizen made some alteration in the legal position of Anglo-American Governments inevitable. This has taken the form of subjecting them haltingly, and with serious reservations, to private law. Other public authorities have remained, meanwhile, subject to private law to the same extent, substantially, as the private citizen. Their very nature as organs of administration has compelled some changes from private law, but these have not been accompanied by any recognition in theory that they are or should be placed in a category separate from private individuals. There is, then, no separate law of administrative liability, although there are very important differences between the liability of governmental and other public bodies. No satisfactory reasons for these differences are adduced; most of them are either personal prerogative powers or reservations insisted on by the Executive as the price of their acquiescence in the imposition of statutory liability. Judges too, at least in the United Kingdom, appear to have thought it indelicate to attempt to tamper with these privileges, even though the issues involved are in no sense personal to the reigning monarch.

It is suggested that the Anglo-American countries ought to copy the French by subjecting all administrative authorities to a uniform law. In

1 Maitland, *Collected Papers*, III, 246-7.

so far as private law rules are appropriate there is no reason why those rules should not be adopted. In the residuary circumstances where private law is inadequate, then uniform principles of public law in accordance with the proposals made herein[1] should be evolved.[2] There seems no need for separate administrative courts, which would be out of harmony with Anglo-American constitutional notions of the judges as independent persons securing a due observance of the law by the legislative and executive organs of state.

It may be that the content of the changes ought not to be finally and fully decided until more statistical data about governmental liability have been made available. English lawyers, both inside the courts and outside, have long been distrustful of social scientists; but that the Committee on Limitation of Actions should use statistical evidence from the Treasury Solicitor was an encouraging step in the right direction. What are wanted are surveys similar to those made in California in the field of municipal liability:[3] e.g. what claims are made, for what sums, how many and in what amounts are paid; what types of activity give rise to claims. Similarly, in the field of contract, there is a lack of information, for example, on the attitude of contractors to present arrangements, what disputes go to administration and what decisions are reached there, and how approved torts are settled.

This comparative survey of the field of State liability shows that English law has not yet made a full contribution to the reconciliation of the freedom of the individual and the authority of the State. Much reform is called for before the individual has adequate legal protection against the Administration. The law's part in settling this conflict of authority and freedom which now confronts democracy is probably an easier one than that of many of the other social sciences. The lawyer at least should not fail to perform his share of the task.

1 *Passim*, but see in particular the proposals in tort at 76 *et seq.*
2 Paton, *op. cit.* VI.
3 See 9 *L. & C.P.* (1942) *passim.*

LIST OF WORKS CITED

PAGE

Allen, C. K., *Law and Orders* (London, 1945) 5, 29, 132, 140

Ambrose, T. R., 'Claims against the Crown' in 8 *Australian L.J.* (1935) 214 6

Anderson, L. L., 'Tort and Implied Contract Liability of the Federal
Government' in 30 *Minnesota L.R.* (1946) 133 11, 122, 127

—— 'The Disputes Article in Government Contracts' in 44 *Michigan L.R.*
(1945) 211 101

Andréades, S., *La Juridiction Administrative en Grèce* (Paris, 1932) 22

Anson, Sir William, *The Law and Custom of the Constitution*, vol. 2 (4th ed.
Sir Arthur Keith, Oxford, 1935) 116

Anstey, T. C., *Letter to Lord Cottenham as to the Petition of Right* (London,
1845) 3

Appleton, J., *Traité Elémentaire de Contentieux Administratif* (Paris, 1927)
60, 73, 82, 83, 184

Arlet, *De la Responsabilité de l'Etat Législateur* (Bordeaux, 1908) 70

Aron, H. G., 'Federal Tort Claims Act' in 33 *American Bar Association Journal*
(1947) 226 130

Aucoc, L., *Conférences sur l'Administration et le Droit Administratif* (Paris,
1869) 73

Bacon, M., *New Abridgement of the Law* (7th ed.; London, 1832) 146

Baecque, F. de, 'Règles de la Jurisprudence Administrative Relatives à la
Réparation du Préjudice en Cas en Mise en Œuvre de la Responsabilité
de la Puissance Publique' in 60 *Revue de Droit Public* (1944) 197 62, 63

Baer, H. R., 'Suing Uncle Sam in Tort' in 29 *North Carolina L.R.* (1946)
119 at 126 54

Barlow, T. B., *The South African Law of Vicarious Liability in Delict
and a Comparison of the Principles of Other Legal Systems* (Capetown,
1939) 7

Barnes, Sir Thomas, 'The Crown Proceedings Act 1947' in 26 *Canadian
B.R.* (1948) 387 39, 43, 142

Baudry, G., *L'Expropriation pour Cause d'Utilité Publique* (2nd ed.;
Paris, 1947) 123, 124

Bennett, R., The Termination of War Contracts in the United States and
Great Britain (1948, unpublished) 100, 102

Bentham, J., *Traité de Législation Civile et Pénale* (Paris, 1802) 44

Benton, R. C., 'The Distinction between Legislative and Judicial Functions'
in 8 *American Bar Association Reports* (1885) 261 10

Berthélemy, H., Note in 24 *Revue de Droit Public* (1907) 92 70

—— 'The Conseil d'Etat in France' in 12 *Journal of Comparative Legislation*
(1930) 23 17, 56

—— *Traité Elémentaire de Droit Administratif* (13th ed.; Paris, 1933) 17, 58, 124

PAGE

Berthélemy, J., 'L'Obligation de Faire ou de ne pas Faire et Son Exécution
    dans le Droit Public' in 29 *Revue de Droit Public* (1912) 513   183
Beutel, F. K. & Billig, T. C., *Government Contracts* (unpublished, 1946) 82, 96
Beven, T., *Negligence* (4th ed.; London: W.J. Byrne and A. D. Gibb, 1928) 33
Bickford Smith, J. R., *The Crown Proceedings Act 1947* (London, 1948)
                                        45, 47, 160, 180
Birdsall, P., 'Non Obstante' in *Essays in History and Political Theory in*
    Honour of Charles Howard McIlwain (Cambridge, Mass., 1936)   145
Black, H. C., *Construction and Interpretation of the Laws* (2nd ed.; St Paul,
    1911)   150
Blackstone, Sir William, *Commentaries on the Laws of England* (1789)   49
Bodenstein, H. D. J., 'The Liability of the Crown for Torts of its Servants'
    in *South Africa L.J.* (1923) 277   7
Bonnard, R., 'La Réparation de Préjudice Moral' in 60 *Revue de Droit*
    Public (1943) 80   63
Borchard, E. M., *Convicting the Innocent* (Newhaven, 1932)   43
—— *Declaratory Judgments* (2nd ed.; Cleveland, 1941)   131, 134
—— 'Declaratory Judgments in Administrative Law' in 11 *New York*
    University L.Q.R. (1933) 139   131
—— *Diplomatic Privileges of Citizens Abroad* (New York, 1915)   52
—— 'French Administrative Law' in 18 *Iowa L.R.* (1932) 133   79
—— 'Governmental Liability in Tort' in 26 *Canadian B.R.* (1948) 399   13
—— 'Governmental Responsibility in Tort' in 36 *Yale L.J.* (1926) 1, 799;
    and in 28 *Columbia L.R.* (1928) 577   3, 9, 13, 14, 20, 58
—— 'State Indemnity for Errors' in 21 *Boston University L.R.* (1941) 201   44
Bower, G. Spencer, *The Doctrine of Res Judicata* (London, 1924)   156
Bowstead, W., *Law of Agency* (10th ed.; London: A. H. Forbes, 1944)   85
Brodeur, J., 'The Injunction in French Jurisprudence' in 14 *Tulane L.R.*
    (1940) 211   142
Brooke, Sir Robert, *Graunde Abridgement* (1586)   49, 120, 144, 157
Broom, H., *Legal Maxims* (10th ed.; London: R. H. Kersley, 1939) 145, 148, 151
Cambier, C., *La Responsabilité de la Puissance Publique et de ses Agents*
    (Brussels, 1947)   22
Chariotis, C. L., *Conseil d'Etat en Grèce de 1830 à 1930* (Paris, 1930)   22
Cherne, L. M., *Government Contract Problems* (New York, 1941)   82, 103
Chitty, J., *Prerogatives of the Crown* (London, 1820)   5, 49, 128, 146, 156
Chrimes, S. B., *English Constitutional Ideas in the Fifteenth Century* (Cam-
    bridge, 1936)   143
Chubb, B., *The Control of Public Expenditure* (Oxford, 1952)   95
Clerk, J. F. & Lindsell, W. H. B., *Law of Torts* (10th ed.; London: H. Potter,
    1947)   33, 42, 51, 216
Clode, W., *Petition of Right* (London, 1887)   3, 49, 81, 133
Cohen, A., *Des Contrats par Correspondance en Droit Français, en Droit*
    Anglais et en Droit Anglo-Américain (Paris, 1921)   118

PAGE

Colliard, C. A., 'Comparison between English and French Administrative
Law' in 25 *Transactions of the Grotius Society* (1940) 119   59
Comyns, Sir J., *Digest of the Laws of England* (5th ed.; London, 1822)   146
Corbin, A. L., 'Waiver of Tort and Suit in Assumpsit' in 19 *Yale L.J.*
(1910) 221   126
Corry, A. J., 'Administrative Law and the Interpretation of Statutes'
in 1 *University of Toronto L.J.* (1936) 286   147
Cot, P., *La Responsabilité Civile des Fonctionnaires Publics* (Paris, 1922)   17
Couzinet, P., *La Réparation des Atteintes Portées à la Propriété Privée
Immobilière par les Groupements Administratifs* (Paris, 1928)   75
Cowen, Z., 'The Consequences of *The Commonwealth* v. *Quince*' in 19
Australian L.J. (1945) 2   28
Craies, W. F., *Statute Law* (4th ed.; London: W. S. Scott, 1936)   148
Crane, J. A., 'Jurisdiction of the United States Court of Claims' in 34
Harvard L.R. (1920) 161   11, 127
Croquez, J. A., *Le Code de l'Expropriation* (Paris, 1940)   123
Debeyre, G., *La Responsabilité de la Puissance Publique en France et en
Belgique* (Lille, 1936)   22, 77
Defert, A., *L'Exécution des Jugements contre les Personnes Morales de Droit
Administratif* (Paris, 1910)   184
Denning, Sir Alfred, *Freedom under the Law* (London, 1949)   31, 40, 42
Dicey, A. V., *Law of the Constitution* (9th ed.; London: E. C. S. Wade,
1939)   5, 15, 85
Doddridge, D. W., 'Distinction between Governmental and Proprietary
Functions of Municipal Corporations' in 23 *Michigan L.R.* (1925)
325   16
Duez, P., *Les Actes de Gouvernement* (Paris, 1935)   73
—— *La Responsabilité de la Puissance Publique* (Paris, 1927)   61, 66, 67, 69, 75, 77
—— 'La Théorie de la Gestion Privée' in 44 *Revue Critique* (n.s.) 337   17
Dufour, *Traité Général de Droit Administratif Appliqué* (Paris, 1856)   72
Duguit, L., *Les Transformations de Droit Public* (Paris, 1913)   18, 19, 58, 69, 70
—— *Traité de Droit Constitutionnel* (3rd ed.; Paris, 1930)
2, 59, 61, 62, 65, 67, 68, 70, 71, 74, 105
Dupeyroux, H., *Faute Personnelle et Faute du Service Public* (Paris, 1922)   59
Durell, A. J. V., *Parliamentary Grants* (London, 1917)   90
Dwarris, F., *General Treatise on Statutes* (1st ed.; London, 1831)   148
Ehrlich, L., *Proceedings against the Crown* (1216–1377), Oxford Studies in
Social and Legal History, vol. VI, no. 12 (Oxford, 1913)   1, 2
Emden, C. S., 'Documents Privileged in Public Interest' in 39 *L.Q.R.*
(1923) 476   167
—— *The Civil Servant and the Law of the Constitution* (London, 1923)
51, 113, 138, 140
Everest, L. F. & Strode, E., *Law of Estoppel* (3rd ed.; London: L. F. Everest,
1923)   156

PAGE

Fabian Publications, *The Reform of the Higher Civil Service* (London, 1947) 117

Farrer, F. E., 'A Prerogative Fallacy—"That the King is not Bound by Estoppel"' in 49 *L.Q.R.* (1933) 511 156

—— 'Equitable Set-Off against the Crown' in 72 *Solicitors Journal* (1928) 262 181

Fayolle, M. M., *La Force Exécutoire des Décisions de Justice à l'Encontre des Administrations Publiques* 183

Fernando, S. E. J., *Actions against Public Servants in Ceylon* (Colombo, 1946) 7

Field, O. P., *Civil Service* (Minneapolis, 1939) 117

—— *Research in Administrative Law* (New York, 1938) 82

Finkelman, J., 'Separation of Powers: A Study in Administrative Law' in I *University of Toronto L.J.* (1935–6) 313 42

Fitzherbert, Sir Anthony, *Nouvelle Natura Brevium* (London, 1531) 49, 144

Foley, C. F. & Hauser, M. M., 'The First Year under the Federal Tort Claims Act' in 9 *Federal Bar Journal* (1947) 23 32

Foster, R. M., 'General Accounting Office and Government Claims' in 16 *Journal of the Bar Association of District of Columbia* (1949) 275 103

Fox, H. A., 'British Government Contract Requirements' in 2 *Comparative Law Services* (U.S. Dept. of Commerce) (1939) 507 95

Freund, E., 'La Responsabilité de l'Etat en Droit Interne' in General Report in *Mémoires de l'Académie Internationale de Droit Comparé*, Book II, Pt. III (Paris, 1935) 20, 120

—— 'Private Claims against the State' in 8 *Political Science Quarterly* (1893) 625 10, 182

Friedmann, W., *Australian Administrative Law* (Melbourne, 1951) 7

—— 'Changing Functions of Contract in the Common Law' in 10 *University of Toronto L.J.* (1951) 15 82

—— 'Legal Status of Incorporated Authorities' in 22 *Australian L.J.* (1948) 7 29

—— 'Public Welfare Offences, Statutory Duties, and the Legal Status of the Crown' in 13 *Modern L.R.* (1950) 24 32

—— 'Statute Law and its Interpretation in the Modern State' in 26 *Canadian B.R.* (1948) 1277 25

—— 'The New Public Corporations and the Law' in 10 *Modern L.R.* (1947) 233, 377 31, 35, 45

Friedrich, C. J., 'Responsible Government Service under the American Constitution' in *Problems of the American Civil Service* (New York, 1935) 1 111

Gahan, F., *The Law of Damages* (London, 1936) 53

Garner, J. W., 'Anglo-American and Continental European Administrative Law' in 7 *New York University L.Q.R.* (1929) 387 21

—— 'French Administrative Law' in 33 *Yale L.J.* (1924) 597 58, 59

Garraud, R., *Précis de Droit Criminel* (9th ed.; Paris, 1908) 69

PAGE

Gaudemet, P. M., 'Le Statut des Agents de l'Etat en Belgique' in 66 *Revue de Droit Public* (1949) 326   119

Gellhorn, W., *Administrative Law* (2nd ed.; Brooklyn, 1947)   43, 95, 137

Gellhorn, W. & Schenck, C. N., 'Tort Actions against the Federal Government' in 47 *Columbia L.R.* (1947) 722   9, 27, 71

Gierke, O., *Das Deutsche Genossenschaftsrecht* (Berlin, 1877)   14

—— *Die Deutsche Genossenschafttheorie und die Deutsche Rechtsprechung* (Berlin, 1887)   20

Giraud, E., *De la Responsabilité de l'Etat à Raison des Dommages Naissant de la Loi* (Paris, 1917)   70

Glanville Williams, L., *Crown Proceedings* (London, 1948)
        25, 29, 32, 35, 36, 38, 40, 49, 93, 94, 113, 121, 125, 126, 160, 168, 180

—— *Joint Torts and Contributory Negligence* (London, 1951)   38

—— 'The Aims of the Law of Tort' in 4 *Current Legal Problems* (1951) 137   53

Goodnow, F. J., 'Interest in Mandamus Cases' in 8 *Political Science Quarterly* (1893) 48   140

Gordon, D. M., 'How Far Privative or Restrictive Enactment Binds the Crown?' in 18 *Canadian B.R.* (1940) 751   155

Gordon, J. W., 'The Crown as Litigant' in 45 *L.Q.R.* (1929) 186   38

Gordon, S., 'La Théorie des "Acts of State" en Droit Anglais' in 53 *Revue de Droit Public* (1936) 5   50

Gottlieb, I. M., 'Federal Tort Claims Act—A Statutory Interpretation' in 35 *Georgetown L.J.* (1946) 1   32

Goutagny, J., *La Théorie des Voies de Fait* (Paris, 1945)   74, 75

Griffith, J. A. G., 'Public Corporations as Crown Servants' in 12 *Modern L.R.* (1949) 496   30

—— 'Public Corporations as Crown Servants' in 9 *University of Toronto L.J.* (1952) 169   32

Griffits, J. O., *Guide to Crown Office Practice* (London, 1947)   137

Halsbury, *Laws of England* (2nd ed.; London, 1933)
        3, 45, 85, 93, 104, 112, 113, 156

Hamson, C. J., 'Illegal Contracts and Limited Interests' in 10 *Cambridge L.J.* (1949) 249   35

—— 'Le Conseil d'Etat Statuant au Contentieux' in 68 *L.Q.R.* (1952) 60   56

Hanbury, H. G., *Essays in Equity* (Oxford, 1934)   129, 133

—— *Modern Equity* (6th ed., London, 1952)   128, 129

Hardcastle, H., *The Construction and Effect of Statutory Law* (London, 1879)   146

Hargreaves, A. D., 'The Crown as Litigant' in 122 *Nineteenth Century* (1937) 98   29

Hart, J., *An Introduction to Administrative Law* (New York, 1947)
        30, 92, 95, 110, 117, 136

Hart, J. M., *The British Police* (London, 1951)   34

Hatschek, J., *Die Rechtliche Stellung des Fiskus* (Berlin, 1899)   14, 15

PAGE

Hauriou, M., *Précis de Droit Administratif et de Droit Public* (11th ed., Paris,
1927)   17, 59, 60, 66, 72, 73, 74, 118, 128

Hawkins, W., *Pleas of the Crown* (London, 1824)   146

Haydock, R., 'Some Evidentiary Problems Posed by Atomic Energy
Security Requirements' in 61 *Harvard L.R.* (1948) 468   169, 177

Hersant, M., 'Esquisse de Recours Contentieux contre l'Abus de Pouvoir
Administratif' in Anglo-French Legal Conference (London, 1947)   72, 135

High, J. L., *Extraordinary Legal Remedies* (3rd ed.; Chicago, 1896)   135

Holdsworth, Sir William, 'A Case Book on Constitutional Law' in
45 *L.Q.R.* (1929) 162   99

—— *History of English Law* (London, 1922–38)
                1, 5, 120, 121, 131, 133, 148, 156, 160, 164

—— 'Immunity for Judicial Acts' in *Journal of the Society of Public Teachers
of Law* (1924) 17   41

—— Note in 38 *L.Q.R.* (1922) 11   51

—— 'The History of Acts of State in English Law' in 41 *Columbia L.R.*
(1941) 1313   50

Holmes, O. W., 'The Path of the Law' in 10 *Harvard L.R.* (1897) 457   101

Hotchkiss, W. E., *The Judicial Work of the Comptroller of the Treasury*
(Cornell, 1911)   103

Hulen, R. M., 'Suits on Tort Claims against the United States' in 7 *F.R.D.*
(1948) 689   26

Ilosvay, T., 'La Responsabilité de la Puissance Publique et de ses Agents en
Hongrie' in *Revue Internationale des Sciences Administratives* (1949) 269   22

Inskip, Sir Thomas, 'Proceedings by and against the Crown' in 4 *Cambridge
L.J.* (1930) 1   175

Iyer, D. R., *Law of Torts* (4th ed. Calcutta, 1950)   7

Jacobs, A. C., *Cases and Materials on Domestic Relations* (Chicago, 2nd ed.;
1939)   38

James, H. G., *The Protection of the Public Interests in Public Contracts* (Chicago,
1946)   97

Jamieson, D. P., 'Proceedings by and against the Crown in Canada' in
26 *Canadian B.R.* (1948) 373   7, 166

Jellinek, G., *System der Subjektiven Öffentlichen Rechte* (2nd ed.; Berlin,
1905)   20

Jennings, E. G., 'Tort Liability of Administrative Officers' in 21 *Minnesota
L.R.* (1937) 263   41

Jennings, Sir Ivor, *Cabinet Government* (2nd ed.; Cambridge, 1951)   90

—— 'Declaratory Judgments against Public Authorities in England' in
41 *Yale L.J.* (1932) 407   131

—— *Principles of Local Government Law* (3rd ed.; London, 1947) 299   136

—— *The Law Relating to Local Authorities* (London, 1935)   33, 36

—— 'The Report on Ministers' Powers' in 10 *Public Administration* (1932)
333   25, 178

PAGE

Jèze, G., 'Le Contrat Administratif de Louage de Services Personnels'
in 43 *Revue de Droit Public* (1926) 5   118

—— 'Préjudice Causé par une Loi' in 60 *Revue de Droit Public* (1945) 366   71

—— *Principes Généraux du Droit Administratif* (3rd ed.; Paris, 1925)   73, 74, 82

—— 'Théorie du Contrat Administratif' in 60 *Revue de Droit Administratif*
(1945) 251   83

—— Note in 26 *Revue de Droit Public* (1909) 267   59

—— Note in 31 *Revue de Droit Public* (1914) 572   64

—— Note in 35 *Revue de Droit Public* (1918) 42   64

Jones, J. W., *Historical Introduction to the Theory of Law* (Oxford, 1940)   13

—— 'The Early History of Fiscus' in 43 *L.Q.R.* (1927) 499   13, 14

Julliot de la Morandière et Byé, *Les Nationalisations en France* (Paris, 1948)   106

Kahn-Freund, O., 'Legislation through Adjudication. The Legal Aspect
of Fair Wages Clauses and Recognised Conditions' in 11 *Modern L.R.*
(1948) 269   82

—— *The Law of Carriage by Inland Transport* (2nd ed.; London, 1949)   105

Kaminski, L., 'Torts—Application of Discretionary Function Exception of
Federal Tort Claims Act' in 36 *Marquette L.R.* (1952) 88   40

Katz, M., *Cases and Materials on Administrative Law* (St Paul, 1947)   84

Keedy, E. R., 'A Petition of Right: *Archer-Slee* v. *R.*' in 87 *University of
Pennsylvania L.R.* (1938) 895   112

Keeton, G.W., 'The Crown as Agent' in 77 *Law Journal Newspaper* (1934) 268   129

Keir, Sir David & Lawson, F. H., *Cases in Constitutional Law* (3rd ed.;
Oxford, 1948)   85, 113, 168

Keith, Sir Arthur, *The Constitutional Law of the British Dominions* (London,
1933)   85

Kennedy, W. P. M., 'Suits by and against the Crown' in 6 *Canadian B.R.*
(1929) 329   6

Kessler, F., 'Contracts of Adhesion' in 43 *Columbia L.R.* (1943) 629   101

Kingsbury, H. T., 'The "Act of State" Doctrine' in 4 *American Journal of
International Law* (1910) 359   51

Knight, F. F., 'Attachment of Monies in the Hands of the Crown' in
3 *Australian L.J.* (1930) 323   183

Laferrière, L., *Traité de la Juridiction Administrative* (Paris, 1887)   58, 59, 73

Laski, H. J., 'The Responsibility of the State in England' in 32 *Harvard
L.R.* (1919) 447   182

Latournerie, R., 'Dommages Causés par des Travaux Publics' in 60 *Revue
de Droit Public* (1945) 1   67, 69

Laubadère, A. de, *Manuel de Droit Administratif* (Paris, 1946) 59, 60, 62, 67, 75, 151

Lawton, J. P., 'Vicarious Liability of Hospital Authorities' in 10 *Modern
L.R.* (1947) 425   36

Le Conseil d'Etat, *Le Livre Jubilaire*   56, 76

Lenhoff, A., 'Scope of Compulsory Contracts Proper' in 43 *Columbia L.R.*
(1943) 586   106

PAGE

Lewin, T., *Practical Treatise on the Law of Trusts* (15th ed.; London:
R. Cozens-Hardy Horne, 1950)   130

Lloyd, W. J., 'Municipal Tort Liability in New York' in 23 *New York
University L.Q.R.* (1948) 278   16

Logan, D. W., 'A Civil Servant and his Pay' in 61 *L.Q.R.* (1945) 240   112

Lorenzen, E. G., 'Tort Liability and the Conflict of Laws' in 47 *L.Q.R.*
(1931) 483   49

Lowe, C. J., 'The Liability of the Crown in Tort' in 11 *Australia L.J.*
(1938) 402   6

Lucas, W. W., *The Primordial Functions of Government and the Legal Status
of Sovereignty* (Cambridge, 1938)   136, 140

Luce, R., 'Petty Business in Congress' in 26 *American Political Science Review*
(1932) 815   11

McDonald, J. W., 'Court of Claims: The Administration of a Tort Liability
Law in New York' in 9 *Law and Contemporary Problems* (1942) 262   184

McFarland, C. & Vanderbilt, A. T., *Cases and Materials on Administrative
Law* (New York, 1947)   30

McGuire, O. R., *Matters of Procedure under Government Contracts*
(Washington, 1935)   102

McIlwaine, C. H., *The Growth of Political Thought in the West* (New York,
1932)   143

McIntire, J. A., 'Government Corporations as Administrative Agencies'
in 4 *George Washington L.R.* (1936) 161   30

Mack, W. H., 'Compulsory Process to the Comptroller-General' in 3
George Washington L.R. (1934) 97   138

McNair, Sir Arnold, Note in 43 *L.Q.R.* (1927) 9   121

Maitland, F. W., *Collected Papers* (Cambridge, 1911)   3, 184

—— *Constitutional History of England* (Cambridge, 1908)   2

Manning, J., *Exchequer Practice* (London, 1827)   3

Mansfield, H. C., *The Comptroller-General* (Newhaven, 1939)   103, 137

Marcq, R., *La Responsabilité de la Puissance Publique* (Paris, 1911)   16, 17

Martindale, C., 'The State and its Creditors' in 7 *Southern L.R.* (1882) 544   182

Mathiot, *Les Accidents Causés par les Travaux Publics* (Paris, 1934)   67

Maxwell, Sir P. B., *Interpretation of Statutes* (9th ed.; London: Sir G. H. B.
Jackson, 1946)   153

May, H. J., *The South African Constitution* (2nd ed.; Capetown, 1949)   34

Mayne, J. D., *Damages* (11th ed.; London: W. G. Earengay, 1946)   53

Meachem, F. R., *A Treatise on the Law of Public Offices and Officers* (Chicago,
1890)   111

—— *The Law of Agency* (2nd ed.; Chicago, 1914)   92, 93

Michoud, 'De la Responsabilité de l'Etat à Raison des Fautes de ses
Agents' in 32 *Revue de Droit Public* (1895) 401   17

Mitchell, J. D. B., 'A General Theory of Public Contracts' in 63 *Juridical
Review* (1951) 60   82

PAGE

Mitchell, J. D. B., 'Limitations on the Contractual Liability of Public
   Authorities' in 13 *Modern Law Review* (1950) 318, 455   98, 115
—— 'The Assumption of Authority by Crown Servants' in 100 *Law
   Journal* (1950) 493   158
—— 'The Treatment of Public Contracts in the United States' in 9 *U. of
   Toronto L.J.* (1952) 194   99
Mitteis, L., *Römisches Privatrecht* (Berlin, 1908)   14
Mommsen, T., *Römisches Staatrecht* (Berlin, 1877)   14
Moore, J. W., *Federal Practice* (Albany, 1938)   169
Moore, W. H., *Act of State in English Law* (London, 1906)   50
—— 'Liability for Acts of Public Servants' in 23 *L.Q.R.* (1907) 12   27, 29, 33
Morgan, J. H., Introductory Chapter on Remedies against the Crown to
   G. E. Robinson, *Public Authorities and Legal Liability* (London,
   1925)   2, 5, 140
Mustoe, N. E., *The Law and Organisation of the Civil Service* (London,
   1932)   93, 116, 138, 140
Naylor, E. E., 'Liability of the United States Government in Contract'
   in 14 *Tulane L.R.* (1940) 580   84
Negulesco, P., 'La Responsabilité de la Puissance Publique' in 10 *Rivista
   de Drept Public* (1935) 233   77
—— *Traité du Droit Administratif* (3rd ed.; Bucharest, 1925)   183
Nesmes-Desmarets, *De la Responsabilité Civile des Fonctionnaires de l'Ordre
   Administratif et Judiciaire* (Paris, 1910)   69
Nokes, G. D., 'Professional Privilege' in 66 *L.Q.R.* (1949) 88   174
Nove, A., 'Some Aspects of Soviet Constitutional Theory' in 12 *Modern
   L.R.* (1949) 12   22
O'Reilly, J. D., 'Discovery against the United States—a New Aspect of
   Sovereign Immunity?' in 26 *North Carolina L.R.* (1942) 1   169
O'Sullivan, J. K., 'The Defence of Act of State in respect of Acts Com-
   mitted on British Territories' in 4 *Res Gestae* (1950) 245   51
Oroveanu, P., *La Séparation des Pouvoirs Administrative et Judiciaire et le
   Contentieux Administratif en Roumanie* (Paris, 1936)   21
Paton, G. W., *A Text Book of Jurisprudence* (Oxford, 1946)   53, 185
Patterson, E. W., 'Compulsory Contracts in the Crystal Ball' in 43
   Columbia L.R. (1943) 731   110
Péquignot, G., *Théorie Générale du Contrat Administratif* (Paris, 1945)
             19, 82, 83, 85, 101, 110
Péritch, J. M., 'La Responsabilité de l'Etat en Droit Interne', General
   Report in *Memoirés de l'Académie Internationale de Droit Comparé*, Book II,
   Pt. III (Paris, 1935)   15
Perry, J. W., *Trusts and Trustees* (7th ed.; Boston: R. C. Balders, 1929)   130
Picot, *De la Responsabilité de l'Etat du Fait de ses Préposés* (Paris, 1920)   16
Pike, J. A. & Fischer, H. G., 'Discovery against Federal Administrative
   Agencies' in 56 *Harvard L.R.* (1943) 1125   169

PAGE

Pollock, Sir Frederick, *Principles of Contract* (13th ed.; London: Sir Percy
  Winfield, 1950)   93
Pollock, Sir Frederick & Maitland, F. W., *History of English Law* (Cam-
  bridge, 1895)   1
Ponthus, M., 'Compétence et Rôle des Tribunaux Administratifs' in
  Anglo-French Legal Conference 1947 (London, 1947) 81   67, 69, 75, 76
Pound, R., 'A Survey of Public Interests' in 58 *Harvard L.R.* (1944) 909   10
—— 'A Survey of Social Interests' in 57 *Harvard L.R.* (1943) 1   175
Prausnitz, O., *The Standardisation of Commercial Contracts* (London, 1937)   99
Preston, C. H. S. & Newsom, G. H., *Limitation of Actions* (2nd ed.; London,
  1943)   159, 160
Prosser, W. L., *Handbook of the Law of Torts* (St Paul, 1941)   107
Puente, J. I. Y., 'The Responsibility of the State as a Juristic Person in Latin
  America' in 18 *Tulane L.R.* (1944), 408, 554   22
Radin, M., 'Contract Obligation and the Human Will' in 43 *Columbia
  L.R.* (1943) 575   107, 110
Ravà, P. B., 'Italian Administrative Courts under Fascism' in 40 *Michigan
  L.R.* (1941) 654   21, 73
Renfree, H. E., 'A Brief Conspectus of Commonwealth Liability in Tort'
  in 22 *Australian L.J.* (1948) 102   6
Richardson, W. A., 'History, Jurisdiction and Practice of the Court of
  Claims in the United States' in 7 *Southern L.R.* (1882) 781   10, 81
Ridges, E. W., *Constitutional Law* (18th ed.; London: G. W. Forrest,
  1950)   112
Robertson, G. S., *Civil Proceedings by and against the Crown* (London,
  1908)   3, 49, 81, 125, 134, 137, 140, 157, 183
Robinson, G. E., *Public Authorities and Legal Liability* (London, 1925)   137
Rokham, W. & Pratt, O. C., *Studies in French Administrative Law*, Studies
  in the Social Sciences, vol. 28, no. 3 (Urbana, 1947)   56, 61
Rolland, L., Note in 26 *Revue de Droit Public* (1909) 727   69
Romilly, Sir Samuel, *Memoirs* (2nd ed.; London, 1840)   44
Roque, M. de la, 'Essai sur la Responsabilité du Juge Administratif' in
  67 *Revue de Droit Public* (1952) 609   69
Salmond, Sir John, *Law of Torts* (10th ed.; London: W. T. S. Stallybrass,
  1945)   33, 36, 53, 107
Sawer, G., 'Law and Orders' in 3 *Res Judicatae* (1947) 80   132
Schwartz, B., *Law and the Executive in Britain* (New York, 1949)   169
—— 'The Administrative Courts in France' in 29 *Canadian B.R.* (1951)
  381   56
Scott, F. R., 'Administrative Law' in 26 *Canadian B.R.* (1948) 268   29
Scott, Sir Leslie & Hildesley, A., *The Case of Requisition* (Oxford, 1920)   4
Sears, K. G., *Cases and Materials on Administrative Law* (St Paul, 1938)   102
Sellar, W., 'Government Corporations' in 24 *Canadian B.R.* (1946) 393,
  489   29

PAGE

Shealey, *The Law of Government Contracts* (3rd ed.; 1938)   81, 82, 123

Sherwood, F. H., 'Mandamus to Review Administrative Action' in 45 *Michigan L.R.* (1946) 123   136

Shulman, H. & James, F., *Cases and Materials on the Law of Torts* (Chicago, 1942)   53

Shumate, R. V., 'Tort Claims against State Governments' in 9 *Law and Contemporary Problems* (1942) 242   11, 13

Sieghart, M. A., *Government by Decree* (London, 1950)   135

Singewalde, K., *The Doctrine of Non-Suability of the State in the United States* (Baltimore, 1910)   8

Smith, A., 'Liability to Suit of an Agent of the Crown' in 8 *University of Toronto L.J.* (1950) 218   93

Spence, G., *Equitable Jurisdiction* (London, 1846)   128

Spilman, E., 'Evidence and Admissions of Government Employees under the Act' in 33 *American Bar Association Journal* (1947) 958   159

Staunford, Sir William, *Exposition of the King's Prerogative* (London, 1567)   1, 49, 120

Stemp, L. F. & Wing, R. A., *The Gas Act* (London, 1949)   106

Stone, J., *The Province and Function of Law* (London, 1947)   41, 53, 175, 176

Street, H., 'The Crown Proceedings Act' in 11 *Modern L.R.* (1948) 129   37, 94

—— 'The Effect of Statutes upon the Rights and Liabilities of the Crown' in 7 *University of Toronto L.J.* (1948) 357   143

—— 'The Provision of Funds in Satisfaction of Governmental Liabilities' in 8 *University of Toronto L.J.* (1949) 32   84, 182

—— Note in 26 *Canadian B.R.* (1948) 994   155

—— 'Tort Liability of the State: The Federal Tort Claims Act and the Crown Proceedings Act' in 47 *Michigan L.R.* (1949) 341   25, 123

Tapping, T., *Law and Practice of the Prerogative Writ of Mandamus* (London, 1853)   136

Tari, G., *Des Moyens d'Assurer l'Exécution des Jugements Rendus contre l'Administration* (Paris, 1933)   183

Teissier, G., *La Responsabilité de la Puissance Publique* (Paris, 1906)   66

—— *Répertoire de Droit Administratif* (Paris, 1908)   69

Téodoresco, A., 'Le Fondement Juridique de la Responsabilité dans le Droit Administratif' in *Mélanges Paul Negulesco* (Bucharest, 1935) 751   77

Thorne, S. E., *Discourse upon Exposicion and Understandinge of Statutes* (California, 1942)   144

Thurlow, P. E., 'Some Aspects of the Law of Government Contracts' in 21 *Chicago-Kent L.R.* (1942–3) 300   84

Thurston, J., 'Government Proprietary Corporations' in 21 *Virginia L.R.* (1935) 351, 465   30

Treves, G. E., 'Administrative Discretion and Judicial Control' in 10 *Modern L.R.* (1947) 276   135

PAGE

Trotabas, L., 'La Responsabilité de l'Etat en Droit Interne' in General
Report in *Mémoires de l'Académie Internationale de Droit Comparé*, Book II,
Pt. III (Paris, 1935)   13

—— 'Les Actes de Gouvernement en Matières Diplomatiques' in *Revue
Critique de Législation et de Jurisprudence* (1925) 342   73

—— 'Liability in Damages under French Administrative Law' in 12
Journal of Comparative Legislation (1930) 44, 213   15, 18, 59, 60, 62, 65, 66, 67

Uhler, A., *Review of Administrative Acts* (Chicago, 1942)   17, 56, 74

Uhlman, R. E. & Rupp, H. G., 'The German System of Administrative
Courts' in 31 *Illinois L.R.* (1937) 847   20

Vaulx, H. de, *La Responsabilité de l'Etat Français à Cause des Dommages
Causés par les Faits de Guerre* (Verdun, 1913)   76

Vauthier, A. M., *Précis du Droit Administratif de la Belgique* (2nd ed.;
Brussels, 1937)   23, 77

Vauthier, P., *Etudes sur les Personnes Morales* (Brussels, 1887)   15

Velge, H., *Le Conseil d'Etat* (Brussels, 1947)   24

Viner, C., General Abridgement (2nd ed.; London, 1791–5)   146

Wade, E. C. S., 'Act of State in English Law: Its Relations with International
Law' in 15 *British Year Book of International Law* (1934) 98   50

—— 'The Constitutional Aspect of the Public Corporation' in *Current
Legal Problems*, vol. II, (ed. G. W. Keeton and G. Schwarzenberger;
London, 1949) 172   30

—— 'The Courts and the Administrative Process' in 63 *L.Q.R.* (1947)
164   136, 139

Wade, E. C. S. & Phillips, G. G., *Constitutional Law* (4th ed.; London,
1950)   29

Wade, H. R. W., 'Quasi-Judicial and its Background' in 10 *Cambridge L.J.*
(1949) 216   42

Waline, M., *Manuel Elémentaire de Droit Administratif* (6th ed.; Paris, 1951)
   57, 59, 60, 61, 67, 68, 69, 72, 74, 82, 85, 110, 128

Walkup, H. A., 'Immunity of the State from Suit by its Citizens—Towards
a More Enlightened Concept' in 36 *Georgetown L.J.* (1948) 310   1, 152

Watkins, R. D., *The State as a Party Litigant* (Baltimore, 1927)   65

Watson, E. R., *Trial of Adolf Beck* (London, 1924)   43

White, L. D., *Introduction to the Study of Public Administration* (2nd ed.;
New York, 1939)   118

Wienshink, R. & Feldman, F., 'The Current Challenge of Military Contract
Domination' in 66 *Har. L.R.* (1952) 47   100

Wigmore, J. H., *Evidence* (Boston, 1940)   159, 169, 170, 175

Willis, J., 'Three Approaches to Administrative Law: the Judicial, the
Conceptual, and the Functional' in 1 *University of Toronto L.J.*
(1935–6) 53   42

Williston, S., *Law of Contracts*, vol. IX (revised ed.; Boston: T. W. Graske,
1945)   82, 103, 127

PAGE

Willoughby, W. F., *The Legal Status and Functions of the General Accounting Office of the National Government* (Baltimore, 1927) 103

Winfield, Sir Percy, *Law of Tort* (5th ed.; London, 1950) 36, 51

—— *Province of the Law of Tort* (Cambridge, 1931) 107, 130

—— *The Present Law of Abuse of Legal Procedure* (Cambridge, 1911) 41

Wodon, L., *Le Contrôle Juridictionnel de l'Administration et la Responsabilité des Services Publics en Belgique* (Brussels, 1920) 23

Wooddeson, R., *Lectures on the Law of England* (London, 1842) 146

Wright, Lord, 'Public Policy' in *Legal Essays and Addresses* (London, 1939) 66 176

LIST OF UNSIGNED ARTICLES

TABLE OF CASES

ENGLAND

Table of Cases 209

PAGE

Enever v. Rex (1906), 3 C.L.R. 969 — 33
Field v. Nott (1939), 62 C.L.R. 660 — 34
Griffin v. South Australia (1925), 36 C.L.R. 378 — 168
Hollett v. Rex, [1949] 4 D.L.R. 225 — 157
King v. King, [1944] Q.W.N. (Aust.) 25 — 174
Ex parte Krefft (1876), 1 S.C.R. (N.S.W.) 446 — 138
Minister for Works for Western Australia v. Gulson (1944), 69 C.L.R. 338 — 149, 150
New South Wales v. Bardolph, [1934] 52 C.L.R. 455 — 89, 90
North Sydney Municipal Council v. Housing Corporation (1948), 48 S.R. (N.S.W.) 281 — 149
Randwick Municipal Council v. Nott (1940), 14 L.G.R. 222 — 141
Roberts v. Ahern (1904), 1 C.L.R. 406 — 149
Seeney v. Seeney, [1945] Q.W.N. (Aust.) 20 — 174
Sharp v. Board of Land & Works (1947), 5 A.L.R. (Current Notes) 81 — 141
Shaw Savill & Albion Co. Ltd. v. Commonwealth (1940), 66 C.L.R. 344 — 28
In re Sooka Nand Verna (1905), 7 W.A.L.R. 225 — 138
Victoria Railway Commissioners v. Herbert, [1949] V.L.R. 211 — 29

CANADA

Attorney-General for British Columbia v. Parker, [1937] 4 D.L.R. 242 — 152
Attorney-General for British Columbia v. The Royal Bank of Canada and Island Amusement Co. Ltd. (1936), 51 B.C.R. 241 — 148, 155
Attorney-General for Ontario v. Toronto Junction Recreation Club (1904), 8 Ont. L.R. 440 — 140
Bender v. Rex, [1949] 2 D.L.R. 318 — 29
Bradley v. M'Intosh (1884), 5 Ont. R. 227 — 174
C.P.R. Co. v. A. G. Saskatchewan, [1951] 3 D.L.R. 362 — 141
Canadian Domestic Engineering Co. v. Ray, [1919] 2 W.W.R. 762 — 90
Chipman v. Rex, [1934] Ex. C.R. 152 — 129
Cooke v. Rex, [1929] Ex. C.R. 20 — 112
Crombie v. Rex, [1923] 2 D.L.R. 542 — 166
Dusfresne Construction Co. Ltd. v. Rex, [1935] Ex. 77 — 175
Re Excelsior Electric Dairy Machinery Ltd. (1923), 52 Ont. L.R. 225 — 155
Farthing v. Rex, [1948] 1 D.L.R. 385 — 34
Genois v. Rex, [1937] Ex. C.R. 176 — 114
Gillies Bros Ltd. v. Rex, [1947] 2 D.L.R. 769 — 157
Greenlees v. Attorney-General (Canada), [1945] 2 D.L.R. 641 — 133
Gruen Watch Co. v. Attorney-General (Canada), [1950] 4 D.L.R. 156 — 133, 134
Hall v. Reg. (1893), 3 Ex. C.R. 373 — 91
Henry v. Rex, [1905] Ex. C.R. 417 — 130
Hereford Ry. Co. v. Reg. (1894), 24 S.C.R. 1 — 129
Hollett v. Rex, [1949] 4 D.L.R. 225 — 157

SGL — 14

TABLE OF STATUTES

AUSTRALIAN

CANADIAN

INDEX

For EU product safety concerns, contact us at Calle de José Abascal, 56–1°,
28003 Madrid, Spain or eugpsr@cambridge.org.

www.ingramcontent.com/pod-product-compliance
Ingram Content Group UK Ltd.
Pitfield, Milton Keynes, MK11 3LW, UK
UKHW010336140625
459647UK00010B/638